CAPTAINS TO THE NORTHWARD

CAPTAIN ABRAHAM WHIPPLE

From a water color in the possession of the Rhode Island Historical Society.
Courtesy Naval History Division, U.S. Navy Department.

CAPTAINS
TO THE
NORTHWARD

*The New England Captains
In The
Continental Navy*

By WILLIAM JAMES MORGAN

BARRE GAZETTE
BARRE, MASSACHUSETTS
1959

To My Dear Wife
Arline Hanlon Morgan

CONTENTS

ILLUSTRATIONS

FOREWORD

William Bell Clark, author and outstanding authority on the naval and military history of the American Revolution, has stated:

> Upon military and diplomatic and economic phases, I could find anything I desired from Paul Revere's ride to Yorktown, from the French Alliance to the Peace Treaty, from Tom Payne's "Common Sense" to the inflation of the Continental dollar. But of the naval phases, printed history has had little to say except of the exploits of John Paul Jones . . . . There were many men who performed most meritorious services but their deeds have been lost in oblivion.

I believe that the correctness of these views will be evident to anyone who has made a study of this period. For example, a recently published volume in the New American Nation series dealing with the Revolution allots about one page to naval operations and that page is chiefly devoted to what was done by the French Navy. Historians, past and present, all too often have omitted completely the naval history of the American Revolution or they have passed over it with superficial attention.

Dr. Morgan has devoted this history to the Continental Naval captains from New England. He has produced a scholarly study based on extensive and careful research and has succeeded in rescuing from oblivion a number of patriotic sailors who deserve to be better known. He has produced an interesting and well written narrative which is a real addition to the history of the period.

The author has not prepared a series of biographical sketches. Instead, he has written a history of the services of these Yankee merchant captains who donned the uniform of the Continental Navy and fought for American independence. He has evaluated the collective contribution of these New England captains and has given us an objective account of their seagoing background, their sectionalism and their abilities. My considered opinion of Dr. Morgan's work is that it is a significant contribution to the most neglected aspect of American Revolutionary history.

John B. Heffernan

Rear Admiral, USN (Ret.)

Former Director of Naval History

Navy Department
Washington, D.C.

PREFACE

The documents connected with the early history of the navy of the country were never kept with sufficient method, and the few that did exist have become much scattered and lost.

J. FENIMORE COOPER

It was in the spring of 1952 that a book by Bryce Metcalf entitled *Original Members and Other Officers Eligible to the Society of the Cincinnati* came to my desk in the Naval History Division, Navy Department. The Cincinnati, oldest patriotic society in the United States, was organized by Continental Army officers in 1783 at the encampment on the Hudson River, near Newburgh, New York, just before the victorious soldiers of the Revolution disbanded. It is a military and social order intended by the founders as a way of retaining old comradeships made in the field. All active officers at the end of the war, as well as those who had resigned with honor after three years service in the capacity of officers, or had been mustered out by resolution of Congress, and the sons of officers who died in service were declared eligible. Hereditary succession to the Cincinnati was provided for through the eldest male branches of original members.

The thing that struck me most about Colonel Metcalf's book was that only 45 Continental Naval officers of all grades from chaplain to captain were listed in 319 pages of eligible names. I felt certain that the war service of numerous additional naval officers entitled them to a place in this select group. Following a discussion with Admiral Heffernan, then Director of Naval History, I was encouraged to pursue the subject. I called at the headquarters of the Cincinnati, which is maintained in beautiful Anderson House, Washington, D.C., and talked with the gracious and well-informed guardian of the Society's records, Miss Blanche Girard. She recognized that the number of naval names was very small, and readily admitted that the Society had virtually no information about the sea officers of the Revolution. Miss Girard kindly put her archives and library at my disposal, and expressed pleasure at the prospect of being able to add some naval officers to the Cincinnati list.

Next I corresponded with Bryce Metcalf who answered that when compiling his book he was disappointed to find "so few naval officers." He concurred that "there must be others, but they are difficult to find and only personal research will bring them to light." Metcalf proved right on all counts.

After deliberation I decided to confine the study to captains in the Continental Navy. In 1794 Secretary of War Knox sent to President Washington a "List of the Commissioned Officers who served in the Navy of the United States in the late War." This list which is now in the custody of the National Archives contains the names of 45 individuals who received captains' commissions during the American Revolution. I have used it as a basis on which to proceed.

John Paul Jones has had, of course, extensive biographical coverage. The naval historian William Bell Clark has authoritatively written the stories of John Barry, Nicholas Biddle, Lambert Wickes, and John Young, as he gradually works his way through the notable naval figures from Maryland and Pennsylvania. With this consideration in mind, I finally resolved to leave the southerners to Clark's capable pen, and further narrow my investigations to the New England captains in the Continental Navy. Why New England? Perhaps I was unwittingly drawn to the area by a Connecticut ancestry. Actually, after British occupation of New York and then Philadelphia, New England, particularly Boston harbor, was the focal point of American naval and maritime enterprise. Therefore, from the service records, the successes and failures of commanders from the northern provinces, a good picture of the overall effort should emerge, and general conclusions take form.

From the file materials in the Early Naval Records Section of the National Archives, it could be established that 22 naval captains were natives of, or resided in, the four New England colonies. They were:

Massachusetts
  John Ayers
  William Burke
  Henry Johnson
  John Manley
  Hector McNeill
  John Peck Rathbun
  John Skimmer
  Samuel Tucker
  Daniel Waters

New Hampshire
  Thomas Simpson
  Thomas Thompson

Rhode Island
  Hoysted Hacker
  John Hazard
  John B. Hopkins
  Joseph Olney
  Silas Talbot
  Elisha Warner
  Abraham Whipple

Connecticut
  Samuel Chew
  Seth Harding
  Elisha Hinman
  Dudley Saltonstall

These little-known and unknown Yankee "Captains to the Northward," so styled by the naval authorities, are my central figures. Although Esek Hopkins of Rhode Island was designated Commander in Chief of the Fleet, he was never commissioned a captain and technically does not come within our purview. Nevertheless, his role in the Navy's first days was too prominent to pass over without notice.

There is no intention to present a complete biographical study on any of the officers. Rather it is the object of this work to trace their active naval careers in the public service through the Revolutionary period. When they are not in actual Continental employ no attempt is made to follow the captains into privateers beyond mention of the fact, for privateering is a subject unto itself. An appraisal, and what I trust the reader finds an objective analysis of the New England mariners' individual and collective contributions to the eight-year fight for American independence, has been made.

Surviving correspondence, ship logs, letter books, journals and similar primary source materials of an official or personal nature are too often fragmentary, but from the pieces I have striven to weave a whole cloth. More than a hundred years ago Cooper, in the words which open this preface, succinctly stated the obstacle confronting an investigator in early American naval history. The few documents are still "much scattered" and some that Cooper seems to have used are now lost. But on the credit side, new material has come to light since Cooper was writing, and historical societies and libraries have gathered, and in some instances have published, valuable collections. One outstanding example is the indispensable *Out Letters of the Continental Marine Committee and Board of Admiralty, August* 1776 - *September* 1780 printed in 1914 under the sponsorship of the Naval History Society. The Navy Department is collecting naval and maritime documents of the Revolution preparatory to publication in a series of volumes.

With Washington, D.C., as "home port," research has taken me to state historical societies, museums, libraries, and private individuals, as far south as Charleston, South Carolina, north to Concord, New Hampshire, and west to San Marino, California. Everywhere I have encountered full cooperation, unstinted assistance, and genuine interest. I have fortunately been able to profit all along the line from Admiral Heffernan's deep knowledge. Several distinguished naval historians, Commodore Dudley W. Knox, USN, Samuel Eliot Morison, and Walter Muir Whitehill, have done me the honor of examining and commenting on the manuscript. I have incorporated a number of their recommendations, but the final results are my own responsibility. The Navy Department Library benevolently allowed me to denude their shelves of Revolutionary War material. Officers assigned to the Historical Research Section, particularly Lieutenant H. P. Deeley, Jr., USN, and Lieutenant H. A. Vadnais, Jr., USNR, have been a captive audience and have listened to me read numerous passages for comment and reaction. Miss Nancy Lindemuth's uncanny ability to decipher my writing proved invaluable. I must also cast one appreciation vote for the legislators who annually appropriate funds to perpetuate and enhance that great mecca, the Library of Congress. And lastly, a special kind of thanks is reserved for Arline and three boys who have had to accept a husband and father devoting leave periods to document hunting and evenings and week ends at the writing desk.

William James Morgan

Washington, D.C.
June, 1959

CHAPTER I

A NAVAL IMPULSE

*We cannot with all the naval force we collect
be able to cope with the British Navy. Our great
Aim should be to destroy the trade of Britain.*

WILLIAM ELLERY

IN A LAND where settlement in the main clung to the coast, and whose people lived, died and were buried within sight of salt water, the sea could not be a stranger. Rather it was an intimate and well traveled avenue, a source of food, and a battlefield. Moreover, as waters which foamed against Connecticut's rocks and washed the sands of the Carolinas found their way to the Cornish coast and gentle Bahama beaches, the distance from America to Europe and the West Indies was bridged.

The sea held a particular significance to the four New England provinces where it was the very blood stream of existence. New England's coast is scalloped by numberless harbors and laced with navigable rivers where tall pine, long prized by the Royal Navy for masts and spars, grew to the water's edge. A country not particularly inviting to agriculture, New England is bountifully endowed with the elements incident to widespread shipbuilding industry and maritime trade. New England sailors, in New England built ships, spread the products of Yankee enterprise, while other New England men took the cod and whale from the sea. They played their part well in the naval service and privateers during England's 18th cen-

1

tury wars with France and Spain. Colonial-manned ships were in action at Louisbourg, Havana, and Quebec, where the lethal art of serving a carriage gun and swivel was amply demonstrated. Many merchantmen habitually went armed and frequently had to fight for defense. What could be more natural, therefore, when open fighting started between Britain and her North American colonies, than that there would be no shortage of New England mariners trained and anxious to turn to the sea to defend the coastal towns, protect trade, make a profit, and cause maximum annoyance to the enemy. This reflex action came hard on the heels of Lexington and Concord.

After tangling with the surprising Massachusetts farmers, the harassed British regulars fell back on Boston whereupon the town was tightly besieged by rebel militia. Excepting those necessities which could be bought at exorbitant prices from Tories or mammonish patriots, the townspeople and "Ministerial Forces" in Boston were totally dependent on water transport for supply.

Several of the small islands which studded Boston harbor, Hog and Noddle's Islands in the northeast side near Chelsea among them, had been stocked with cattle and planted in pasturage for many years. Attempts by British troops to take off the hay and livestock during May 1775 met with a prompt and most determined resistance. Web-footed American soldiers in small boats made a series of commando-style raids on the islands, burning the forage, slaughtering and running off the cattle rather than suffer the beef to grace enemy mess tables. A British author tells how the success of these bold attacks both annoyed and surprised his bedeviled countrymen.

> That the rebels should be well informed of the exact situation of the fleet and army at Boston is little to be wondered at, considering the number of avowed friends which they had in the town; but it is a matter of surprise, that notwithstanding the number of professed friends, which Government was supposed to have on the continent of America, either the inclination or the power was wanting in them,

to transmit such intelligence of the designs of the enemy, as might be the means of frustrating any of their depredatory excursions. With such secrecy and dispatch did they conduct their expeditions to the islands in the bay, that the flames of the houses and the hay generally gave the first intimation of the attack.[1]

British men-of-war were stationed off New England ports and cruising in adjacent waters ready to pounce on home-ward bound colonial trading vessels, and divert their cargo to General Thomas Gage in Boston. Captain John Lynzee in His Majesty's sloop-of-war *Falcon,* patrolling off Cape Cod, watching for the expected arrival of a heavily-laden American sloop from the West Indies, fell in with and took a timber sloop, unarmed and in ballast. Holding out a promise of release, the English captain wrung informaton from the craft's master that the West Indiaman had eluded Lynzee and was already safe within the harbor at Dartmouth, Massachusetts. Instead of releasing the timber sloop the Britisher put guns and men on board and dispatched her to look over the situa-tion at Dartmouth. Finding the Indiaman riding at anchor, cargo ashore, the English sailors seized her and made off.

This action so aroused the Dartmouth citizenry that some thirty of them in a vessel mounting two swivel guns set out in hot pursuit. The "royal pirates" were spotted near Martha's Vineyard preparing to load the timber sloop and Indiaman with "a parcel of sheep" for Boston. "The Bedford people resented the conduct in such a manner as to immediately fit out two sloops, with thirty men on board and . . . retook them both with fifteen men on board. In the action there were three of the men-of-war sailors badly wounded, one of whom is since dead. The other thirteen they immediately sent to Taunton Jail."[2]

Still another of the early and colorful incidents fore-shadowing greater efforts against the enemy at sea is worthy of the telling. Ichabod Jones, a Boston loyalist not averse to turning a quick profit, loaded two sloops with provisions which he intended to trade off for wood at the town of

Machias in Maine, then the easternmost shore of Massachusetts Bay colony. Jones had interests and property in Machias, and being well known expected to be able to deal with the hardy woodsmen. But as a precaution, in the event of trouble, his two sloops were accompanied by HBM *Margaretta,* an armed schooner, Midshipman Moore commanding.

Jones arrived in the Machias River on June 2, 1775, and the following day circulated a paper in the town setting forth his proposition, asking cooperation, and soliciting signatures of approval. Following the accustomed pattern of New England local government a town meeting was called to decide whether or not Machias would do business with Jones. To rush along the machinery of direct democracy, Jones caused the *Margaretta* to move so close to the town that "her guns would reach the houses." The majority gave their affirmative; for, as the town clerk later related to the Massachusetts Congress, "the people considered themselves as nearly prisoners of war in the hands of the common enemy."

Having received his "vote of confidence," Jones brought the vessels alongside the wharf and commenced a brisk sale. But with rash vindictiveness he would deal only with those who had cast an "aye" in his favor.

Among those left out were a young fire-eater, Jeremiah O'Brien, and Benjamin Foster, older than O'Brien and a veteran of the Seven Years War. Together with men of like mind from the nearby settlements of Mispecka and Pleasant River who were invited to join the fun, O'Brien and Foster laid plans to seize Jones and Mr. Moore of the *Margaretta.* The strategy was sound for they plotted to take the gentlemen while they were attending church when such a move would be least suspected and the victims quite vulnerable. Tactics must have been faulty because both escaped the trap. Moore scurried to his vessel and Jones to the woods. O'Brien and company marched off to the wharf, helped themselves to the cargo which had been denied them, and took possession of the Jones' sloops.

Meanwhile Midshipman Moore sent a message ashore threatening to pour hot shot on the town if any harm came to Jones or his property. People armed with muskets began to gather on the shore, while some menacingly approached the *Margaretta* in rowboats and canoes. "Surrender to America," shouted one Maine boatsman with more bravado than logic. "Fire, and be damn'd," replied Moore, whereupon a "smart engagement ensued" between Machias canoes and a King's schooner. This was the evening of June 11, 1775.

The morning next, Moore, having had some hours to reflect upon the warm reception his threat to put Machias to the torch had prompted, viewed his duty differently. With tide and wind right, he crowded on all sail to get off for Boston, and in his haste carried away the *Margaretta's* main boom and gaff. Not to be thwarted by this misfortune, the enterprising midshipman helped himself to the spars he needed from a sloop which happened to be nearby, and for good measure took along the vessel's hapless captain, a Mr. Robert Avery of Norwich, Connecticut.

O'Brien's band now pursued a dictum of sound military strategy which teaches that once you have your enemy on the run, keep right after him. Forty men, including O'Brien, armed with "guns, swords, axes, and pitchforks" manned the better of Jones' two craft, and, together with about twenty people under Foster in a small schooner, started the chase. As they sailed, the Americans made a use of the pine board Jones had loaded into his vessel which the Tory could not have foreseen. They threw up hasty breastworks to screen against enemy fire.

The *Margaretta* was apparently a dull sailer, a defect not improved by her jury rig. The distance rapidly closed and "a most obstinate engagement ensued, both sides being determined to conquer or die." Midshipman Moore fell with two balls in the breast, and Mr. Avery, unfortunate victim of circumstance, was also killed. The *Margaretta,* boarded and taken, became the first vessel of the Royal Navy forced to lower her flag to the rebellion.[3]

While the episode of the Dartmouth sloop and the Machias excitement were unfolding, Washington had arrived to take command before Boston. The General at once came face to face with the problem that was to be his constant companion — an acute shortage of munitions of all description, and most particularly powder. "I am now, Sir," he wrote to Governor Nicholas Cooke of Rhode Island, "in strict Confidence to acquaint you, that our Necessities in the Articles of Powder and Lead are so great as to require an immediate supply. I must earnestly intreat you will fall upon some Measure to forward every Pound of each in the Colony which can possibly be spared . . . the Case calls loudly for the most strenuous Exertions of every friend of his Country and does not admit of the least delay. No Quantity, however Small, is beneath notice...." Washington informed the Governor that he had reason to believe in the existence of a considerable powder magazine in Bermuda, and because the inhabitants were not unfriendly to the American cause, it could be had practically for the taking. He proposed that one of the two Rhode Island armed ships be sent south without delay on the urgent mission. Cooke agreed, and the sloop *Katy,* Captain Abraham Whipple, was selected. Whipple carried a spirited appeal from General Washington to the island people, but he was too late, the powder had been removed.[4]

In mid-August 1775 the Massachusetts legislature passed on to Washington a proposal sponsored by the zealots at Machias calling for a punitive expedition accompanied by four armed vessels to be launched against Nova Scotia. Without hesitation, Washington vetoed the plan on the moral basis that the colony of Nova Scotia was not hostile, and for the practical consideration that not "a single ounce" of powder could be spared. He pointed out to the gentlemen of the legis-

lature "our weakness and the Enemy's Strength at Sea."⁵ This
was the General's attitude on August 11, yet within a matter
of days, that is, by the beginning of the next month, he had
reached a decision to spare the ammunition for outfitting
vessels to gamble against the enemy's sea strength.

From headquarters at Cambridge, Washington could watch
the unhindered and regular passage into Boston harbor of
British supply ships laden with the sinews of war. The tempt-
ingly pleasing, and not impossible prospect of capturing some
of these transports and precious cargoes must have crossed the
thoughts of any number of adherents to the American cause.
Whether the Commander in Chief had the scheme put before
him by John Glover, colonel of a Marblehead regiment of sailors and fishermen from which the crews of Washington's
"fleet" were largely drawn, or anyone else, or whether he
acted without outside suggestions, is of little moment. The
fact remains that the General had the vision to see the possibilities and the courage to set the enterprise in motion.

On September 2, 1775, Washington appointed Nicholson
Broughton, of Marblehead, a captain in the Army, and directed
him "to take the command of a detachment of said Army,
and proceed on board the Schooner *Hannah,* at Beverly, lately
fitted-out and equipped with arms, ammunition, and provisions
at the Continental expense." Broughton was ordered to enter
on a cruise immediately "against such vessels as may be found
on the high seas or elsewhere . . . in the service of the Ministerial
Army, and to take and seize all such vessels, laden with soldiers, arms, ammunition, or provisions," and to send them to
the port nearest the American camp. As an added encouragement over and above their pay in the Continental Army,
Captain Broughton, his officers and men would receive one
third of the cargo of each vessel taken, military and naval
stores excepted. The one third was divided as follows: captain,
six shares; first lieutenant, five; second lieutenant, four;
ship's master, three; steward, two; mate, one and a half; gun-

ner's mate and sergeant, one and a half; privates, one share. Never for one moment forgetting the precarious state of his powder resources, Washington cautioned Broughton "to avoid any engagement with any armed vessel . . . the design of this enterprise being to intercept the supplies of the enemy," and "to be extremely careful and frugal of your ammunition; by no means to waste any of it in salutes, or for any purpose, but what is absolutely necessary."[6]

The *Hannah*, running before a fair wind, got to sea in the forenoon of 5 September. Twice British men-of-war chased Broughton back into port but on the 7th he brought a captured ship into Cape Ann harbor. The prize, taken without a fight, was the *Unity*, laden with naval stores, timber, fish and provisions.[7] No powder or guns this time, but a fruitful and extremely cheering two-day cruise.

Heartened by Broughton's easy success, Washington ordered other vessels to be outfitted during the fall and winter. His "fleet" included seven schooners and one brigantine by the time the British evacuated Boston in March 1776.[8]

In spite of troublesome and often mutinous crews which caused Washington much concern, his vessels met with considerable success and occasioned no little discomfort for the enemy.[9] Attesting to that fact we have the account of none other than General Howe who confided to the Earl of Dartmouth: "I am also concerned to observe that the uncertainty of defenceless vessels getting in this harbour is rendered more precarious, by the rebel privateers infesting the bay, who can take the advantage of many inlets on the coast, where His Majesty's ships cannot pursue them, and from whence they can safely avail themselves of any favourable opportunities that offer." Howe recommended that hereafter valuable stores be sent over in ships-of-war with their lower deck guns removed to make cargo space.[10]

The English general's uneasiness was further aggravated by news of the spectacular capture of the fully-loaded ord-

nance ship *Nancy* on November 29, 1775, by Washington's
72-ton schooner *Lee,* Captain John Manley.   Among other
things, the *Nancy* was found to contain two thousand muskets,
31 tons of musket shot, three thousand round shot, barrels of
powder, and a 13-inch brass mortar.[11] It has been estimated
that the quantity of munitions in this one prize alone would
have taken the colonists 18 months to manufacture.[12]   An
English poet lamented the loss in verse.

> Retarded by a tedious long delay,
> The live stock perished on the blust'ring sea,
> And transport ships became provincial prey.
> Laden with apparatus for the train,
> Thrice strove the *Nancy* Boston's port to gain;
> Oft as she came, the wind unfriendly grew,
> (A rough opposing storm against her blew:)
> The *Cerberus* for her protection sail'd;
> But in th' attempt the royal frigate fail'd
> In darkness wrapp'd by tempest rudely tost,
> They parted, and the precious prize was lost;
> This through the royal army spread a damp;
> And fill'd with pleasure the provincial camp.[13]

Colonel Moylan has left us a picture of the pleasure that
"fill'd" the provincial camp. The "G. R.", *George Rex,* em-
bossed on the brass mortar was scratched out, and replaced by
"G. W." for George Washington as the 27-hundred pound
monster was readied to speak out against its erstwhile masters.
"Such universal joy ran through the whole camp as if each
grasped victory in his hand; to crown the glorious scene there
one truly ludicrous, which was Old Put [General Putnam]
mounted on the large mortar, which was fixed in its bed for the
occasion, with a bottle of rum in his hand, standing parson to
christen, while god-father Mifflin gave it the name of Congress. The huzzas on the occasion, I dare say, were heard
through all the territories of our most gracious sovereign in
this province."[14]

Captain Manley, who had taken the *Nancy,* was the most successful of the army captains detailed to sea duty by Washington. Consequently, he enjoyed the General's favor, and was appointed Commodore of the "fleet" on the first of the year 1776 with the hope that some of his victorious ways would rub off on the other captains. "Your general good Behaviour since you first engaged in the Service, merits mine and your Country's Thanks," read Washington's words of commendation. "You may be assured that every Attention will be paid to any reasonable Request of yours, and that you shall have the Command of a stronger Vessel of War. . . I wish you could inspire the Captains of the other armed schooners under your command with some of your Activity and Industry."[15] Manley's early reputation, public acclaim, and Washington's backing would not be forgotten several years later when fortune was not so kind, and the captain faced a naval court martial.

At the time Manley captured the ordnance ship he was about 42 years old and a mariner of long experience. Like so many seafaring New England men who served in the Revolution and then quietly slipped back to their maritime interests, his pre-war years are shrouded in the deepest obscurity. Although some naval historians have called Manley an Englishman, his biographer, Isaac Greenwood, and an early 19th century writer contend that he was probably born in Boston.[16] At any rate, Manley lived in that city for many years prior to the war. When he was married in 1763 to a Miss Hannah Cheevers in Trinity Church, he was captain of a schooner plying the Boston-West Indian trade.[17] He is said to have been a resident of Marblehead when Colonel Glover brought him to Washington's attention, and it may well be that Manley removed his family to that town as the British occupied Boston. His subsequent career as a captain in the Continental Navy is of particular interest.

Washington in seizing the initiative and outfitting cruisers to prey upon the enemy's supply ships acted under the general authority vested in him as Commander in Chief of the Army. He sought no further approval from Congress for his action. The armed vessels were an integral part of the military operations intended to fill his Army's desperate needs and to hasten the British departure from Boston. His commanders were captains in the Army, and their crews were privates, similarly drawn from the military ranks. It seems clear, therefore, that Washington did not intend to create a navy, yet he did just that. The vessels he commissioned were the first to be outfitted at the Continental expense by an official representing the Congress, and to sail for the good of the Continent as a whole. A convincing, and, it seems to this writer, a sound claim can be made that George Washington was not only the father of his country, but has equally strong title to being recognized as the founder of the United States Navy. The General was completely aware of "the great advantage the enemy have . . . by being masters of the sea."[18] But he also recognized, and acted on, the real possibility of hurting the lion by snapping at his flanks; thereby drawing the operational pattern of American naval action throughout the conflict for independence.

While Washington on his own was setting a naval war in motion in the north, Congress in Philadelphia was proceeding slowly and with extreme caution. In mid-1775 a majority in Congress could not accept the break with England as irreparable; the Declaration of Independence was a year away. The artificial line was still drawn between evil ministers and the well-intentioned but duped sovereign, George III, to whom the conservative colonial element looked for a reconciliation. A deliberative body in this frame of mind was now presented with a motion to establish a Continental Naval force.

As might be expected, the movement in Congress for a navy emanated from New England. More specifically, it was the representatives from Rhode Island, a colony which was experiencing the unpleasantness of British cruisers in Narragansett Bay, and had already outfitted two vessels to strike back. The Rhode Island Assembly meeting on the third Monday in August 1775, that is, the 26th of the month, voted:

> That this Colony most ardently wish to see the former friendship, harmony, and intercourse between Britain and these colonies restored, and a happy and lasting connection between both Countries, upon terms of just and equal liberty; and will concur with the other Colonies in all proper measures for obtaining these desirable blessings: And as every principle, divine and human, require us to obey that great and fundamental law of nature, self-preservation, until peace shall be restored upon constitutional principles, this Colony will most heartily exert the whole power of Government, in conjunction with the other Colonies, for carrying on this just and necessary war, and bringing the same to a happy issue. And amongst other measures for obtaining this most desirable purpose, this Assembly is persuaded that the building and equipping an *American* Fleet, as soon as possible, would greatly and essentially conduce to the preservation of the lives, liberty and property of the good people of these Colonies; and therefore instruct their Delegates to use their whole influence, at the ensuing Congress, for building at the Continental expense, a Fleet of sufficient force for the protection of these Colonies, and for employing them in such manner and places as will most effectually annoy our enemies, and contribute to the common defence of these *Colonies*: And they are also instructed to use all their influence for carrying on the war in the most vigorous manner, until peace, liberty and safety be restored and secured to these Colonies upon an equitable and permanent basis.[19]

After passing this revolutionary resolve which is a truly significant pronouncement in the genesis of United States naval power, the Rhode Island Assembly shouted "God save the King," and adjourned.

Congress reconvened on September 5, 1775, after a month's absence from Philadelphia, but with no quorum present, adjournment was called daily until the 13th of the month.[20] A member of the Rhode Island delegation, probably Samuel Ward, presented the naval instructions to Congress on

October 3.[21] Consideration was deferred until the 7th at which time the proposal was debated and condemned by Samuel Chase of Maryland as "the maddest idea in the world to think of building an American fleet . . . we should mortgage the whole Continent." Christopher Gadsden of South Carolina, although not entirely hostile, thought the Rhode Island plan went too far.[22] There was "light skirmishing" on the floor but the New England members, exhibiting their political acumen, did not press for a vote. The Rhode Island motion was still tabled November 16 when Samuel Ward wrote to his brother: "Our instructions for an American fleet has been long upon the table. When it was first presented, it was looked upon as perfectly chimerical; but gentlemen now consider it in a very different light. It is this day to be taken into consideration, and I have great hopes of carrying it. Dr. Franklin, Colonel Lee, the two Adamses and many others, will support it."[23] Actually Congress did not act on the Rhode Island resolve until the 13th of December.

To follow the thread of more pressing events in Congress relative to authorizing armed vessels, we will leave the oft-postponed Rhode Island plan temporarily and go back to the beginning of October 1775. On the fifth of that month the members of Congress had information placed before them from London concerning the sailing of two unarmed brigs for Quebec loaded with powder and other munitions. A motion was made and seconded that a special committee of three be named to prepare a plan immediately for intercepting the two vessels. This action coming within two days of the Rhode Island naval motion gave rise to heated debate along rather clearly defined sectional lines — New England and the South.

Edward Rutledge of South Carolina with all his great eloquence voiced the opposition. The idea of an attempt on the Quebec bound vessels was represented as "the most wild, visionary, mad project that ever had been imagined. It was an infant taking a mad bull by his horns." Furthermore, it would "ruin the character and corrupt the morals of all our seamen. It would make them selfish, piratical, mercenary, bent wholly upon plunder, etc., etc." On the other side the great advantages of distressing the enemy, supplying ourselves, and beginning a system of maritime and naval operations were represented in colors as glowing and animating.[24] The motion carried by a small majority, and Silas Deane of Connecticut, John Langdon of New Hampshire, and John Adams from Massachusetts were named a committee.[25]

The members of this committee obviously had some prior understanding, for they met briefly and on the very same day presented a plan. They recommended that a letter be sent to Washington at once apprising him of the two powder-laden enemy brigs and directing that he apply to the Council of Massachusetts for permission to use that colony's two armed vessels for the purpose of going after them. Similar letters were to go off to Governors Cooke of Rhode Island and Trumbull of Connecticut asking naval assistance for the enterprise. All vessels while engaged in the business were to be "on the continental risque and pay," and their crews to receive "one half of the value of the prizes by them taken."[26] This proposition, like the initial motion to form a committee, touched off a flood of rhetoric. But it passed, again by a slim margin — maritime New England triumphant! It is of interest to note here that on this date, October 5, 1775, just one month to the day after Captain Broughton put to sea in the first of the vessels commissioned by Washington, the legislators resolved to have the General request the use of Massachusetts ships. This seems to indicate that Congress had no knowledge of Washington's naval activity.[27]

After clearing the first barrier, the naval enthusiasts moved forward with more certainty. Friday, October 13, Congress voted to fit out two swift vessels "with all possible despatch" for a three months' cruise eastward for "intercepting such transports as may be laden with warlike stores and other supplies for our enemies."[28] Another three man committee was named to estimate the expense involved. Deane and Langdon were again designated, but John Adams' place was taken by the South Carolinian, Christopher Gadsden; an apparent bid for southern support without sacrificing New England control. Simultaneously with Congressional action on this committee's report, October 30, two additional vessels were authorized. This time the objective was not limited to intercepting enemy transports but the ships were "to be employed in such manner, for the protection and defence of the united Colonies, as the Congress shall hereafter direct." The committee, which now became known as the Naval Committee, was increased to seven by the addition of Stephen Hopkins, John Adams, Joseph Hewes of North Carolina, and Richard Henry Lee of Virginia; a membership of four Yankees and three southerners.[29]

By the end of October 1775, four vessels had been authorized, and the American colonies committed to a definite policy of naval warfare. The lengthy debates in Congress on the state of trade, and enforcement of the Continental Association led even the more cautious members to realize that the schism was not healing but widening daily, and that the issue with England would have to be fought to a conclusion. This, combined with the presence of a British fleet off the Carolinas, and the marauding expeditions along the coasts of Virginia and Maryland by vessels under the roundly despised Governor Dunmore, brought southern delegates to the New England point of view and made passage of naval legislation possible.

The Rhode Island plan for an American fleet, which had been assailed as visionary and fantastic during the first week in October, gained favor and finally on December 13 was acted upon. Perhaps conscious of the date on which the action was voted, but more certainly influenced by the number of colonies in revolt, Congress ordered that 13 ships be "fitted for the sea," five of 32 guns, five of 28 guns, and three of

24 guns. These vessels were not going to be converted merchantmen, but built from the keel up as ships-of-war; one in
New Hampshire, two in Massachusetts Bay, in Rhode Island
two, in Connecticut one, in New York two, in Pennsylvania
four, and in Maryland one, at an average cost of almost 67
thousand dollars per ship.[30]

This was no inconsiderable expenditure, and the naval
armament provided for, if realized and brought to bear against
the enemy, would comprise a force and weight of gun metal
which could not be ignored even by the Mistress of the Seas.
The action was illustrative of how far, and in what direction,
Congress had traveled during the few short months of the
fall session, 1775.

Not even the brashest revolutionary could visualize
America aspiring to a naval force capable of seriously or per-
manently contesting British control of the sea. Yet, the representatives of the United Colonies responded to a naval impulse
which had erupted at Machias in June, and was given form
by General Washington in the waters around Boston.

CHAPTER II

SHIPS, CAPTAINS, AND NAVAL ADMINISTRATION

*The Conduct of the Affairs of a Navy as well
as those of an Army, We are yet to learn.*

WILLIAM ELLERY

EACH EVENING after the close of the day's regular session
seven members of Congress moved through the gathering dusk
and sharp air to a Philadelphia tavern, where, gathered around
the table in a private chamber, they constituted the Naval
Committee under the chairmanship of Stephen Hopkins, the
aged and keen onetime governor of Rhode Island. At these
nightly meetings, reality was given to the October 1775 Congressional decision to arm four vessels with all possible haste as
a striking force against the Crown's commerce. Merchant
vessels were purchased and their metamorphosis to men-of-war
set in motion, the first officers were appointed, and the poli-
cies and regulations for administration of the Continental Navy
were formulated. The Naval Committee accomplished this
with creditable speed during the closing months of 1775, and
John Adams ascribed to himself "at least as great a share in
producing them as any man living or dead."[1]

Adams cherished his association with the Naval Committee
as "the pleasantest part of my labors for the four years I spent
in Congress from 1774 to 1778."[2] Because of his faithfulness
to a diary and fondness for reporting, a glimpse into the
Committee room's relaxed atmosphere has been preserved.

17

Among the Committee members, Adams remembered Mr. Lee and Mr. Gadsden as cheerful sensible men, and he was completely captivated by the charm of Governor Hopkins, "Whose experience and judgment were very useful." When the order of business was ended for the evening, the sage Rhode Islander of more than seventy years would keep his comrades enthralled until midnight. "His custom was to drink nothing all day, nor till eight o'clock in the evening, and then his beverage was Jamaica spirit and water. It gave him wit, humor, anecdotes, science and learning. He had read Greek, Roman, and British history, and was familiar with English poetry, particularly Pope, Thompson, and Milton, and the flow of his soul made all his reading our own, and seemed to bring to recollection in all of us, all we had ever read. Hopkins never drank to excess, but all he drank was immediately not only converted into wit, sense, knowledge, and good humor but inspired us with similar qualities."[3]

Congress authorized its Naval Committee to draw on the Continental Treasury in an amount not exceeding one hundred thousand dollars to purchase and outfit the four vessels. The Committee initially turned north for suitable ships. Silas Deane journeyed to New York and Connecticut, and Adams wrote to Elbridge Gerry in Massachusetts on November 5 to inquire, "What ships, brigantines, schooners, etc., are to be found in any port of the Province, to be sold or hired out, which will be suitable for armed vessels. What their tonnage, the depth of water they draw, their breadth, their decks, etc., and to whom they belong and what is their age." Anticipating favorable Congressional action on the more extensive Rhode Island naval plan by more than a month, Adams asked, "what places in our Province are most secure and best accomodated for building new vessels of force, in case a measure of that kind should be thought of."[4] As it turned out, the Committee did not have to look any farther than the nearby Delaware

River. The four ships were bought in Philadelphia, a decision probably dictated by a combination of immediate availability and pressure from the local shipowner interests.

The first vessel purchased into the Continental Navy was the practically new *Black Prince* of about 450 tons, owned by Robert Morris among others, and commanded during her merchant service by John Barry, both of whom were marked to play leading roles in naval affairs. The *Black Prince* was rechristened *Alfred* to honor the founder of the British Navy, "the greatest navy that ever existed." Even the passions of war did not erase the rebellious colonials' pride in English naval heritage. Within several weeks the *Alfred* was followed into the naval service by the *Columbus*, "after the discoverer of this quarter of the globe"; the *Cabot*, "for the discoverer of this northern part of the continent"; and the *Andrew Doria*, "in memory of the great Genoese admiral."[5]

The *Alfred* and *Columbus*, both "clumsey and crank," were ship-rigged and larger vessels than the brigs *Cabot* and *Andrew Doria*. Virtually nothing is known about the dimensions of the ships, with the exception of the *Cabot* which when captured in 1777 was considered such a fine craft that she was taken into the Royal Navy. English records show that the *Cabot* was a 14 gun brig, manned by a crew of 80, length of deck 74'9½", on the keel 53' 7", beam 24'8", depth in hold 11'4", and displacement 189 tons.[6]

The Naval Committee was indeed fortunate to have John Barry and a young shipbuilder and naval architect, Joshua Humphreys, direct the numerous conversions required to make plodding cargo vessels into a naval force.[7] Hulls were swept clean, altered and strengthened, sides were pierced for gun ports, new masts were stepped, all were rerigged to improve sailing qualities, ammunition and ships stores were gathered and placed on board.

Outfitting proceeded under capable guidance while the Naval Committee and Congress were framing the administrative practices and regulations which are inherent in any naval establishment. The matter of prize shares had been decided at the same time money to procure and arm the vessels was voted. Exclusive of wages, encouragement for officers and men in the Continental Navy was placed at "one half of all ships of war made prizes of by them, and one third of all transport vessels."[8]

The legal ramifications of libeling prize ships and cargoes being brought in by his armed schooners gave Washington cause for thought. On November 8, 1775, he wrote to the President of Congress that these "Captures point out the necessity of establishing proper Courts without loss of time for the decision of Property and the legality of Seizures: otherwise I may be Involved in inextricable difficulties."[9] The General's letter was laid before Congress Friday, November 17, and referred to a committee for examination and recommendation. When the committee reported back on the floor a week later, it had expanded upon Washington's request for a system of admiralty courts, and had used the occasion to prescribe the nature and extent of America's naval war against Britain. Almost apologetically, and as if compelled to justify a very distasteful step, the commitee report opened with an exposition of the "unwarrantable violences" and "unprovoked injuries" committed by the "king's ships" which led Congress to authorize armed vessels. All enemy men-of-war captured by Continental vessels were declared fair game and legitimate prizes. Cargoes could be taken out of transport vessels, but the ships were to be released unless owned by American loyalists (this restriction was eliminated in December, and the seizure of merchant vessels authorized regardless of ownership). Wanton piracy was not to be countenanced. Only ship captains holding commissions from Congress or its authorized agents could cruise and take prizes. Colonial legislatures were urged to set up prize courts as soon as possible or to use existing judicial machinery for the purpose. The committee concluded by placing a legal stamp of approval on Washington's excursion into sea warfare. This lengthy naval policy report won approval November 25, 1775.[10]

On the following Tuesday, the legislators had under consideration still another essential segment of naval organization, *Rules for the Regulation of the Navy of the United Colonies.* The first set of naval regulations spread before Congress by the Naval Committee late in 1775 was the work of John Adams, drawing freely on the rules governing the British Navy. They are a picturesque and concise recital of the duties, rights, and obligations of captain and crew on board ships of the Continental Navy, ranging over such widely scattered topics as divine services at sea, lashes with the "cat," and daily pork ration for seamen. A pay table was included which scales from 32 dollars a month for a captain down to 6-2/3 dollars for an able seaman or Marine private.[11]

"You will perceive by a letter from the Committee dated yesterday, that they have pitched upon you to take the Command of a Small Fleet," wrote Stephen Hopkins on November 6 to his brother Esek in Rhode Island.[12] In "pitching upon" Esek Hopkins, the Naval Committee was acting under authority granted by Congress "to agree with such officers and seamen, as are proper to man and command the vessels of war."[13] December 22, 1775, the Committee submitted to Congress the names of the persons appointed by them to be the first officers in the Continental Navy. Esek Hopkins, Commander in Chief of the Fleet, led the list, followed by Captains Dudley Saltonstall of the *Alfred,* Abraham Whipple, the *Columbus,* Nicholas Biddle, the *Andrew Doria,* and John Burroughs Hopkins of the *Cabot.* Five 1st lieutenants, five 2nd lieutenants, and three 3rd lieutenants were also named. The Commander in Chief's pay was fixed at 125 dollars a month, just under four times that of a captain.[14]

Commodore Esek Hopkins, 57 years old in 1775, impressed General Henry Knox as "antiquated in figure" but "shrewd and sensible." He reminded Knox of the celebrated Dutch Admiral Van Tromp, and apparently carried away with boundless enthusiasm, the General continued panegyrically that he "should have taken him for an angel only he swore now and then."[15] It may be doubted, however, that the Naval Committee weighed the angelic qualities of Esek Hopkins before naming him to be senior naval officer in the Continental service. He was a member of one of the oldest Rhode Island families, descending from Thomas Hopkins, who migrated with Roger Williams from Massachusetts Bay to Providence Plantations. Throughout colonial Rhode Island history, the name Hopkins appears conspicuously in public affairs. Esek, the sixth of William and Ruth Hopkins' nine children, was born on the family farm in a section of Providence later included in the town of Scituate. Giving truth to the common belief that "Rhode Islander" was synonymous with "born sailor," Esek and three of his brothers took to the sea.[16] He rose to master mariner, and commanded the vessels of Moses Brown and leading Providence merchants. During the French and Indian War, Hopkins cruised as a privateer with marked success. When ashore, he took an active hand in Rhode Island politics, and aggressively sponsored the cause of education.[17] Several times he was elected to the General Assembly, but seemed never able to turn his back on the sea for very long. By chance Hopkins was on shore when the Revolution opened and was at once pressed into service, along with other mariners familiar with cannon, to prepare a heavy battery for the defense of Providence. When the battery was completed it became known as the Fox Hill fortification, and Hopkins commanded it. Shortly thereafter, on October 4, 1775, he was commissioned Brigadier General by Rhode Island and ordered to take a militia force to the southern part of the colony to protect Newport against a British squadron lying off the town. It was while he was at Newport that Esek received the letter from his brother with news of his selection as Commander in Chief.

Rhode Island men continued well in the forefront among the first naval captains — two out of the four. Captain John Burroughs Hopkins was the first of ten children born to the Commodore and Desire (Burroughs) Hopkins. Very little is known of his activities prior to service in the Continental Navy, save as a youngster he followed his father to sea, and that in 1768 he married a cousin, Sarah Harris. The marriage was childless. Young Hopkins early identified himself with the Whig element in Rhode Island, and was one of the audacious band who boarded the British revenue cutter *Gaspee* in 1772 and burned her to the water's edge.[18] Abraham Whipple led this violent assault on royal authority, antedating the celebrated tea party in Boston by more than a year.

Captain Abraham Whipple, like Hopkins, was a son of one of Providence's prominent families dating from an original Rhode Island proprietor.[19] He was a neighbor and staunch friend of the Commodore with whom he shared a singularly similar maritime career. Both were active in the lucrative West Indian trade. Whipple had served under Esek Hopkins in privateers during the French war, and had himself been a commander in the same service. At one time Whipple captained the letter of marque *Game Cock,* a name which perhaps may have described the captain better than the ship. A water color in the possession of the Rhode Island Historical Society portrays Whipple as rather short and definitely heavy set. He has a whimsical look about his eyes and mouth, and a heavy touch of humor is in evidence.[20] (See Frontispiece). He looks like the kind of man who might be expected to place himself at the head of a group of hearties determined on direct action to rid themselves of a nuisance. And that is exactly what he did one June night in 1772.

An English schooner, the *Gaspee,* was on patrol duty in Narragansett Bay carrying out the home government's avowed intention to enforce the revenue and navigation laws. Lieutenant Dudingston, the *Gaspee's* commanding officer, determined to carry out his orders to the letter by stopping and searching all ships entering or leaving Rhode Island, was making himself particularly obnoxious to the commercial and maritime community in Providence. Profits decreased in proportion to the vigilance with which the collection of fees was enforced. The *Gaspee* grounded during the day of June 9 presenting Whipple and his friends with a splendid opportunity to carry out their incendiary designs. Slipping silently down the Bay in whale boats, they captured and destroyed the stranded schooner. Whipple, fully aware of the consequences, quickly sought the sanctuary of a voyage to sea. Esek Hopkins cautioned him to stay away until the tempest calmed: "There is now setting a Court of Commissioners setting at Newport in order to take up and send home to England for trial all those that were concerned in burning the schooner *Gaspee* . . . What will be the consequence I can't tell you, but I hope all those concerned will not come by water into this port before the times alter."[21]

Three years later when Whipple was commodore of Rhode Island's two ship navy, he was again making his presence felt by capturing a tender of the British frigate *Rose*. The infuriated British Admiral, Sir James Wallace, well remembered the *Gaspee* incident and wrote — "Sir: You Abraham Whipple on the 10th of June 1772 burned his majesty's vessel the *Gaspee* and I will hang you at the yard arm." The American reportedly answered: "Sir James Wallace Sir Always catch a man before you hang him."[22] Whipple did not fall into British hands until 1780, at Charleston where he was granted his parole instead of the noose.

Dudley Saltonstall, captain of the *Alfred,* was a native of Connecticut. Like the Rhode Island officers, Saltonstall was a son of one of the most influential families in New London and Connecticut colony. He was a direct descendant of Sir Richard Saltonstall, patentee of Massachusetts Bay Colony, and the grandson of Gurdon Saltonstall, clergyman and governor of Connecticut from 1707 until his death in 1724. Governor Saltonstall was active in the movement which led to the establishment of the Collegiate School later renamed Yale College.[23]

Graduating classes at Yale usually included at least one Saltonstall, but not Captain Dudley who chose sailoring rather than academic and clerical training. He was a privateersman in war and a merchant captain in peace. Just as Esek Hopkins had briefly turned artilleryman for the defense of Providence, Saltonstall, at the start of the Revolution, took charge of the battery on the common at New London.

No portrait of Dudley Saltonstall is known to exist. But on the back of a privateer's commission dated 21 May 1781, issued by Governor Trumbull of Connecticut, the following description is found: "age 44 years, Heighth 5 ft. 9 in., Sandy Colored hair, light complexion, light hazel eyes and thick set."[24] His fellow captain, Nicholas Biddle, saw him as "a Sensible indefatigable Morose Man."[25] To his 1st lieutenant and executive officer in the *Alfred*, John Paul Jones, he was a "sleepy gentleman," as well as being "ill-natured and narrow-minded."[26]

Only non-New Englander on the original naval list was the young Philadelphian, Captain Nicholas Biddle, whose brilliantly promising career was cut short on March 7, 1777, when his command, the *Randolph*, blew up during an engagement with His Majesty's 64 gun ship *Yarmouth*.

New England, and especially Rhode Island, domination of the naval scene in 1775 is most readily apparent in the choice of commodore and the four captains. As the wily Stephen Hopkins hypnotized his fellow Naval Committeemen with poetry, anecdote, and grog, it is not difficult to visualize how brother Esek was "pitched upon" to be senior officer, and nephew John Burroughs Hopkins to take command of one of the vessels. The selection of Abraham Whipple not only kept appointments in Rhode Island, but also in the Hopkins family. Whipple's wife was Sarah Hopkins, a niece of the Naval Committee chairman and the Commodore. Dudley Saltonstall was the brother-in-law of Silas Deane, Naval Committee member from Connecticut. John Adams tells us frankly that "At the solicitation of Mr. Deane, we appointed his brother-in-law, Captain Saltonstall."[27] Biddle, the sole representative from outside New England, was well known in Philadelphia, and not without his champions and influence. His brother Edward was in Congress, and other relatives were on the Pennsylvania Committee of Safety.[28]

That influence, whether family, political, geographical, or a combination, was the dominant consideration in naming the Commodore and captains does not alter the fact that the Naval Committee or Congress would have been hard pressed to find a more experienced and better qualified group. All had long experience at sea, and privateering ventures against the French left them no strangers when the cannon spoke. Nicholas Biddle brought the advantages of a tour of duty in the British Navy, where, it may be mentioned, he was a messmate of young Horatio Nelson.

It would seem well at this point, before following the New England captains through the first naval war in United States history, to consider the several administrative committees and boards which governed the affairs of the Continental Navy throughout its existence. The orders, records, and correspondence of these administrators in large measure make it possible to piece together the operational history of the Continental Navy.

The duties assigned to the Naval Committee, which amounted to laying the foundation for a navy, were completed by the beginning of 1776, at which time Commodore Hopkins' fleet was manned and ready for sea. On December 14, 1775, the day after Congress responded to the long delayed Rhode Island instructions, and voted to build 13 frigates, a committee of 13 members of Congress, one from each colony, was appointed to carry out the naval program.[29] This Marine Committee, as it was called, administered the business of the Continental Navy, and directed the operation of the vessels for four years until December 1779. The membership of the original Naval Committee was absorbed into the larger Marine Committee, which, like its predecessor, was presided over by a chairman or president. John Hancock of Massachusetts and Henry Laurens of South Carolina occupied the Marine Committee chair while they served as president of Congress. Since the Marine Committee was a Congressional committee it performed both executive and legislative functions, just as the parent body embodied within itself both spheres of government. As an executive agent of Congress, the Marine Committee was charged with putting naval enactments into effect and giving commands to that end. Acting in a legislative capacity, the Committee made reports to Congress and recommended legislation on all matter of naval subjects from pensions to uniforms.

It has already been noted that the building locations for the 13 frigates were scattered from Maryland to New Hampshire. Local agents were engaged by the Marine Committee to supervise the work at the construction sites. Nevertheless, building did not always progress satisfactorily, and it was impossible for the Marine Committee sitting in Philadelphia to keep abreast of all the details demanding administrative action. Late in 1776 the Committee, unable to cope with the vastly increased naval requirements, recommended and Congress approved "the immediate appointment" of three persons, "well skilled in maritime affairs . . . to execute the business of the navy, under the direction of the Marine Committee."[30] Thus, the Marine Committee was given permanent assistants to take over a large share of the administrative load. Three qualified individuals were appointed, all from the Philadelphia vicinity, each with the title of Commissioner, and collectively designated the Navy Board of the Middle Department. Of prime interest to us here is the authorization on April 19, 1777, of a second group, this one for the New England states; the Navy Board of the Eastern Department. Members of this board were to receive $1500 annual salary, "to reside at or in the neighborhood of Boston," and as directed by the Marine Committee, to "have the superintendance of all naval and marine affairs of these United States, within the four eastern states."[31] John Deshon, of New London, Connecticut, William Vernon of Providence, Rhode Island, and James Warren from Plymouth, Massachusetts, were selected by the Marine Committee from among those John Adams suggested to be the Commissioners of the Navy Board Eastern Department with headquarters at Boston.[32]

The duties of both Navy Boards were similar, but the Boston Board enjoyed greater authority and freedom of action because of its physical separation from Congress and the Marine Committee. The Navy Boards represented the Marine Committee in their areas, and saw to it that the naval resolves of Congress and the orders of the Marine Committee were circulated and complied with. Supervision of building or purchase, manning, provisioning, and repairing of vessels were the Boards' responsibility. They were required to keep statistical records on ships and report their movements, as well as maintain a register of officers, seamen, and marines in their districts.

The Marine Committee furnished blank commissions which the Boards used to appoint warrant officers, and very often the naval lieutenants. Names of prospective captains were submitted by the Boards to the Marine Committee, and Boards were empowered to convene courts of inquiry and courts martial. It is significant that in authorizing the Navy Boards, Congress went outside its own membership for the first time to organize agencies of naval administration.[33]

Beginning in April 1776 resident prize agents were appointed in the more important ports to receive captures sent in by Continental vessels, and to manage the legal details of condemnation, sale, and distribution of prize money to the crews. Prize agents were required to make quarterly reports of their transactions to the Marine Committee. More often than not the prize agents doubled as Continental agents in which capacity they represented Congress in other than naval affairs. Although the prize agents may be considered as responsible to the Navy Boards, very frequently they dealt directly with the Marine Committee and *vice versa;* a practice not calculated to lend itself to harmony and efficient administration.

As the war progressed and strains increased, the acute shortcomings of administration by legislative committee became more and more evident. The Marine Committee was much criticized for inefficiency and slowness. Yet the fault lay not with the Committee but within the system. Service on the Marine Committee was an added duty for Congressmen already heavily burdened. All too often they brought with them to the Committee room little interest and no knowledge of maritime affairs. Moreover in addition to suffering from a dearth of technical skill, the Committee was further hampered by a membership subject to frequent change as delegates entered or left Congress. Robert Morris, John Jay, and William Ellery, were conspicuous among those who urged that the Marine Committee be replaced by a responsible and competent Board of Admiralty patterned on the British naval system. Congress established a Board of War in 1777 and a Board of Treasury in the summer of 1779, thus paving the way for a Board of Admiralty which was voted in October 1779.

The Board of Admiralty's authority and duties were the same as the superseded Marine Committee. There were to be five members on the Board, each from a different state — three appointed commissioners, and two members of Congress. This is a composition which reflects that Congress was not yet ready to turn loose all the strings of executive power. The Board of Admiralty could maintain its office and carry on business only in the town or city where Congress was sitting. Clerks would be appointed by the Board but the secretary, a more important position, was named by Congress. It was expected, but not realized, that this reorganization which placed full time paid commissioners on the governing body of the Navy would bring efficiency.

At the end of 1779, as the Board of Admiralty was being formed, the fortunes of the Continental Navy were low indeed. Few were anxious to ride a dead horse, and Congress experienced insurmountable difficulty in finding three men willing to serve as Admiralty commissioners. Francis Lewis of New York and William Ellery of Rhode Island accepted appointments, but it proved impossible to fill the third vacancy.

After an inauspicious start, the Board of Admiralty staggered through an inglorious tenure lasting until mid-1781. If anything the Board of Admiralty proved more dependent on Congress than its predecessor, the Marine Committee, had been. The legislators were disposed to grant more freedom of action to an administrative group drawn entirely from Congressional membership than they were to one including "outsiders." Congressional members of the Board of Admiralty were at best irregular in their attendance with the result that all too often vital naval business was suspended for lack of a quorum. It was a thankless and uncompensating job for Commissioners Ellery and Lewis, but both stuck it out until July 1781 before resigning. The naval department was then left without executive direction.

By 1780 exponents of the single executive system, Washington and Hamilton among them, were running ahead of the Partick Henry, Samuel Adams school, which above all feared a concentration of power, and cherished government by committees and boards. In January 1781 Congress voted to appoint a Secretary for Foreign Affairs, and a month later, February 7, 1781, resolved that there should be a Superintendent of Finance, a Secretary of War, and a Secretary of Marine.

Finding a qualified individual willing to be Secretary of Marine proved equally as difficult as getting commissioners for the Board of Admiralty. Congress offered the place to Major General Alexander McDougall of New York. He politely refused on the patriotic grounds of a desire to remain in the field with the Army. No further effort seems to have been made to name a Secretary of Marine, most probably because the Continental Navy had dwindled to insignificance.

Robert Morris became steward of an empty treasury in May of 1781 as Superintendent of Finance. The control of naval affairs fell to Morris by default while the defunct Board of Admiralty expired without replacement. After being *de facto* head of the naval department during the summer, Morris was officially vested with dual maritime and financial responsibility when Congress named him Agent of Marine on September 7, 1781. He filled this post until November 1784. Morris was eminently well qualified for the assignment by experience and training. He had owned numerous merchant vessels, including the *Alfred,* and was an active member of the Marine Committee in 1776 and 1777. At a time when the war was drawing to a close, and the knotty problems of settling naval accounts and claims were multiplying, Morris brought to the naval department a business-like executive authority which it had heretofore not known.

A few final lines are in order about still another arm of naval administration, namely, the marine duties performed by the American representatives resident in France. Throughout the war, Continental vessels and American privateers sailed forth from Nantes, Bordeaux, Dunkirk, and other French ports against enemy commerce. Prior to 1778, while France was nominally neutral, His Most Christian Majesty did not place the royal seal on Americans using his country for a naval base, but the practice was winked at and the embarrassment to Britain thoroughly enjoyed.

Silas Deane at first, and later Franklin, Arthur Lee, and John Adams were involved in "the renting, purchase, and building of naval vessels; officering, manning and fitting out of vessels; the directing of cruises; the purchase of naval supplies; the disciplining of officers; the paying of officers and crews; the disposing of prizes; the devising of naval plans; the commissioning of privateers; the caring for naval prisoners and the negotiating for their exchange; and the disseminating of naval intelligence."[34] Although an American naval board or office as such never formally existed in Paris, all the duties of same, and more, were performed by our representatives at the French Court.

It has been intended that the foregoing paragraphs devoted to a review of the administrative agencies which founded, directed, and shaped, the course of the Continenal Navy will prove a valuable aid to clearer understanding of the chapters to follow as the naval careers of the captains from New England are charted. And now we must return in time to the winter of 1775-76, and to Commodore Hopkins' fleet in the ice-choked river Delaware.

CHAPTER III

THE FIRST FLEET CRUISE — 1776

---

*No great things are to be expected at first, but
out of a little a great deal may grow.*

JOHN ADAMS

LIEUTENANT JAMES JOSIAH penned the first entry in the brig
Andrew Doria's journal, Thursday, January 4, 1776: "At 2
P.M. Cast off from ye. Warf In Company with ye. Commodore
Ship Alfred, Columbus & Cabot, Light airs from ye. West-
ward and much Ice in ye. River, at 6 Do. Came to at ye.
Pierse at Liberty Iland, and was there Detain'd by ye. Ice till
the 17th."[1] A Philadelphia loyalist drew the same scene for
Molyneux Shuldham, Vice Admiral of the Blue and Commander
in Chief of His Britannic Majesty's ships in North America:
"This day about one o'Clock sailed the Ship Alfred and the Ship
Columbus with Two Brigs, . . . Hopkins commands the Alfred,
she has Yellow sides, her Head the figure of a Man, English
Colours but more Striped; — The Columbus is all Black,
except white bottom, with no Head, Commanded by one
Whipple. . . . A Sloop of 12 Guns is to sail this Evening, she
is a Sloop that came from Rhode Island."[2]

The Rhode Island sloop noted by the British informer
was none other than the *Katy* which we first met in the summer of 1775 when, at the urging of General Washington, she
was sent on a fruitless cruise to Bermuda in search of gunpowder.[3] Whipple sailed the *Katy* from Providence loaded with

Yankee seamen for the Commodore's fleet. While she was in passage to Philadelphia, on December 2, 1775, Congress directed the Naval Committee "to employ the armed sloop," and to "despatch her forthwith to aid the marine business to the southward."[4] Thus, upon arrival the *Katy* was promptly taken into the Continental Navy and renamed *Providence.* Should the reader conclude that by choosing this name the Naval Committee was courting beneficent Divine favor, let John Adams tell us how she was named "for the town where she was purchased, the residence of Governor Hopkins, and his brother Esek, whom we appointed first captain."[5] Command of the *Providence* was given to John Hazard.

Prior to his appearance in Philadelphia in December 1775 the record is silent on Captain John Hazard. Since he was given a captain's commission, he was unquestionably trained to the sea. It seems reasonable that Hazard arrived with Abraham Whipple in the *Katy,* and may have been the sloop's first lieutenant. Captain Nicholas Biddle of the *Andrew Doria,* upon meeting Hazard for the first time, saw him as "A Stout Man Very Vain and Ignorant — as much low Cunning as Capacity."[6] Hazard's place of origin is uncertain. William Bell Clark, without documentation, calls him a Rhode Islander. However, Hazard himself writing from Providence spoke of being "in a Strange place."[7] An inquiry to the Rhode Island Historical Society brought the following reply:

> I had always assumed that Captain Hazard was a Rhode Islander; since the Hazard family was not only prominent but very numerous in the southern part of Rhode Island during the 18th century. There was a John Hazard of the proper age, but if he were the one in question his family have been very successful in concealing his record as a naval officer. Another thing that makes me think that he was not perhaps a Rhode Islander, is the fact that I can find no record of a John Hazard from Rhode Island having served either as a privateersman or merchant captain previous to the Revolution. Ordinarily our Revolutionary officers had had some such career before the War.[8]

It is most likely that Hazard, if not from Rhode Island, was from one of the New England colonies, and we shall accept him as such.

When the lines were cast off on the 4th of January, the fleet was not yet ready to put to sea. The Commodore was only shifting position from the shore line piers, where heavy ice was dangerously piling up, to Liberty Island in the river channel, thereby lessening the possibility of being solidly frozen. The move gave each ship an opportunity to muster and exercise its crew. Sensing that a goodly number of officers and seamen, finding it distasteful to leave the charms of Philadelphia, would turn up missing the Naval Committee had a notice conspicuously posted in all taprooms and public houses — "every Officer in the Sea and Marine Service, and all the Common Men belonging to each, who have enlisted into the Service of the United Colonies on board the Ships now fitting out, that they immediately repair on board their respective Ships as they would avoid being deemed deserters . . . Boats will Constantly Attend at Messrs. Welling and Morris's Wharf to Carry all people on board the Ships."[9] The next day, January 5, the Naval Committee prepared its instructions to the Commodore.

Hopkins was issued two sets of orders. The first, which he was at liberty to issue to his officers, was a series of directions for the conduct of the fleet. The Commodore was enjoined to "take care that proper discipline good order and peace be preserved amongst all the ships, and their companies," and that all men "be properly fed and taken care of when they are in health, as well as when they are sick or wounded." Prisoners were to be "humanely treated," and all arms, powder, shot, and cartridges be kept "always fit for immediate Service."[10] In a second set of instructions, the Committee, expressing a fervent wish to see "our unnatural enemies . . . meet with all possible distress on the sea," issued specific sailing orders which Hopkins for the time being kept to himself.

> . . . you are instructed with the utmost diligence to proceed with
> the said fleet to sea and if the winds and weather will possibly admit

of it to proceed directly for Chesapeak Bay in Virginia and when nearly arrived there you will send forward a small swift sailing vessel to gain intelligence of the enemies situation and strength. If by such intelligence you find that they are not greatly superior to your own you are immediately to enter the said bay search out and attack, take or destroy all the naval force of our enemies that you may find there. If you should be so fortunate as to execute this business successfully in Virginia you are then to proceed immediately to the southward and make yourself master of such forces as the enemy may have both in North and South Carolina in such manner as you may think most prudent from the intelligence you shall receive; either by dividing your fleet or keeping it together.

Having completed your business in the Carolinas you are without delay to proceed northward directly to Rhode Island, and attack, take and destroy all the enemies naval force that you may find there . . .

Notwithstanding these particular orders, which it is hoped you will be able to execute, if bad winds or stormy weather, or any other unforseen accident or disaster disable you so to do, you are then to follow such courses as your best judgment shall suggest to you as most useful to the American cause and to distress the enemy by all means in your power.[11]

Here was no small mission to assign an undisciplined and untried collection of merchant sailors manning a converted cargo ship squadron.

When one reflects upon the dominant part played by New England in sponsoring a Navy, and it is remembered that in January 1776 the British still occupied Boston, and enemy ships were infesting adjacent waters, the fact that the first services of the Continental fleet were directed to the southward requires examination. The appearance and activities of British vessels on the southern coasts in the autumn of 1775, caused the Congressional delegates from that section to line up in support of New England's demand for a Continental naval force. In return for their support the southerners extracted first call on the services of Hopkins' squadron. Then again, just as operational orders were being written, the news of Lord Dunmore's New Years' Day cannonade and burning of Norfolk, Virginia, was received and widely circulated in the Philadelphia press. Alarm and concern over Dunmore, and the prospect of having him enter Delaware Bay next, most certainly shaped the thinking of the Naval Committee.

Christopher Gadsden, a Naval Committee member who was himself to leave Congress shortly and join his South Carolina militia regiment as colonel, was particularly enthusiastic about Hopkins' chances of success in the south. He kept up a running correspondence with the Commodore, encouraging the venture and supplying him with the names of Charleston people who could be called on for assistance. "I flatter myself," pleaded Gadsden, "we shall have your Assistance at Carolina, when you may depend on an easy Conquest, or at least be able to know without Loss of Time when off our Bar the Strength of the Enemy, & shou'd it be too much for you prudently to encounter wch. I hardly think probable if soon attempted wth. the Assistance to be depended on from us you may in such Case Retreat with great Ease, Safety, & Expedition." He asked Hopkins to set a secret signal which would identify the fleet, "Shou'd you come our way." Hopkins replied, "Som one of the Fleet if to gather or the Small Sloop if a Lone will higst a striped flagg half up the flying Stay."[12] It never became necessary to show this signal.

Ice married the ships to Liberty Island until mid-January during which time the *Providence,* Captain Hazard, joined her consorts. Hazard brought with him a personal flag or standard for the Commodore as a token from Colonel Gadsden. It was a yellow flag depicting a rattlesnake, and bearing the words "Don't Tread On Me."[13] On the 17th the ice had thinned sufficiently for the fleet to fall down the river to Reedy Island near Port Penn, Delaware, where winter closed in anew. The Naval Committee penned a final summary to Hopkins bringing him up to date on the latest news including the death of General Montgomery before Quebec, naval intelligence from New York and from Virginia where, "we have heard nothing but what you are well acquainted with." Spurring the Commodore on to heroism worthy of immortality in marble and bronze, the Committee ended with the inspirational note that, "The Congress have determined to erect a Splendid Monument to the Memory of the Gallant Montgomery and to every other commanding officer, bravely fighting and falling in his country's cause." There is nothing in this letter which would even vaguely suggest a change in Naval Committee plans for the cruise. On the contrary, the Committee expressed every expectation that should Hopkins go as far south as Savannah, Georgia, he could make prisoners of three Royal governors who had sought a haven on board British ships, and also increase his naval strength by capture of the vessels *Tamar, Scorpion,* and *Cherokee.*[14]

The fleet was held in the ice at Reedy Island from 17 January until Sunday, 11 February. Supplies came down by wagon from Philadelphia, and the small schooner *Fly* with additional New England seamen managed to beat her way up the Bay. Congress had authorized a tender or small dispatch vessel for the fleet, and so Hopkins designated the *Fly*, purchased by the Naval Committee in Baltimore, for that service.[15] Lieutenant Hoysted Hacker, another Rhode Islander on the original list of naval officers, was given the schooner's command.[16]

On February 13 at anchor inside Cape Henlopen awaiting a favorable wind, the squadron was strengthened by the Continental sloop, *Hornet,* 10 guns, Captain William Stone, and the 8 gun schooner *Wasp,* Captain William Hallock.[17] Both vessels and their captains were from Baltimore. Hopkins' fleet now included *Alfred,* 24 guns, *Columbus,* 24 guns, *Cabot,* 14 guns, *Andrew Doria,* 14 guns, *Providence,* 12 guns, *Fly,* 8 guns, plus the two most recent arrivals, giving the Commodore a respectable eight vessel force mounting a total of 114 guns.

The captains were ordered to report on board the Commodore where each was issued a set of signals and the following sailing instructions:

You are hereby Ordered to keep Company with me if possible, and truly observe the Signals given by the Ship I am in — but in case you should be separated in a gale of Wind or otherwise, you then are to use all possible means to join the Fleet as soon as possible — but if you cannot in four days after you leave the Fleet, you are to make the best of your way to the Southern part of Abacco (one of the Bahama Islands) and there wait for the Fleet fourteen days — but if the Fleet does not join you in that time, You are to Cruise in such Places as you think will most annoy the Enemy — and you are to Send into Port for Tryal, all British Vessels or Property or other Vessels with any Supplies for the Ministerial Forces, who you may make Yourself Master of to such Places as you may think best within the United Colonies.

In Case you are in very great danger of being taken you are to destroy these Orders and your Signals.[18]

By setting the place of rendezvous for stragglers in the Bahama Islands, the Commodore's choice to ignore the wish of the Naval Committee and Congress that he strike in Chesapeake Bay and on the Carolina coast was unfolded. There is no indication that his captains were consulted in the decision, or that they were aware of their destination before gathering in the *Alfred's* flag quarters on February 14 to receive their orders. In coming to the conviction that the fleet should go directly to the West Indies, Hopkins was exercising the discretion granted by the Naval Committee which, under certain circumstances, allowed him "to follow such courses as your best judgment shall suggest to you."[19] Some months after, in a report to John Hancock, President of Congress, the Commodore set forth as the basis for his decision the large number of seamen sick with the smallpox which left his fleet in no condition "to keep on a cold Coast." Still later he confided to brother Stephen his opinion that the enemy off Virginia and south along the coast to Georgia was too strong.[20]

All preliminaries were complete, and the wind was right. Lookouts in the tops of each ship fixed their eyes on the *Alfred's* foremast to pass the word immediately when seamen in the flagship were seen to "loose the Fore topSail and sheet it home"—the Commodore's sailing signal.   About one o'clock Sunday afternoon, February 18, 1776, the signal was given, all ships weighed, and the first American fleet stood out to sea.[21]

Thick weather and gale winds parted *Hornet* and *Fly* from the main body of the fleet on the second night out, and the two small vessels remained separated playing no part in the ensuing operations. Otherwise passage to the Bahamas was without notable incident, and the squadron came to anchor in 12 fathoms under the lee of Abaco Island on the 1st of March.   Here the Commodore spent two days watering and otherwise readying for his planned assault on New Providence Island, a short sailing distance to the south.   The expedition's object was to seize upon the gunpowder reportedly cached on that island.   Before departing Abaco, Hopkins transferred his Marine assault force into the *Providence* and two small sloops which were commandeered locally[22]

At two o'clock Sunday afternoon, March 3, 1776, ships' boats, covered by guns of the *Wasp* and Captain Hazard's *Providence*, beached on the northeast tip of New Providence, and some 250 Marines and sailors commanded by Marine Captain Samuel Nicholas stormed ashore through the surf. The first Naval-Marine amphibious operation in American history was handsomely executed. Ships' cannon were shotted and runout, but the landing was unopposed and firing was not called for.

Marine Nicholas and his men moved rapidly along the coast toward nearby Fort Montague. The few defenders at that place fired several rounds in token resistance, ineffectively spiked their cannon, and retired to Nassau town without further fight. The Americans passed the night at the fort. Commodore Hopkins sent a friendly message ashore to the island inhabitants guaranteeing their property and safety, and assuring them that his only interest was in the "Kings Stores." At daybreak the landing party marched on Nassau whereupon the Governor promptly surrendered both town and fort without a shot being fired.   The fleet now entered the harbor, and the Commodore and captains came ashore to survey the fruits of an easy conquest.[23]

The captured material which included a goodly number of cannon, was otherwise very considerable and remarkably varied.   The inventory of stores taken has enough flavor and sufficient interest value to justify listing in full.

From Fort Nassau:
- 71 Cannon from 9 to 32 Pounders
- 15 Mortars from 4 to 11 Inches
- 5337 Shells
- 9831 Round Shott — and 165 Chain & doubleheaded, ditto
- 140 hand Grenadoes
- 816 Fuzees or false Fires
- 99 Spunges Rammers and Worms
- 46 Copper Ladles
- 407 Copper Hoops & 5 Copper Powder Measures
- 220 Iron Trucks for Carriages
- 3 Bells
- 24 Casks Powder
- A Quantity of Match Rope not Weigh'd
- 2 double Blocks with brass Sheafs
- 1 Scale Beam - 1 Hammer
- 3 Tann'd Hides
- 2 Boxes Tallow Candles
- 4 Barrels Flour, 4 ditto Bread, 4 ditto Beef
- Part of a Cask Spirit
- 1 Sun Dial and 1 English Flag

And at Fort Montague:
- 17 Cannon from 9 to 36 Pounders
- 1240 Round Shott
- 121 Shells
- 81 Iron Trucks for Carriages
- 22 Copper Hoops - 2 Copper Powder Measures
- 1 Worm, 1 Laddle
- Some old Iron, Copper and Lead not Weigh'd.[24]

To take only 24 casks of gunpowder from Nassau, the seat of British administration in the Bahama Islands, was certainly a disappointing and meager catch of the one item which was the aim of the New Providence attack. The explanation is that while Nicholas' party bivouacked at Fort Montague over the night of 2-3 March, and Commodore Hopkins' manifesto dispelled any doubts about what the Americans were after, Governor Montfort Brown directed that 150 barrels of powder be loaded into a small sloop which made good her escape in the darkness.²⁵

The American fleet remained off New Providence for two weeks loading the booty. It was necessary to press an additional sloop into service to accommodate everything that was being carried off.²⁶ During this time the *Fly,* missing since the squadron left the Delaware Capes, rejoined. Captain Hacker gave the Commodore the details of how he had fallen afoul of *Hornet* carrying away "her Boom and head of her Mast."²⁷

Sickness of epidemic proportions ran wild through each ship, "our people takeing very Sickly with the fever."²⁸ The fleet cast off on March 17, 1776, for the homeward voyage. Hopkins later asserted that it was his intention to go from New Providence to Georgia for the relief of that colony, but intelligence which the Commodore claimed to have come by several days before sailing convinced him that the enemy to be found in that quarter was too strong for him.²⁹ He ordered his captains to keep company with the *Alfred* if possible, but if they were to be separated they should make their way to Block Island Channel.³⁰ Governor Brown and his lieutenant governor were carried along as prisoners. Perhaps Hopkins took these dignitaries to soothe a spirit graveled by the 150 barrels of precious powder slipping through his fingers, or maybe he remembered the Naval Committee's parting words before leaving the Delaware, expressing the hope that a royal governor or so might be bagged to adorn the flagship's wardroom.

The voyage northward was routine. In fair weather the crews exercised at the guns, and the captains enjoyed the mild luxury of exchanging visits and dining with each other. Foul weather demanded full attention of officers and men and left no time for pleasantries. Some men died of fever, and were committed to the Atlantic with the ritual of seafarers. Several small prizes were made, all in the Block Island area. Captain Whipple in the *Columbus* captured a schooner on April 4, and the next day Captain Saltonstall took a bomb-brig. Both of these vessels were attached to the British fleet at Newport, Rhode Island. A second prize for Whipple, this one a brig, was seized after a chase, and a sloop was taken at the same time by the *Cabot*, Captain Hopkins.[31]

Two sail were sighted in a calm sea at about the first hour of the mid watch, 6 April. All hands were called to quarters as the distance closed, and it became clear that one of the strangers was a vessel of considerable size. She was in fact the *Glasgow*, 20 gun ship of the Royal Navy, Captain Tyringham Howe commanding, accompanied by a tender. The *Cabot*, Captain John B. Hopkins, in the van, was first to range within pistol shot of the Britisher. Captain Howe hailed and was answered by Hopkins, and by a hand grenade thrown from high in the *Cabot's* rigging. Both ships opened with broadsides. The *Glasgow's* greater weight of metal forced the *Cabot* to sheer off. On board the American brig four men were killed and seven wounded including Captain Hopkins. Now Captain Saltonstall brought the *Alfred* into action. After exchanging several broadsides, a shot from the *Glasgow* carried away *Alfred's* wheel-block and ropes making the ship unmanageable and causing her to broach to. Captain Howe alertly taking advantage of his opponent's situation raked the American flagship several times doing considerable damage to hull and rigging. The *Glasgow* made all possible sail for Newport harbor, all the while firing her stern guns, and being answered by the pursuing rebels. Even in a shattered condition, the *Glasgow* was a faster sailer than any of the ships in the American squadron, heavy in the water with the weight of the New Providence stores. After a futile stern chase of some seven glasses, Hopkins' squadron had approached close enough to Newport to arouse apprehension over the prospect of bringing on an engagement with the British fleet based there. The Commodore signaled all ships to give over the chase. Captain Howe had made good his escape, and the Americans got nothing but the *Glasgow's* tender.

It appears that only the *Alfred* and *Cabot* came to close grips with the Englishman. Captain Biddle in the *Andrew Doria* was forced to tack to avoid collision with the *Cabot,* thus allowing the *Glasgow* to run ahead.[32] *Columbus* was unable to engage closely because, as Captain Whipple explained to the Commodore, "the *Glasgow* suddenly hauling to the northward, brought me to the southward of her, and brought her directly into your and Captain Hopkins's wake. I hauled up for her, and made all sail with my three topgallant sails. Captain Hopkins then beginning the fire, the *Glasgow* returning the same, and my being in her wake, and as far to the leeward as she, it instantly deadened all the wind, which put it entirely out of my power to get up with her. I used my utmost endeavour, but in vain."[33] As for the sloop *Providence,* Captain Hazard appears to have kept her well out of range.

The Continental Navy's baptism of fire could hardly be called a success. British Captain Howe brilliantly fought his ship and eluded a vastly superior force. At the same time the *Glasgow* handed out as much punishment as she received. While the King's ship was able to outsail the fully-laden clumsy American vessels further handicapped by sickness and the absence of officers and men as prize crews, a proper disposition by the Commodore might have prevented escape. Captain John B. Hopkins in the *Cabot* opened the engagement on his own responsibility without receiving an attack signal from the Commodore. Once the action was joined each captain was on his own, no orders or direction came from the flagship. There was no effort to cooperate in a coordinated attack which could have easily taken the *Glasgow*. The American gunnery was high and not notably effective. Casualties on board the *Glasgow,* one killed and three men wounded, were caused by small arms fire and not by cannon metal.[34] The action disclosed all too clearly that men, guns, and ships alone do not make a Navy, and that the elements of training, experience, discipline, and *esprit* are essentials which cannot be legislated, but must be acquired. Hopkins reported to the President of Congress that during the fight the *Alfred's* officers had "behaved well," and of his son's ship he said, "too much Praise cannot be given to the Officers of the Cabot, who gave and Sustain'd the whole Fire for some considerable time within pistol Shot."[35] He was silent about his other ships.

After breaking off the *Glasgow* chase, the American squadron and prizes turned to the southwest and came to anchor in the harbor at New London, Connecticut on April 8, 1776 — the first cruise in Continental Naval history was at an end. The sick crewmen numbering several hundred were brought ashore and billeted among the townspeople. Unloading of the New Providence stores started, and the Commodore penned his operational report to Congress. On the same day, it is significant to note in the light of future happenings, Hopkins also wrote to Governor Cooke of Rhode Island and Governor Trumbull of Connecticut. Although Hopkins held his authority from the Congress, and he operated at the general expense, he did not consult Congress or its Marine Committee on the disposition of the captured stores which were, after all, Continental property. Instead he offered them to the Rhode Island and Connecticut governors for the defense of their colonies.[36]

Hopkins' report of the cruise was enthusiastically hailed by Congress which directed John Hancock to send official congratulations. "Your letter of the 9th of March (*sic*), with the enclosure was duly received, and laid before Congress, in whose name I beg leave to congratulate you on the success of your expedition. Your account of the spirit and bravery shown by the men affords them the greatest satisfaction, and encourage them to expect similar exertions of courage on every future occasion. Though it is to be regretted that the Glasgow man-of-war made her escape, yet, as it was not through any misconduct, the praise due to you and the other officers is undoubtedly the same."[37] The vision of a British man-of-war put to flight by the Continental fleet was reveled in, but more sober reflection put the engagement in sharper focus. How could one 20 gun enemy ship do such damage, and escape a squadron mounting better than five times as many cannon? This embarrassing question stood high among the causes for a growing dissatisfaction, both in and out of Congress, with the conduct of naval affairs.

Not long after the fleet arrived at New London, the night battle with the *Glasgow* was the universal topic on the streets and in the taverns. Sailors with grievances, some real and others imagined, and those with rum-flexed tongues freely spoke of certain captains as being "backward" when it came to meeting an enemy, and the still more directly damning indictment, "coward," was frequently applied. Captains Nicholas Biddle and John B. Hopkins (a wounded commander is rarely criticized) alone seem to have escaped without smear. For Captain Abraham Whipple of the *Columbus* the situation became unbearable. On April 30, 1776, he wrote with much passion and eloquence to Commodore Hopkins requesting a court martial.

> Honoured Sir: I have had the honour to serve under you in the last French war, and I believe to your satisfaction; and since my arrival at Philadelphia, where I was appointed by the honourable Continental Congress to the command of the ship Columbus. I have strictly obeyed your commands, and done all in my power for the honour of the fleet, to the best of my knowledge . . . on our arrival at New London, I found that a report was spread, (from the Alfred and Cabot) that I was a coward, and many other ill-natured and false aspersions. If I did not do my duty, it proceeded not from cowardice, but from want of judgement. The inhabitants of New-London, and others, by means of those cruel aspersions, look on me with contempt, as a man not serving the country in my station. The circumstances of having a family of children to be upbraided with my supposed cowardice, and my own character rendered infamous through the Thirteen United Colonies, is an indignity I cannot bear. If I am a coward, I

have no business in the service of this Continent. I therefore request that there may be a Court-Martial called, that I may be tried by my brother officers of the fleet, and either acquitted with honour, or broken with disgrace. I ask no favour of them. If I should be broken, the publick will then have a right to despise me. If I can obtain no satisfaction in this way, I should be under a necessity to return you my commission. I will then thank the Congress for the honour they intended me, and curse those who first spread the infamous report. I have nevet yet mentioned the matter to anyone. If your Honour had let me come to Newport when the Scarborough man-of-war lay there, as was my request, I might perhaps have convinced the world that I am not a coward; but this is now out of my power.[38]

Hopkins approved his old shipmate's demand, and Captain Whipple's inquiry was held on board the *Alfred* May 6, 1776, at Providence, Rhode Island.[39] Captain Saltonstall presided over a court consisting of naval captains Nicholas Biddle and John Hazard, Marine captains Samuel Nicholas and John Welch, naval lieutenants John Paul Jones, Rhoades Arnold, Hoysted Hacker, Elisha Hinman, and Jonathan Maltbie, Marine lieutenants Matthew Parke and Henry Dayton. Whipple told his fellow officers essentially what he had previously written to the Commodore; that on the night of the *Glasgow* engagement the want of wind made it impossible to press a closer attack. Sundry eyewitnesses from the several vessels were heard, and the court quickly gave the opinion that Captain Whipple had erred in judgement, but was no coward.[40]

Two days after Whipple was cleared he found himself sitting as judge on another court martial convened on board the *Alfred* by Commodore Hopkins' order. The defendant was Captain John Hazard who stood accused by his junior officers and others in the *Providence* of gross misconduct. Hazard pleaded not guilty to charges of neglect of duty on the night the fleet took on the *Glasgow*, embezzlement of ships stores and two counts of breach of orders. The court, whose membership was the same at both trials except that Hazard and Whipple changed places, unanimously agreed that Hazard was

guilty of all charges brought against him and unworthy of
holding a commission in the Navy of the United Colonies. The
verdict was confirmed on 9 May by Hopkins who ordered
Hazard to surrender his commission to Captain Saltonstall.[41]

Before he realized the court martial findings had the Commodore's endorsement, Hazard wrote him a lengthy appeal
for clemency and consideration. One instance of disobedience
of orders was Hazard's failure to deliver wood to Reedy Island
as directed before the fleet left the Delaware. The deposed
captain said he thought that matter had been settled on the
spot and nothing more would be said about it. Relative to the
failure of the *Providence* to stay with the fleet and follow the
flagship up the Providence River, Hazard contended that this
was no disobedience of orders but rather a misunderstanding
since he believed the *Alfred* to be going to Newport. He wrote
that once awakened and on deck the night of the *Glasgow*
fiasco, he was far from "Backwards in fighting." Hazard
thought embezzlement the most heinous crime of all he stood
accused of. He did not deny his guilt, however, but called
it a "Mear Triffle indeed." Hazard claimed his trial was unfair,
and the blame for this he placed on the court's president,
Captain Saltonstall. He bitterly accused Saltonstall of depriv-
ing him of legal rights and in every way exhibiting prejudice.
"I am ready," he declared, "to face my Antagonist any day
and to let him and the world know I am no Coward." He
asked for another trial, and begged Hopkins for a recommendation to the Naval Committee.[42] The Commodore remained unmoved, and John Hazard became the first officer
cashiered from the Continental Navy. Command of the
Providence passed to John Paul Jones.

The same day as Hazard's trial was underway in Providence, May 8, 1776, Congress ordered that the Naval Committee's sailing instructions to Commodore Hopkins be reread
on the floor. This being done, a committee of seven was
appointed to determine in what degree Hopkins had complied with his orders, and how far he had departed from

them.[43] The bitter disappointment felt in the southern colonies over the failure of the Continental fleet to appear off their coasts and operate for their protection, congealed into torrid anti-Hopkins and anti-New England sentiment in Congress. Had Hopkins planned to do so, it is doubtful if he could have done a better job of widening this rift. Not only did he sail from the Delaware to the Bahamas without attempting to aid Virginia or the Carolinas, but on the northward passage he went directly to New England, ignoring the south once more. And, as if this was not sufficient to guarantee him further troubles, he took it upon himself, without a moment's hesitation, to distribute the cannon and other captured stores in New England much to the resentment of all outside the favored provinces. "But," wrote the Commodore to brother Stephen, "if they think I am partial in favour of the Northern Colonies they are greatly mistaken."[44]

Congressional disapproval of Hopkins was sharpened by an apparent inability or lack of desire to put the fleet to sea after the maiden cruise, in spite of persistent urgings to come south or to attack the Newfoundland fishery. Here, however, the blame was not the Commodore's. The fleet was idle for want of able seamen which just could not be had. Even at this early period of the war the attractive wages and prize shares of the privateering service were proving impossible for the Continental marine recruiters to compete against. Then again, many experienced sailors had engaged in the Army before a naval establishment was formed and were not then available.[45] Washington lent Hopkins 170 soldiers to fill out the crews thinned by sickness, but the General soon demanded their return for the campaign shaping up around New York. Sailors, British or neutral, taken in the prizes during the New Providence cruise were pressed into Continental service by the desperate Commodore.[46]

Slow pay and idleness are never conducive to good order and discipline in a navy, more markedly so in one newborn and lacking the adhesion of tradition and a heritage of victory.

Such was the situation in the Continental ships riding at anchor in Narragansett Bay in the spring of 1776. Complaints of mal-practices and abusive treatment flooded in upon the Marine Committee and Congress. Officers with a "friend" at court did not hesitate to bolster their own interests through criticism of their senior officers. John Paul Jones gave vent to his undisguised contempt for the "narrow-minded" Captain Saltonstall to Daniel Tillinghast, and ventured "some free thoughts on certain characters in the fleet" to his patron in Congress, Joseph Hewes.[47] Whipple's officers in the *Columbus* were resentful of their captain's attitude toward them, and told the lawmakers so.

On June 14 John Hancock explained to Washington: "The shameful Inactivity of our Fleet for some time past; the frequent neglect or disobedience of Orders in Commodore Hopkins, the numberless Complaints exhibited to the Marine Committee agt. him, and also against Captains Saltonstall and Whipple, have induced the Congress, in Consequence of a Representation from the Marine Committee, to order them to repair immediately to this City to answer for their Conduct."[48] Terse summonses were sent off to the Commodore and two captains.

> Sir: The present inactive state of the Navy of the United Colonies, the many complaints exhibited to the Marine Board against some of the officers of the ships, and the daily applications of both officers and men who have left the fleet in consequence of very severe usage, have constrained the Marine Board to make a representation of our Naval concerns to the Congress, which require a speedy reform. And in order that the true and just reasons of this very great uneasiness and inactivity may be fully investigated, it is necessary that the officers against whom complaints have been lodged should be fully heard.
>
> I have it in command, therefore, from Congress to direct you, immediately upon receipt of this, to repair to the city of Philadelphia by land, and on your arrival here to give notice to me as President of the Marine Board. The command of the ship will naturally devolve upon the next officer. And you are to bring with you an exact state

of the ship under your command, the list of the men remaining, what number of effective and non-effective, the state of the stores of every kind belonging to the ship, and everything relative to your ship.

As you will be called upon in general to answer for your conduct since you left this city, I give you this notice that you may come prepared for that purpose. I am to repeat to you that Congress expect your immediate compliance with this order.[49]

The very definite stipulation that the naval Commander in Chief and two captains come "by land" may be considered as official concern lest a vessel fall to the British, but more likely it was an expression of how strong feeling was running against these three sailors.

Hopkins, Saltonstall, and Whipple arrived in Philadelphia as the city was vibrant over events which dwarfed their hearings into insignificance — Congress was drafting the Declaration of Independence. Nevertheless, the Marine Committee in its regular nightly sessions got on with the inquiry at once. Officers who served in the fleet, and were available to do so, were called to testify before the Committee. By July 11 a decision was reached on Captains Saltonstall and Whipple. The charge against Saltonstall did not appear to the Committee to be "well founded," and that against Whipple to be nothing more than a "rough, indelicate mode of behaviour to his marine officers." Congress accepted the opinion, and directed the Committee to order both captains "to repair to their respective commands." A mild rebuff went to Whipple who was told "to cultivate harmony with his officers."[50] The verdicts must have been a little less than pleasing to star witness John Paul Jones.

Commodore Hopkins' investigation was not carried out with the same alacrity as the captains. He was kept on in uncertainty until mid-August. John Adams, who believed that Hopkins had rendered great service, was the accused Rhode Islander's staunchest defender against the "gentlemen from the Southern and Middle States, and of many from New England."[51] The Commodore presented his own case on the

floor of Congress August 12, and the same day the Marine
Committee findings were submitted. Congress deferred a decision for several more days, and then on August 16 resolved
that the "conduct of Commodore Hopkins deserves the censure
of this house, and the house does accordingly censure him."[52]
Hopkins was ordered to return to Rhode Island and resume
command of the fleet.   But official and public rebuke of a
military commander destroys confidence and weakens authority over subordinate officers.   Although in titular command
of the Navy, Hopkins never again went to sea in a Continental
vessel.   Agitated by the censure vote, the political storm continued to swirl about the Commodore who reportedly characterized Congress as "a pack of ignorant lawyers clerks who
know nothing at all."[53]   On March 26, 1777, Hopkins was suspended from his command, and January 2, 1778, the "lawyers
clerks" decided that "having no further occasion for the
service of Esek Hopkins, esq., who on the 22nd of December,
1775, was appointed commander in chief of the fleet fitted
out for the naval committee . . . the said Esek Hopkins, esq.
be dismissed from the service of the United States."[54]

It appeared to section-conscious John Adams that Hopkins was sacrificed to "that anti-New-England spirit which
haunted Congress...."[55] Hopkins may have been lacking in experience or skill, but that he was not corrupt or wanting in inte-
grity, was the firmly expressed Adams' conviction. However,
Congress did not question Hopkins' honesty, but condemned
him for not paying due regard to the tenor of his orders which
expressly directed him to attack the enemy on the coasts of the
southern colonies. The Commodore's explanations for his decisions were by no means satisfactory to the legislators.[56] There
is no doubt that anti-New England sentiment worked against
him, but his actions did nothing to dispel the feeling, but
rather entrenched it. Hopkins was a brusque unpolished seafaring man who either would not or could not accept the con-
cept that the Navy had been created for the good of the Continent as a whole rather than for the exclusive benefit of the

northern provinces. This provincialism and his attitude toward Congressional authority militated against his usefulness. Hopkins' descent on New Providence was a well carried out amphibious assault, and as subsequent events will show, it was one of the most successful fleet operations undertaken by the Continental Navy. The *Glasgow* affair illustrated all too well the Commodore's lack of experience in handling a group of ships in action, but he cannot be blamed for inexperience. It may be that Hopkins, given the opportunity, could have served the nation better as a ship's captain than as Commander in Chief.

The Continental fleet, as such, did not put to sea again, but by taking crewmen out of some of the vessels, particularly *Alfred,* other ships cruised singly or in pairs and otherwise rendered service during 1776. Those which New Englanders commanded must be here recorded.

In April and May the swift sailing vessel *Fly* was sent out by Hopkins to report British strength and movements in Block Island Sound and off the eastern end of Long Island. Lieutenant Hoysted Hacker had commanded the *Fly* since the little Baltimore schooner was taken into naval service. Hacker's career in the Continental Navy, it is recalled, began gloomily when the *Fly* fell foul of the *Hornet* just as the cruise to New Providence was getting underway. The unhappy incident in no way injured Hacker's reputation with his fellow Rhode Islander; the Commodore characterized him to the Marine Committee as having "behaved so well that I think he deserves a Captain's Commissn from you."[57]

The Pennsylvania Committee of Safety, very much out of sympathy with the idea of retaining all the captured New Providence stores in New England, applied to Congress for twenty of the heaviest cannon to be brought to Philadelphia. It was agreed, and on May 10 the Marine Committee directed Hopkins to remove the cannon from Newport and put them on board "the *Fly,* or any other of your vessels."[58] Hopkins thought New London could spare the cannon better than Newport; naturally so did Rhode Island Governor Cooke. Con-

necticut was asked to meet the Pennsylvania needs. Governor
Trumbull disagreed and expressed his conviction to Congress
that the cannon were vital to the defense of New London,
a harbor essential to the navigation of Long Island Sound
and communications between New England and New York.
Cooke and Hopkins retorted with reasons why Newport could
not give up the cannon.   Finally in a compromise move Congress resolved, "That six of the heaviest cannon at Newport and
fourteen of the heaviest cannon at New-London belonging
to the Continent, be transported to Philadelphia as soon as
possible."[59]

This squabble meant considerable delay so that Hacker
did not receive orders to proceed with the cannon until June
14. He was to call at New York for any orders General Washington might have, or to deliver the cannon there to be sent
overland by wagon to Philadelphia as directed by Messrs. Hol-
lingsworth and Richardson, representing the   Pennsylvania
Committee of Safety in the matter.[60] The *Fly* departed Newport June 24 escorted by *Andrew Doria,* Captain Biddle, as far
as New London. But Governor Trumbull was not yet ready
to give up his fight to retain the cannon, and when Hacker
sailed down the Thames River with a fair wind during the
forenoon of June 27, *Fly* carried only the six Newport cannon.[61]

Hugging the Connecticut shoreline for protection, Hacker passed through Long Island Sound to New York and put
into Amboy, New Jersey, just across from Staten Island. The
guns were loaded into carriages for the remaining journey to
Philadelphia.

Very shortly after the *Fly's* arrival, Lord Howe and about
10,000 British troops landed on Staten Island (July 2). Hacker
found himself hemmed in at Amboy and got off a dispatch
telling the Commodore of his plight. Hopkins, who was at
Philadelphia in compliance with the Congressional summons,
answered Hacker on July 9 directing him to remain in the
New York-New Jersey vicinity to "assist the Common Cause,"

and in the last extremity to destroy his vessel rather than have her fall into enemy hands.[62] The *Fly* somehow managed to get out, run down the coast into Delaware Bay, and come up the river to Philadelphia. The schooner now passed from Commodore Hopkins' orders to direct Marine Committee control, and Hoysted Hacker turned over command to Lieutenant Elisha Warner.

The *Fly's* new skipper was still another in the long line of Rhode Island naval officers. He was named a second lieutenant December 22, 1775, on the original list. Warner saw duty in the *Andrew Doria*, Captain Biddle, through the New Providence campaign and until transferred to his own command.

During the fall months of 1776 the Marine Committee ordered Warner to take station off Shrewsbury, New Jersey, in company with the *Wasp*, to maintain a close watch on British vessels entering or leaving New York, and to seize on any opportunity for making prize of transports and supply ships. "You must be careful," Warner was cautioned, "not to let any british frigate between you and the land, and then there's no danger for they cannot pursue you in shore, and they have no boats or Tenders that can take you, besides the Country people will assist in driving them off shore if they should attempt to follow you in." A sound *modus operandi* was also spelt out for the *Fly's* captain, "altho we recommend your taking good care of your Vessel and people, yet we should deem it most praiseworthy in an officer to loose his vessel in a bold enterprise, than to loose a good Prize by too timid a Conduct."[63] It is immediately apparent from the foregoing that the Marine Committee went beyond administrative functions to plunge into the professional business of shiphandling and naval tactics.

Alarming intelligence reached Philadelphia early in November 1776 that the British were once again preparing to use the mobility and tremendous advantage given to them by control of the seas. Some 15,000 enemy troops at New York were about to embark in transports for an assault elsewhere on the coast, but where the blow would fall was unknown.[64] To Captain Warner and the *Fly* went the important assignment of preventing the enemy "from coming by Surprize on any part of this Continent." The moment the British fleet appeared outside Sandy Hook and set a course, Warner was to send a boat ashore with an express letter for the Marine Committee. This done, the swifter between *Fly* and *Wasp* was to run ahead of the enemy force, and the dullest sailer was to follow after it, both sending intelligence reports ashore as British intentions became clearer.[65]

The *Fly* was not on station to see and report the departure of the escorted British transports on 1 December. For sometime between 11 and 26 November the *Fly* was engaged by an enemy ship or ships and driven severely damaged into an inlet on the New Jersey shore, probably Egg Harbor or Toms River. A surgeon was sent up by the Marine Committee to care for the *Fly's* wounded, and because the schooner was in no condition to cruise, Warner was ordered to return to Philadelphia where he remained as the year ended.[66]

After being detached from the *Fly*, Hoysted Hacker was directed by the Marine Committee to return to New England to assume command of the *Hampden*. This was in the form of a promotion for Hacker since his new ship was larger and heavier gunned than the *Fly*. The *Hampden* was a brig-rigged, 14 gun vessel, formerly in the West Indian trade and converted to the naval service at New Haven, Connecticut. On her final merchant voyage before being purchased by the Continent *Hampden* carried military stores from Santo Domingo, and was brought safely into New York in June 1776 under convoy of the *Providence*, Lieutenant John Paul Jones.[67]

As Commodore Hopkins passed through New Haven on his way north after the Congressional hearings he inspected the *Hampden* on August 28, 1776, and found her about fit for sea except that the vessel still wanted officers and men. Hopkins left orders for Hacker, who had not as yet arrived, to enlist men as necessary to bring the brig to New London.

Hacker appeared in New Haven shortly thereafter, for by the first week in September he was already at New London and had the *Hampden* graved. He conferred with the Commodore who instructed him to take in five or six months provisions, and, as soon as his ship was cleaned, to join the *Alfred* at Newport, Rhode Island, preparatory to cruising in concert.[68]

Toward the end of September the *Alfred* and *Hampden* were ready to cruise save for the chronic complaint, shortage of men, which delayed sailing for another month. Not only was it becoming constantly more difficult to enlist sailors in the Continental service, but the vicious habit of jumping ship for the more lucrative privateering was rapidly gaining favor.

Sailing orders were forthcoming on October 22 for Hacker and his senior, Captain Jones, who had been transferred to command the *Alfred,* the ship of his original naval service as first lieutenant. The objects of the joint expedition were to capture or destroy all British vessels encountered, raise as much havoc as possible with the Newfoundland fisheries, and to do everything possible to liberate American prisoners of war forced to work the coal mines on Cape Breton Island.[69]

The *Alfred* and *Hampden* were under sail going out from Newport on October 27 when again Captain Hacker showed himself no master navigator; he ran the *Hampden* on a rock ledge doing serious damage to the keel and causing her to take water.[70] Jones was infuriated by this unexpected delay, and immediately sent a report to the Commodore scorching Hacker. But New England blood was still flowing thicker than winter molasses, and Hopkins' reaction to Jones' "disagreeable letter" was to order Hacker to transfer his command, crew, and provisions to the *Providence* and continue under the same orders.[71]

At a season far advanced for an extended cruise to the northward, November 1, 1776, *Alfred* and *Providence* put to sea as the frigid atmosphere between the captains complemented the weather. Before turning Cape Cod, an American privateer was boarded and several naval deserters ferreted out. Jones took them into the *Alfred* plus 20 other men for good measure.[72]   Shortly after arrival in the cruising area off Cape Breton an enemy merchant brig, *Active,* was captured, and on November 12 a most valuable prize was taken. This was the *Mellish,* a large British ship carrying a company of soldiers and a cargo of ten thousand uniforms for General Burgoyne's army in Canada.[73]   Red or not these woolen coats brought warmth to many a Continental soldier.

Quick success did not make "Jack" any fonder of duty in a cold climate, nor was there a great display of enthusiasm for a shore assault to liberate his brethren from the Nova Scotia coal mines. "We have a quarter part of our hands sick," petitioned *Providence* crew members to Captain Hacker, "and the prizes we have taken will reduce our number, as they are of great value. Should you think proper to continue further to the northward, we are ready and willing to do anything in our power for the good of the expedition, but we are of opinion it will too much endanger the vessel."[74] Hacker subscribed to these voices of timidity, and on the night of November 18 he deserted Jones, put before the wind, and headed the *Providence* toward Rhode Island.[75] This confirmed Jones' low opinion of Hacker, and bitterly sarcastic he wrote some time later: "If such things are permitted the Navy will never rise above contempt. The aforesaid noble captain doth not understand the first case of plain trigonometry, yet it is averred that he had the honor and that his abilities have enabled him to command a passage boat between Rhode Island and Providence long before the war began."[76] What reasons Captain Hacker gave for returning to Providence against orders, and without as much as signaling departure to his senior officer, are unknown. However, he must have satisfied Hopkins that his conduct was in order. He suffered no disciplinary action, and the end of the year found Hacker still commanding the hopelessly blockaded sloop. Commodore Sir Peter Parker's strong force had arrived on December 7 under convoy of 16 warships to occupy Newport and the entire island of Rhode Island.[77]

To pick up the narrative of other New England captains during 1776 we retrace our steps once again to April, immediately after the *Glasgow* engagement.   Captain John B. Hopkins of the *Cabot,* wounded in the battle, was ashore in New London recuperating at the home of Mr. Nathaniel Shaw, Jr., Continental Agent. The extent of young Hopkins' injury we do not know, but it was his father's opinion on April 21 that he would not return to duty in less than three or four weeks.[78] In the meantime the *Cabot* was needed to carry guns to Newport, and command of her was given to the first lieutenant, Elisha Hinman, whom we first encountered when placed in charge of a commandeered sloop at New Providence. Hinman continued in the *Cabot* after Captain Hopkins' recovery. The Commodore thought him "a good Officer, and I can't tell where you can mend it if you should give him a Captains Commission."[79]   The Marine Committee accepted Hopkins' judgement and put Hinman before Congress for a captain's commission and permanent command of the *Cabot*.   The recommendation was approved August 13, 1776.[80]

Hinman was a Connecticut man being born in 1734 at Stonington, a beautiful little fishing village near the Rhode Island line.   He settled in New London about 1760 and married a local belle, Abigail Dolebear.   By the period of the Revolution, Hinman was a veteran of the West Indian and European trade, and is believed to have commanded a merchant brig when but 19 years old.   He prospered, and in due course owned considerable New London property.   Benedict Arnold was numbered among the Captain's pre-war friends and frequent dinner guests.   It is said that after Arnold's defection when he and his Hessians burned New London in 1781 three buildings belonging to Hinman were spared.[81]

Hinman got underway in the *Cabot* from Newport on May 19 in company with *Andrew Doria,* Captain Biddle, with orders to cruise "in such places as you think will most annoy the Enemy" for a period of "three or four weeks."[82]   But on the second night out, when about five leagues southeast of No

Mans Land Island, the 28 gun British frigate *Cerberus* gave chase to the Continental ships. Since both were no match for the enemy warship which was "coming up fast," the *Andrew Doria* and *Cabot* parted company. Biddle made sail southward, while Hinman bore off toward Nantucket Shoals.[83]

About one week after separating from Biddle, Hinman took his first prize, the *True Blue*. She was a 200 ton ship bound from Jamaica to Lancaster, England, loaded with rum, sugar, coffee, pimento, ginger, cotton, and hides. The *True Blue* was manned and sent into Rhode Island where she was libeled against in Admiralty Court at Providence on July 4 in favor of her captors.[84]

The *Cabot* kept the sea for several more weeks without event before putting into New London toward the end of June. There Hinman learned that Hopkins had been called to Philadelphia, and that command of the fleet had devolved on Captain Biddle as the senior officer present during the Commodore's absence. Biddle had Hopkins' specific instructions to "be careful that you take no Steps with the Ships 'till further Orders from Congress."[85] This meant a considerable stretch of idleness for Hinman, although it must not have been altogether unpleasant being in his home port and ashore with his family.

"The Cabot has been lying here ever since Commodore Hopkins set out for Philadelphia," Nathaniel Shaw informed John Hancock, "with a fine brave crew waiting for orders."[86] But no orders were forthcoming. The monotony was broken briefly on July 29 when the *Cabot* went to the assistance of one of Captain Biddle's prizes run on the rocks between Stonington and Watch Hill, Rhode Island, by the *Cerberus*. Hinman and his crew, in a perilous enterprise, got out 90 hogsheads of rum and seven of sugar before the merchantman broke up.[87]

A ship in harbor captures no prizes and puts no silver in a tar's pocket. As the days passed the *Cabot's* men became increasingly restive and disgruntled with forced inactivity.

Some answered the urge to run off in privateers. Finally Captain Hinman decided to act, and about August 25 the *Cabot* slipped her cable and took the wind for the North Atlantic. The following week Hopkins was back in Providence much disturbed by Hinman's action and soliciting the Marine Committee's sentiments, "as I believe he has gone without Orders from any Person."⁸⁸ While it was in fact true that Hinman had no orders, he had not acted entirely on his own initiative. We have already seen that the presence of the *Cabot* so long in port, although manned and ready for sea, bothered the Continental Agent, Nathaniel Shaw, to the point where he wrote to John Hancock about it. Shaw also informed Governor Trumbull of the circumstances, and the Governor in turn "advised Captain Hinman to go on a cruise."⁸⁹ This was authority enough for Hinman who grasped the suggestion. Naturally, the Marine Committee did not look too kindly on a state governor recommending that a Continental vessel cruise. However, the Committee was "desposed to pass it by in silence," being convinced that the good Governor and Captain meant only to render service when the ship would be otherwise idle.⁹⁰

For Hinman far out to sea and totally unaware of the furor his departure had stirred, this was to prove the most fortunate cruise in his naval career. Prowling the regular sea lane between the West Indies and the British Isles, the *Cabot*, by October 5, had captured six Jamaicamen heavily laden with sugar, rum, and indigo. Four of the prizes were bagged in a single day, September 27.⁹¹ All but one of the English ships were manned by prize crews and sent into various New England ports. The exception was the last capture, a brig called *Georgiana*. When this capture was made Hinman's own crew was dangerously thinned by earlier prizes, and the *Cabot* was jammed full of prisoners. Hinman decided to use *Georgiana* as a cartel vessel and thereby unburden the *Cabot* of her unwilling passengers. The *Georgiana* was released under her own master, Captain Kentish, and in due course arrived in Dover, England, after a passage which began in Jamaica thirteen weeks and four days earlier. Announcement of her arrival included the British merchant captain's account of his capture and subsequent events.

> On the 5th of October the Georgiana was chased, and taken by an American brig-of-war called the Cabot, Captain Hinman, mounting fourteen six pounders, as many swivels, and one hundred and fifty men. After being plundered of all their arms, powder, and as much sugar, rum, cotton, etc., as the Americans could conveniently get out, they put on board the officers and seamen belonging to . . . prizes which they had taken . . . They sent on board for the maintenance of the people three barrels of pork, two hundred weight of bread, and two puncheons of water, which were not sufficient, as they have been at very short allowance ever since parting from the American pirates, which was the next day. Captain Kentish spoke with the Betsy . . . who spared him some bread and water, or they must all have perished.[92]

The somewhat unusual predicament in which the captain of one of Hinman's other prizes found himself has preserved for us a human and domestic sidelight to war at sea in the 18th century. This was Captain John Harvey of the ship *Esther*, captured while enroute to London and sent into Dartmouth, Massachusetts. Captain Harvey was not removed to the *Cabot*, but allowed by Hinman to stay in his own vessel for reasons which become clear as one reads Harvey's petition addressed to the Massachusetts Council:

> . . . and that your petitioner had on board his ship at the time he was captured, his wife and family, which consists of four orphan children, under the care of your petitioner, the eldest of which is between six and seven years of age, and five servants — four whites and one black — all which are now at said Dartmouth. This being the situation of your petitioner and his family, he prays the indulgence of the honourable Court that they, in their great goodness and humanity, would grant leave to their unfortunate petitioner to purchase some small vessel, such as he may be able, and also to grant him a permit to depart with his said family, in said vessel, from Dartmouth, back again to Jamaica . . . The situation of your petitioner's family being so peculiarly unhappy, by reason of his having his wife with him, who is now pregnant and very near her time, and so many small children

and servants, induces him to believe the honourable Court will indulge him in his requests, or otherwise grant him relief such as they, in their great wisdom, shall think proper and best. And their petitioner as in duty bound, will ever pray, etc.[93]

Prize-master for the *Esther*, Thomas Weaver, second lieutenant of the *Cabot*, testified in Harvey's behalf, and the Massachusetts Council ordered "that the prayer thereof be granted," and "recommended to all American cruisers to suffer the said Captain Harvey to pass with his vessel, company, and passengers, unmolested."[94]

The *Cabot* continued to cruise through October but no captures were made after the first week. Returning to the American coast, Hinman touched at Cape Ann near Gloucester, Massachusetts, where he got off a report to Commodore Hopkins before continuing to New London. After an absence of slightly over two months, Hinman reentered the Thames River considerably enriched in prize money and reputation.[95] The successful, if unordered, cruise and the knowledge that it was prompted by Governor Trumbull softened the Commodore's attitude toward the *Cabot*'s captain. He congratulated Hinman and passed on the news that the Marine Committee was also impressed, and, thinking him worthy of a larger ship, had appointed him to command the *Alfred*. Because his new command was presently out under Captain Jones, he was to remain temporarily in the *Cabot*.[96]

The Marine Committee still harbored hope of seeing the Continental vessels operate again in fleet strength, particularly along the southern coast. Hopkins was ordered to ready an expedition to destroy the enemy vessels cruising with impunity off the Virginia Capes and North Carolina.[97] Although enemy occupation of Newport and his blockade of Narragansett Bay in December doomed this plan to stillbirth, Hinman, immediately upon returning to New London, was directed to take in provisions and ready the *Cabot* to participate.[98] To that end he brought the *Cabot* around to Boston where she remained until the close of the year. Here we leave the *Cabot* and Elisha

Hinman for the time, and turn next to Captain Abraham Whipple and his ship *Columbus*.

All the Congressional inquiry could find Whipple guilty of was "a rough indelicate mode of behavior to his marine officers," and he was so eager to show no lack of spirit that he had the *Columbus* manned with a crew of 178 men and on a cruise to the eastward within four days after returning from Philadelphia.[99] "On the 10th of August following, I ran the gauntlet amidst the enemy, got to sea from New London, and soon after took five sugar-ships, two of which arrived in Boston and Portsmouth, the others were retaken."[100] The prize sent to Boston was a brig out of Antigua loaded with 250 hogsheads of rum.[101] The prize ship *Royal Exchange,* captured August 29 in passage from Granada to London, was by far the most valuable. She carried a cargo of 284 hogsheads and two tierces of sugar, 55 hogsheads of rum, 11 hogsheads of coffee, two bales of cotton, and some Madeira wine.[102] Before coming to anchor at Portsmouth, New Hampshire, on September 26, the *Royal Exchange* was the scene of high adventure. Two of the prize crew, Samuel Erlom and Thomas Donehoe, mutinied in an abortive attempt to put the ship back into English hands. Their trial revealed that Lawrence Bowden, late master of the *Royal Exchange,* had promised them twenty guineas each and half the value of ship and cargo should they succeed and bring her into England. Bowden denied any part in the plot, and Commodore Hopkins was inclined to go along with the Englishman on the belief that he was being censured "for a few dirty fellows that we know to be Villains."[103]

Although at one time chased by a 60 gun enemy warship, the *Columbus* outran her, and Whipple was back in Providence on September 29, his ship very foul and in sorry need of rigging and hull overhaul.[104] She did not cruise again in 1776, but in December ran up the Providence River for safety when the British arrived to dominate the Bay. As for Whipple himself, he was given command of one of the new ships building in Rhode Island.

If John Hazard broken by court martial, be disregarded, then the only New England captains who rendered no further naval service in 1776 after the New Providence adventure were Dudley Saltonstall and John B. Hopkins. Saltonstall, of course, had been called to account in Philadelphia and his damaged command, the *Alfred,* was virtually stripped to man other ships. Young Hopkins may not have recovered from his wounds as rapidly as expected making it impossible for him to return to active duty in the *Cabot.* Then again, it may not have been considered wise to be away at sea when commands for the new frigates, real men-of-war, were being handed out. The applicants for these choice plums were many, the politics unbridled, and the jealousies furious. Many aspirants came to press their claims in person at Philadelphia.

It will be remembered that while Commodore Hopkins was gathering his flock of made-over merchantmen in the Delaware River, Congress on December 13, 1775 enacted naval legislation for 13 frigates to be built as warships from the keel up. Six of the vessels were to be raised in New England: two in Massachusetts, two in Rhode Island, one in Connecticut, and one in New Hampshire. Plans for the frigates were drawn up in Philadelphia and laid before the Marine Committee one month after Congress approved the ship construction program.[105] Selection of the builders was entrusted to the Marine Committeemen from the colonies where the ships were to be built, and copies of the master plans were sent out.

Silas Deane gave over direction of building the Connecticut frigate *Trumbull* to his brother, Barnabas Deane. The *Trumbull,* 28 guns, was built under the direct supervision of John Cotton in a shipyard at Chatham, some 20 miles up the Connecticut River from Long Island Sound.[106] She was launched September 5, 1776, two weeks after Congress had certified the Deanes' brother-in-law, Dudley Saltonstall, to the command.[107]

Both Rhode Island frigates, *Providence,* 28 guns, and *Warren,* 32 guns, were built at Providence.[108]   Here Marine Committeeman Stephen Hopkins turned over construction to an 11 man committee of prominent merchants and ship owners, under the chairmanship of Governor Cooke. The larger ship was launched Wednesday, May 15, 1776, and the "28" took the water the next Saturday.[109]   Once again two local favorites had the inside track to command of the frigates. Captain John B. Hopkins was working closely with the building committee at least as early as May 27.[110]   He was rewarded with command of the *Warren* in June.[111]   On September 2 Governor Cooke's committee resolved "that a letter be wrote to the Navy Board at Philadelphia Recommending Abraham Whipple, Esq., now of the Columbus to be appointed Captain of the ship Providence — write by the next post."[112]   This got results, and Congress gave Whipple the frigate *Providence.*[113]

Up the coast in neighboring Massachusetts two more frigates were scheduled. John Hancock passed this handsome bit of patronage to an old political crony, Thomas Cushing, who contracted for both ships to be built at Newburyport.[114]   *Boston,* 24 guns, slid off the ways into the Merrimack River "in view of a great number of spectators" on June 3, 1776, and *Hancock,* 32 guns, was launched slightly over one month later.[115]

Unlike Connecticut and Rhode Island, no Massachusetts men were captains with Commodore Hopkins, and therefore no pretensions to command the Bay Colony ships could be based on previous service in the Continental Navy. John Manley, successful commodore of Washington's schooner "fleet," aspired to the larger frigate. Reinforced with the General's early promise, "that you shall have the Command of a stronger Vessel of War," Manley journeyed to Philadelphia[116]   The Marine Committee placed his name before Congress where, on April 17, 1776, "John Manley and Isaac Cazneau were elected captains of the two frigates now building in Massachusetts bay."[117]   Cazneau never served, and his place was given to Hector McNeill.[118]

Captain McNeill, a 47 year old long time seafarer of Scotch ancestry and Irish birth, was living in Quebec with his family when the Revolution began. At the earliest opportunity he seems to have embraced rebellion against the King he had served in the French War.   April 1776 found McNeill in the St. Lawrence River operating with the American troops before Quebec.[119] Soon thereafter McNeill was in Boston where he was quite at home. It was here he had arrived from Europe as a child, he married in the town's First Presbyterian Church, and when not at sea he resided in Boston for many years.   Undoubtedly it was McNeill's early mercantile connection with Cushing and Hancock which led to a naval commission in June 1776 and command of the frigate *Boston*.

Josiah Bartlett, representing New Hampshire on the Marine Committee, believing that shipbuilding was out of his sphere, asked the Committee of Safety in that Colony to pick the proper person as overseer for the construction of a 32 gun frigate.[120] John Langdon, prominent Portsmouth merchant, former Congressman, member of the first Naval Committee, and soon to be appointed naval agent for New Hampshire, was named.   The *Raleigh's* keel was laid in Portsmouth, and the vessel touched the water of the Piscataqua River on May 21, 1776. A contemporary reporter filled with local pride allows us to relive that launch.

> On Tuesday the 21 instant, the continental Frigate of thirty-two guns, built at this place under the direction of John Langdon, Esq., was launched amidst the acclamations of many thousand spectators. She is esteemed by all those who are judges that have seen her to be one of the compleatest ships ever built in America. The unwearied diligence and care of the three Master Builders, Mess. Hacket, Hill and Paul together with Mr. Thompson under whose inspection she was built, and the good order and industry of the Carpenters, deserve particular notice; scarcely a single instance of a person's being in

liquor, or any difference among the men in the yard, during the time of her building, every man with pleasure exerting himself to the utmost; and altho' the greatest care was taken that only the best of timber was used, and the work performed in a most masterly manner, the whole time from her raising to the day she launched did not exceed sixty working days, and what afforded a most pleasing view (which was manifest in the countenances of the Spectators) this noble fabrick was completely to her anchors in the main channel, in less than six minutes from the time she run, without the least hurt; and what is truly remarkable, not a single person met with the least accident in launching, tho' near five hundred men were employed in and about her when run off.[121]

The Mr. Thompson mentioned in the newspaper account as building inspector for the *Raleigh* was Thomas Thompson, English sailor and shipbuilder who had settled in Portsmouth, New Hampshire, about 1767.[122] A French nobleman, the Marquis de Castelleaux, traveling in New Hampshire in 1782 called Thompson "a sensible man, greatly attached to his new country, which it is only 15 years since he adopted."[123] His close friendship with John Langdon accounts for Thompson's selection to supervise the frigate's construction and his subsequent nomination to her command which Congress approved on June 6, 1776.[124]

The last of the six New England frigates to launch, *Trumbull*, was in the water by September. All were fitting out and striving to sign on crews. Some of the busy commanding officers may have found time to have a tailor fit them for a coat of blue cloth with red lapels and flat yellow buttons, blue breeches, and a red waistcoat with narrow lace — the uniform but recently prescribed by the Marine Committee to give naval captains a "regular" appearance and set them off from those in private service.[125]

Congress had yet to settle the thorny question of relative rank among the captains. Whatever the decision in that regard, it would inevitably cause friction and generate vitriolic criticism among those officers who felt themselves slighted in favor of others. When granting appointments Congress had side stepped the rank issue. But in the fall of 1776 with the new frigates readying for sea and plans formulating to cruise two or more of them together, it became imperative that a seniority order be established.

A most remarkable list it was that the Marine Committee prepared and which Congress accepted on October 10. The names of twenty-four captains were placed in rank order with the vessel to which assigned as of that date next to each name. Here are the ten New Englanders on the list and how they fared:

2. John Manly, *Hancock*
3. Hector McNeil, *Boston*
4. Dudley Saltonstall, *Trumbull*
6. Thomas Thompson, *Raleigh*
12. Abraham Whipple, *Providence*
13. John Hopkins, *Warren*
16. Hoysted Hacker, *Hampden*
20. Elisha Hinman, *Alfred*
21. Joseph Olney, *Cabot*
24. Elisha Warner, *Fly*[126]

How can one view the evident injustice of disregarding previous service other than in terms of favoritism, politics, and sectional feeling? Neither number two, Manley, although conspicuous in Washington's "fleet," nor McNeill, number three, had as yet been to sea in a Continental naval vessel. On the other hand, Saltonstall, captain of the *Alfred* in Commodore Hopkins' squadron, fared no better than fourth. Manley and McNeill were Massachusetts appointees, and John Hancock, political boss of that state, was President of Congress and chairman of the Marine Committee; whereas Saltonstall's benefactor, Silas Deane, had by this time left for France.

Evidence of strong dissatisfaction with Commodore Hopkins, the frigate building committee, and reaction against Rhode Island's domination in naval affairs are perceptible in the list. The first Rhode Island name to appear is Abraham

Whipple down in the 12th position. And it was this same Whipple who had chanced the hangman's noose to burn a British revenue vessel three years before Lexington and Concord, and who since had fervently waged the patriotic fight on the ocean. Rhode Islander Elisha Warner was anchor man on the captain's list.

The placement of Captain James Nicholson of Maryland at the head of the list was a victory for southern influence, and largely a personal triumph for the Virginian, Richard Henry Lee. Nicholson supporters in Baltimore were assured as early as June 1776 by Joseph Hewes, North Carolina member of the Marine Committee, that "Captain Nicholson has been strongly recommended, and Congress has high opinion of his abilities and merit and I have no doubt of his standing pretty high in rank."[127] Samuel Purviance, Jr., lawyer, merchant, chairman of the Baltimore Committee of Correspondence, and staunch Nicholson backer, suggested to Lee that Nicholson would be the proper person to be named commodore. Lee replied that Nicholson's merit "will not be forgotten," but "It is not probable that the frigates will sail in fleets for some time; and therefore, 'tis likely that no higher appointment than that of Captain will soon take place." On October 11, Lee could with pleasure write to Purviance — "the Congress have placed Captain Nicholson at the head, he being the first Captain."[128]

The senior captain of the Continental Navy was the eldest son of a well-to-do eastern shore of Maryland family. He ingratiated himself with Chesapeake Bay communities in March of 1776, when, as captain of the Maryland ship *Defence*, he drove off the tender of the enemy's sloop-of-war *Otter* and retook a merchant prize from the Britisher. Congress, on June 6, 1776, appointed Nicholson commander of the frigate *Virginia* building in Baltimore. Nicholson played a leading role in Baltimore politics and the local Whig club. On one occasion he is reputed to have caned a fiery newspaper man, William Goddard, through the streets for having sarcastically described him in print as a "Commodore snug in harbour."[129]

Nicholson's elevation to position of senior captain could not help but be acrid to those officers who had been out in the service of Congress months before him and now found themselves his junior.

The Marine Committee entertained the thought that at least some of the new ships would be cruising before the year ended. For one or more reasons, however, none of the New England frigates got to sea in 1776. A vessel's condition when launched may be likened to the outer shell of a new house requiring many weeks or months of tedious interior work before it is usable. Outfitting, rigging, and arming the frigates was no easy task particularly since such large quantities of ships' stores and skilled shipwrights were absorbed by privateers. Getting and keeping sailors was by all odds the greatest obstacle. Commodore Hopkins summed up the climate when he said: "The whole attention of Merchants and Seamen at present seems to be on Privateering through the whole New England Colonies."[130] He figured that about one third of the men who signed on in the Continental Navy had, after drawing one month's bounty pay, "been one way or another carried away in the Privateers." He asked the Marine Committee for, but did not receive, authority which would have allowed him whenever finding a deserter on board a privateer "not only to take him out, but all the rest of the Men."[131]

The scarcity was not confined to willing and able seamen, for not even a chaplain could be found. When the pastor of the First Congregational Church at Newport, Rev. Samuel Hopkins, complained to his namesake, the Commodore, about the lack of piety shown by the sailors, he received this answer which may afford the reader a chuckle:

Sir

I receiv'd yours of the 20th Septembr. (yesterday) and am very much Oblig'd to you for your Address and advice, and as to your Complaints of the Morals of the People belonging to the Navy I am now to let you know that I did not enter into the Navy as a Divine, and that I am not qualified to Act nor give directions in that matter,

the Congress whom I serve made provisions for a Chaplain to perform that necessary duty, but to my Mortification I have not been
able to get a single Man to act in that Character although I have
applied to many. If you know of any that has the good of Man-
kind at heart Sufficient to expose himself to necessary Danger of
that Service should be glad you would Send him who you may
depend shall be treated with due Respect. And if none can be
procured I cannot but Condole with you the depravity of the times.[132]

As a further solution to the manpower problem, Hopkins urged
that a more liberal prize share be offered, and this was accepted
by Congress. After November 1, 1776, officers and crews of
Continental vessels would be entitled to one half the value of
merchantmen, transports, and store ships taken, and the whole
value of warships and enemy privateers captured.[133] How
much this revision helped is problematical. This we do know,
that there were many times throughout the war when Continental ships were idle for want of crews, but this writer has
found no record of a privateer being in like straits.

At the end of 1776 the Continental Navy closed the book
on its first year of operations. It was the year in which New
England's virtually uncontested domination of naval affairs
reached the summit and began to decline. Inexperience, sometimes timidity, and often a lack of unity were evidenced.
There was long and loud criticism from several quarters. Nevertheless, the year's achievements, as a whole, merit a "well
done" for the neophyte naval captains from New England. As
we have seen, the New Providence attack was carried out with
the smoothness of a veteran service. Numerous valuable prizes
were made during the year, and in waters infested with enemy
sea-might, not one Continental vessel commanded by a New
Englander was lost. The added strength of the new frigates
gave every expectation of enhanced success.

British naval units on the North American station had
practically doubled in number during the year. Admiral
Shuldham reported 43 vessels of all classes in March and 54
in July.[134] A November 1776 letter from London printed

in the *Boston Gazette* revealed that, "the Marine Force of England now in America consists of two ships of the line, ten fifties, and seventy-one frigates and armed vessels, amounting in the whole to eighty-three ships and vessels of war and 15,000 seamen."[135]

The disparity between the Continental and British navies is staggering. Yet it must be noted that the enemy was also having manning problems and had resorted to the press. Moreover, numerous English vessels, unseaworthy for want of repairs, were unable to meet the arduous demands of blockading a long hostile coast, transporting an army, and escorting across great stretches of ocean. Inefficiency at the Admiralty in London further reduced operating effectiveness.

Before leaving 1776, I cannot forbear mention of the naval battle fought by the Army on Lake Champlain which was to prove a determinant in the course and end result of the Revolution. Control of this vital waterway, Lake Champlain, was essential to Britain's plans for invasion from Canada aimed at isolating New England. The Americans built a small flotilla on the Lake, and the enemy did the same. Near Valcour Island on the morning of October 11 the opposing lake navies joined battle. General Benedict Arnold's force was destroyed, but he had so delayed the British that they went into winter quarters and postponed the invasion until the following year. This set a chain of fortuitous events in motion. Washington used the breathing spell to strengthen the force which defeated Burgoyne at Saratoga. The Saratoga victory cast a deciding vote to bring France into the war; and with France came indispensable sea power to the American side.

CHAPTER IV

NEW FRIGATES IN ACTION — 1777

The several commanders . . . will have . . . a
chance of immortalizing their own names besides
inriching all the brave Fellows under their
command.

RESOLUTION OF THE MARINE COMMITTEE,
April 29, 1777

THE YEAR of Independence just over had seen the British evacuate Boston, and the major land campaign move south to
New York and New Jersey. It culminated in Washington's
coup at Trenton. When the new year 1777 opened there was
in New England a concentrated array of actual and potential
Continental Naval strength which would not again be equalled.
Commodore Hopkins was still in nominal command, but he
had openly broken with Rhode Island men of influence by
challenging the cupidity of certain mercantile interests while
the frigates were under construction. His suspension from the
Navy was a matter of months away, and the Marine Committee
was regularly bypassing him to give the captains direct orders.
There was disappointment because none of the new frigates
had gone to sea, but hope ran high that they would shortly
make their metal felt in the contest. The Reverend Samuel
Cooper writing from Boston on March 24, 1777, expressed
both moods.

It is astonishing to many here that after so long a Time for Prepe-
ration, not a single Frigate this way has yet been made ready to put
to Sea, while the British Frigates and Cruizers are distressing us
everywhere, cutting off our most necessary Supplies. This has occasioned no small Clamor & uneasiness here. Talk'd Capt McNeal the
other Day, the Occasion of the delay. He laid it upon those who had
the Care & Oversight of the Marine here. I inquired of our friend
here Mr. C----ng [Cushing]. He returned it upon the Captain.
There is Blame somewhere. I know not whether there be any Person
or Persons here fully authorized to conduct and rectify these matters.
I hope however they will soon be ready for sailing.[1]

In Connecticut the *Trumbull*, Dudley Saltonstall's command, was fitting and manning with painful slowness. Upon
dropping down to Saybrook the sickening discovery was made
that the *Trumbull*, drawing too much water to clear the bar,
was trapped in Connecticut River. Her guns, if she had them
in, were removed to lighten ship leaving her in a defenseless
position. When a marauding British force burnt Danbury in
April of 1777, General Benedict Arnold thought it very probable that destruction of the *Trumbull* was contemplated and
could have been easily achieved, "as there is no Battery or
Armed Vessell to Cover her." Arnold, a former sailor with a
trained seaman's eye, saw no reason why the ship couldn't get
over the bar given proper lighters and a good easterly wind.[2]
But the *Trumbull* defied all attempts to get her out and remained in the river which had spawned her, a dead loss, drain-
ing naval resources for over two years.

Apparently the Marine Committee was not immediately
aware of *Trumbull's* sorry predicament, or else they expected
that Saltonstall would soon find the solution. April 4, 1777,
the Committee exhorted him to the "most diligent exertions
in getting immediately manned, and out to sea, there to Cruize
in such Lattitudes as will be most likely to fall in with &
intercept the enemies Transport Vessels coming to reinforce
or to supply their Army at New York."[3]

Now occurred an event which defies full explanation. On April 12 from "on board the Continental ship of war Trumbull" off the Virginia Capes, Saltonstall wrote to the Marine Committee acquainting them "that at one P.M. I fell in with two transports from England, one of eight the other of ten guns. They engaged us three glasses, when they struck their colours. They killed seven of our men and wounded eight more. We shattered them in a terrible manner and killed and wounded numbers of their crews. I have the pleasure to inform you that our people behaved well and with much courage."[4] The transports were sent in as prizes. Saltonstall being at sea in a vessel named *Trumbull* has misled a number of naval historians, including James Fenimore Cooper, to conclude in error that he was out with the frigate *Trumbull*.[5] This, of course, we know was impossible since that frigate was bottled in the Connecticut River. The surviving records provide no answer to what ship Saltonstall had in the action. This writer is inclined to accept Gardner Allen's plausible explanation when he states: "It is likely that, owing to the importance of the service to be performed, a vessel was impressed, chartered, or borrowed for the occasion, perhaps the ten-gun sloop *Trumbull*, a Connecticut privateer."[6] If this is correct, then Saltonstall was showing heretofore undisclosed initiative and vigor. He had not made a cruise since the New Providence exploit more than a year before. Perhaps an acute need for prize money sparked him. Saltonstall performed no further active duty in 1777 after this success against the transports.

At Providence, the frigates *Warren* and *Providence*, together with *Columbus*, the sloop *Providence*, and the *Hampden* brig were sealed in by British ships patrolling lower Narragansett Bay.[7] The enemy blockading squadron as of February 1777 consisted of two 50 and one 40 gun ships and eight smaller vessels.[8] The month previous, intelligence current in Philadelphia, which proved very premature, had the British ready to depart from Rhode Island. With a forlorn hope Rob-

ert Morris wrote to Hopkins, "I long to hear that you contrive
ways and means to get rid of the enemy in your neighbor-
hood"; but he remained for two more years.[9] Neither John B.
Hopkins and Whipple with the frigates, nor the ship *Columbus*, Hoysted Hacker, was able to run the gauntlet to the open
ocean during the whole of 1777. The three captains saw only
some minor local action.

The 2nd of January on board *Warren*, the frigate selected
to fly the Commodore's broad pennant, Esek Hopkins got word
that a large enemy ship, the frigate *Diamond*, Captain Field-
ing, was hard aground near Warwick Neck. Here was a golden
opportunity for Hopkins to refurbish a tarnished reputation.
If he could capture the British man-of-war all past shortcomings would surely be forgiven and forgotten in Philadelphia.
To avoid endangering the new *Warren* in shoal waters, Hopkins took 22 of her crew to man the smaller *Providence* sloop.
Captain Whipple was directed to take charge of the sloop for
this adventure, and he brought along additional men from his
own command.

When the *Providence* ran down to where the enemy lay,
it was discovered that because there was still some water under
her at low tide, and she was on a soft bottom, the *Diamond* had
not careened and could bring stern chasers to bear. The *Providence* crossed the stranded frigate's stern several times, fired
at "a little more than Musket Shott" distance and was answered
by the *Diamond*. In the meantime, two field pieces on shore
brought up within range joined the *Providence* in the attack.
Hopkins went ashore several times to confer with Colonel
Bowen, the militia officer in charge; a very unusual thing
indeed for a commodore to do during an engagement. On his
last trip to the beach, Hopkins' boat drifted away by itself
and he was unable to get back to the *Providence* all night! In
the early morning hours, upon return of the tide, the *Diamond*
floated free and all possibility of taking her ended. The Commodore said that all the while a 50 gun British ship stood a

short way off and could have come to the assistance of the *Diamond* if needed.[10] An English source does not mention the presence of the 50 gun ship but records that, "Fortunately for his Majesty's ship, the enemy took very bad aim. Most of their shot going over her, no one of her crew was either killed or wounded, but seven shot pierced her bottom, and her fore-top-mast and rigging were very much wounded and cut."[11] Hopkins missed a great chance, and the criticism for not bringing to bear against the *Diamond* all of the naval strength he had available drove another spike in his official coffin.

The second week in February an enemy armed schooner was ashore at the northern end of Prudence Island. This time it was John B. Hopkins who took the sloop *Providence* and went after her. Upon the approach of the Americans, the schooner was set afire and shortly thereafter blew up.[12] This was the extent of Captain Hopkins' active cruising in 1777.

In the fall of the year an amphibious attack to drive the British out of Newport and off the Island was planned. General Spencer was named to command the assault, and the landings were to be covered by Captain Whipple with the frigate *Providence,* "the only one that is ready for service." Use of a fire ship to grapple with and destroy an enemy frigate lying off Hog Island in the path of the expeditionary force was included in the plan. The prospects of an active service must have gladdened Whipple's restless spirit. But it came to naught, for the entire scheme had to be cancelled when General Spencer could not muster a militia force strong enough to make the attempt.[13]

Whipple and Captain Hacker journeyed overland from Providence to Point Judith with wagons and crew to salvage the guns and usable stores from HBM *Syren,* 20, wrecked there on November 10.[14] While going about the business Whipple fell from the side of the hulk to some of the guns on the ground thirteen feet below. This mishap crippled Whipple in the leg and ankle for the remainder of his long life.[15]

When Hacker moved up to Whipple's place in the *Colum-bus,* his old command, the sloop *Providence*, was left without a captain. She was offered to a former skipper, John Paul Jones, who found himself without a ship when ordered relieved in the *Alfred* by Hinman.[16] Jones, already smarting under the slight of being passed over when selections were made for the frigates, had no mind to step down to a 12 gun sloop. Congress, April 19, 1777, approved John Peck Rathbun to be captain of the *Providence*.[17]

Rathbun, a Bostonian, had been in the Continental Navy since the beginning. He had served as a lieutenant in the *Providence,* Captain Hazard, during the New Providence attack, and later in 1776 under Jones in the same vessel and in the *Alfred*. At the juncture when Hopkins himself was in need of a friendly word, Rathbun presented the Marine Committee with a letter of recommendation from the Commodore.

> The bearer Lieutt. Rathbun waits on you with this he has served since the Fleet went from Philadelphia there being no Vacancy whereby I could promote him agreeable to his Merits — if there Should be any Vacancy with you I can Recommend him as a man of Courage and I believe Conduct, and a man that is a Friend to his Country — and I believe the most of the Success Capt Jones has had is owing to his Valour and good Conduct, he is likewise of a good Family in Boston — any Service you may do him will be Serving the Cause.[18]

The Marine Committee had no vessel to offer Rathbun, but Jones was also in Philadelphia loudly making it known that he did not want the *Providence*. Rathbun then became the Committee's second choice for the sloop.

After taking part in the attempts against the beached British schooner and frigate *Diamond*, the sloop *Providence,* temporarily in charge of Lieutenant Jonathan Pitcher, successfully ran the enemy blockade in Narragansett Bay and got to sea toward the end of February. She was the only Continental vessel at Providence to do so in 1777. Before reaching relative safety in open water, the *Providence* passed so near a Bri-

tish 50 gun ship in the darkness that the crew could be heard
talking on board, and at sunrise she was becalmed within sight
of the enemy at Newport. Pitcher put into New Bedford,
Massachusetts, where Captain Rathbun took command. To
fill the sloop's complement it became necessary to press some
seamen from Nantucket.[19]

The *Providence* put to sea again in June, and cruised the
New York vicinity. Off Sandy Hook an enemy merchant
ship in company with a brig, schooner, and sloop bound for
Jamaica was sighted. Rathbun decided to engage the ship,
the largest of the lot, for if taken, prizes could leisurely be
made of the others. A bitter broadside cannonade followed.
The smaller enemy vessels coordinated their attack with the
ship, all firing into the *Providence* at once to such effect that
Rathbun had to break off the action to repair sails and rigging. Closing once more, Rathbun determined to lay the Britisher close aboard and carry her by boarding. But once again
"all three of them played their part so well we gave it up."
Rathbun followed the enemy ship overnight intending at daylight to have "the third heat at her," but when morning came
she was out of range. The schooner was captured, and Rathbun learned that the enemy ship carried 16 guns, and was by
herself more than a match for his *Providence*.[20]

Rathbun continued to cruise in the Gulf Stream before
returning to New Bedford in August. One night he gave
chase to a sail which appeared to be acting most erratically. But
what could be better than to have an eyewitness tell this
strange sea story.

> Being in the Gulf Stream it being meridian, saw a sail as far as we
> could descover; stood for her, and at sunset found her to be a ship
> Her crew appeared to act strangely; she decoyed us before the wind,
> and sometimes shaking in the wind top-gallants and all sail out.
> About 1 o'clock A.M., it being star light, we neared her, but received
> no answer. We gave her three shots at once, which made a cracking
> on board of her, but still no answer, and no lights were seen. Captain
> Rathbone ordered the boat out, armed her, and told me to take com-

mand of her, and said for my consolation, if they killed me! he would not spare one of them. I set out and ordered the coxswain to steer under her stern; I held a lantern and saw her rudder was gone, and hailed, but received no answer. I ordered the coxswain to steer around her larboard quarter, and go alongside, and I sent one man up with the lantern and followed him. I found no boats on deck, but saw on the quarter deck a deep sea-lead and line. I went into the cabin and found all the beds and all the trunks full of rich clothing, and chests with their keys in them. One of our men cried out, a man! a man! I asked where, and it proved to be a small dog, that opened all the eyes he had, but could not speak our Yankee tongue. I then went to the hold and found her in ballast; no cargo or provisions, except bread, and 40 casks of nails, and a few of French cordials. I sent the chests, trunks, and what was of value on board our sloop, but we were so lately out we could not stow away much. The ship being destitute of a rudder it would have been difficult to get her into port, so we kept the barge plying all day and until late in the evening, when we took out the dog, and for fear she would fall into the hands of the English (she being a noble ship) we set her on fire and burnt her to the water's edge. She appeared to be a French ship of about three hundred tons. The trunks were full of ladies' rich silk gowns shoes and fancy articles; and gentlemen's fine shirts, all ruffles in French style, French pocket handkerchiefs, etc., etc. She was a tight ship, and we think she must have got on Cape Hatteras Shoals, and the crew and passengers had abandoned her. She was under full sail, top-gallant sails hoisted a taunt o, and sheeted home; they must have left her in great haste.[21]

The *Providence* was active again in November cruising to the south. Off the Charleston bar in bright moonlight Rathbun was surprised by a British privateer. The Englishman ordered "the d--d Yankee beggars to haul down the colors" as he opened the action; his fire was answered by a "yankee welcome with a handsome broadside." Culminating a night long chase the Americans carried the privateer by boarding. Rathbun had now traveled so far to the southward that he and his prize stood for Georgetown in South Carolina where the *Providence* remained until the end of the year.[22]

Providence, Rhode Island, which had been the focal point of New England naval activity in 1776 gave way to Boston the following year. This resulted from several factors fore-most of which was, of course, British occupation of the island of Rhode Island and control of adjacent waters. Commodore Hopkins' suspension by Congress on March 26, and authoriza-tion in April for the Navy Board of the Eastern Department with headquarters at Boston made the shift official. Boston had the added natural advantage of one of the best harbors north of New York.

Early in 1777 the untried Continental frigates *Hancock* and *Boston* were at Boston having been brought around for outfitting from their building sites at Newburyport. The ship *Alfred* and brig *Cabot* had also put in at that port after suc-cessful cruises. The latter vessel was the first of the four to sail from Boston this year. Captain Joseph Olney of Provi-dence commanded the brig. He had received the appointment from Congress in October 1776 at the same time he was placed number 21 on the seniority list.

We met Olney briefly in these pages when Hopkins or-dered him to Newport in charge of getting the stranded *Hamp-den* off a rock ledge.[23] Olney had been in the Continental Navy since its inception. He was commissioned second lieuten-ant on the original list and filled that station in the *Columbus* while under the command of Whipple. His name appears among the junior officers Hopkins recommended for captain-cies when any vacancies should occur.[24]

January 15, 1777, Olney, who had tarried in Rhode Island, was ordered to repair to Boston at once, ready the brig for sea as soon as possible, and cruise "against the Enemys of these States, and Chiefly for Transports."[25] Olney's receipt for the *Cabot's* stores and provisions was given to the departing Captain Hinman, and the change of command was effected. Supplies to complete the brig's allowance were obtained from John Bradford, the Continental Agent. When just about to get underway on February 27, the *Cabot* received damage from a snow storm accompanied by winds of gale strength.[26] The severity or extent of the damage is unknown. However, Olney was still in port on March 9, but he put to sea shortly thereafter setting course to the northeast.

March 28, off a bleak Nova Scotia shore, a sail was sighted rapidly closing the gap. This proved to be the 28 gun enemy frigate *Milford*, Captain John Ford. *Cabot* made a two-day run for it, but there was no escape, and she was chased ashore on a hostile coast near the mouth of the Chebogue River.[27] So close was the *Milford* that Olney and his crew barely had time to abandon their vessel and take to the timber. A Halifax account of the beaching reprinted in Boston tells something of what actually happened liberally sprinkled with interpolation.

> Olney, and his motley crew (including what they call a Captain, two Lieutenants and a numerous party of Marines) fled into the woods in the greatest hurry and confusion, carrying their small arms and ammunition with them, but could not *Spare time* in their fright to set fire to their vessel, which they might very easily have done. Olney himself was the first man in the boat having *jumped* into her whilst they were hoisting her out. A party of 20 seamen and as as many marines were detached from the Milford as soon as possible in quest of them; but the Rebels having started first proved too nimble of foot to be overtaken. Marching along shore to the northward of the Cape, they seized upon a light schooner, plundered the adjacent houses for provisions and set off for N. England, to blaze a broad their heroic exploit.[28]

Upon returning to Boston a court of inquiry called by Captain John Manley, the senior naval officer present, cleared Olney of blame in the loss of the *Cabot*.[29]

After laboring for two weeks the British got *Cabot* off and took her to Halifax where, according to a report in the *Boston Gazette*, "there was a day of general rejoicing; guns firing, drums beating, colours displayed; and the *good, loyal* run-away Tories (from this town) who remain there, were congratulating each other, on the glorious (as they said) acquisition. — Deluded creatures! -- they think the fate of

America depends on a single Brig — Were they to capture the thirteen Frigates fitted out by this Continent, they could not have exulted more."[30] *Cabot*, the first Continental Naval vessel captured by the British, was purchased into the King's service under the same name.[31]

Prior to the series of events just related HBM *Milford* cruised throughout the fall of 1776 in New England waters, particularly in Massachusetts Bay and off Portsmouth where she was able to make a number of captures and generally depress commerce. With the expectation that the annoying Englishman could be destroyed, taken, or at least driven away, the Assemblies of Massachusetts and New Hampshire in September offered to lend guns and render every other assistance to complete fitting out and manning the *Boston*, McNeill, and *Raleigh*, Thompson. Congress through its Marine Committee gladly accepted the proffered aid, and orders went off to McNeill at Boston and Thompson in Portsmouth to join against the *Milford*.[32]

But once again the plan was far removed from the reality as delay followed delay. *Boston* had considerably less difficulty in getting her cannon than the *Raleigh*, but both shared equally the familiar dearth of seamen. "The Boston of twenty-four guns, I expect is at sea before this time commanded by Captain McNeill, a very clever officer," Robert Morris told the American Commissioners in France just before Christmas 1776.[33] Morris was over optimistic, for McNeill was still months away from sailing. When the *Boston* finally stood down the Bay in the spring of 1777 she was not in company with *Raleigh*, but with her sister Massachusetts-built frigate, *Hancock*, Captain Manley. McNeill's and Manley's long, tortuous, and discouraging struggle to man their ships cannot be considered unusual, but rather as illustrative of what every captain in the Continental Navy was up against.

Desertions were routine, and in desperation McNeill appealed to the Council of Massachusetts:

. . . there is scarcely a day passes but instances offer, of desertions from Regiments and Ships in the Continental Service, yet within my Knowledge there has not been a single instance of punishing an offender . . . With what Spirit can an officer advance Monies to Cloathe the Naked Objects, who offer themselves, as willing to serve in their severall Capacity's, if the next moment those Men may with impunity go away in a Privateer, or enter into any other Corps, either by Sea or Land? and run no risque by being detected . . . Would it not be consistent with the Wisdom and Justice of the Legislative body of this State, to do as in like cases has allways been done by prudent people, in time of War in all Countrys; and which is now practiced by our Sister States, to the Southward of us, that is to make some regulations whereby all Travellers, on the Publick Roads, should be obliged to give an account of themselves, to proper persons of the Committee's of Safety, in each Town as they pass? This regulation would not be burthensome to honest Men but would Effectually stop all runaways of every denomination, and prevent many abuses which in our present deplorable Condition happens every day. Had such a regulation been attended to some Months past, I had not been now loitering inactive in this port . . .[34]

Manley petitioned Major General Heath, commanding the Continental troops in Massachusetts, for release of some sea-trained soldiers to duty in the *Hancock.* He offered to pay back personally any advanced wages or bounty received by the soldiers if he could but have the men. Manley also took this occasion to complain about Rhode Islanders recruiting in Boston for the Continental ships at Providence under "the Term of six Weeks or two months in Violation of Congresses Resolves to the great Damage of your Petitioner & to the Damage of the Common Cause."[35] Both Manley and McNeill went heavily in debt advancing money to their men for clothing and common needs. "The very Interest of Money which I have borrowed and advanced to Carry on the Service of this Ship," said McNeill, "would have mentained my Family in Credits."[36]

Continued harassment of the coast by British cruisers sustained local eagerness to see *Boston* and *Hancock* spread canvas for blue water before trade was completely ruined. The Massachusetts General Court, toward the close of April 1777, furnished Manley with £400 and McNeill with more than £1600 to enable them to put the frigates to sea, both captains "being accountable for the several Sums by them received."[37] The state also offered free insurance and several inducements to the owners and commanders of privateer vessels consenting to sail with the Continental ships for a 25-day period. Nine privateers of varying strengths responded.[38] Manley, senior Continental captain, would be the squadron commodore, and to run the *Hancock* while he was occupied with flag duties, he chose Captain Daniel Waters, an old friend and associate from Washington's "fleet."[39]

Waters was a Massachusetts sailor who had commanded the *Lee* schooner under General Washington's orders. In June 1776 the *Lee* together with another of the small vessels captured an enemy transport with upwards to a hundred soldiers on board. On March 15, 1777, Congress approved a Marine Committee request for authority to purchase and arm three prize ships in Massachusetts. The same day they appointed Daniel Waters, who came "strongly recommended" by Washington, a captain in the Navy to command one of the vessels.[40] Probably because Waters' own ship was not ready, and Manley found himself responsible for nine privateers and the two Continental frigates, he agreed to cruise in the *Hancock*. While Waters had a captain's commission, Manley did not turn over command of the frigate to him, rather his station was perhaps more like that of a sailing master.

Following the months of soul-trying labor *Hancock* and *Boston* mustered crews and together with the privateers weighed from Nantasket Road, May 21, 1777, for their maiden endeavor, a cruise to the eastward on St. George's Bank. [41] As the new frigates presented to the land gleaming black and yellow sterns, with rattlesnakes carved thereon, McNeill gave vent to his happiness: "The long wish'd for hour is at last come in which I bid farewell, to the sleepy Agents, disheartened Tradesmen and distress'd Seamen who frequent the Streets of Boston." And, he went on: "For mine own part, I have Suffered so much in fitting out the Ship I am now have the Honour to Command, that I do not think I would undertake such a Task again for any Sum whatever unless I was better Supported then I have been hitherto."[42]

If success is to crown a joint naval operation of this nature, harmony, subordination and complete understanding between the commanders is a positive requisite. However, it was common knowledge that such was not the case here. Doctor Cooper sensed trouble when he informed John Adams, "Manley and McNeal do not agree. It is not, I believe, the Fault of the first . . . . If they are not better united, infinite Damage may accrue."[43]

The habitually unreliable privateers took the first gale to run off in their separate directions, and Commodore Manley suddenly found his fleet reduced to the Continental frigates. A small brig laden with cordage and duck was captured on May 29 and sent into Boston, "a very good market" for the prize cargo.[44] Dawn the following day, the Americans fell in with three large New York bound transports escorted by a 64 gun ship, *Somerset*. According to McNeill, "Capt: Manley was not convinced of the size of our Opponent untill she was within Shott of him, when very Luckily for him Hancocks Heels saved his Bacon." *Somerset* left the transports to give the *Hancock* and *Boston* chase for about six hours before nightfall compelled her return to the convoy.[45]

Manley now ordered a change of course to the northeast in hopes of encountering other transports less heavily escorted. Nothing was sighted except a "few miserable fishermen" until June 7 when they came up with the *Fox*, a 28 gun frigate of His Britannic Majesty's Navy, Captain Fotheringham commanding.

The Englishman made a run for it, but the American ships were both fast sailers, and after several hours the *Hancock* overhauled and drew alongside. "A Spitefull Short Action Ensued," wherein the *Fox* "pegg'd Mr. Manley's ribbs so well that he had his pumps going" as the *Boston* closed to pistol shot range 45 minutes later. A *Boston* man, with a dramatic bend and an ear for phonetics, recorded in his journal, "at Last we Came up and Gave them a Noble Broid Side witch made them to Strike a meadeatly a Bout half after one."[46] When Fotheringham hauled down his colors, according to an English account, the *Hancock* lay on his port bow, the *Boston* on the starboard quarter, so that a few if any of the *Fox's* guns could be brought to play. The *Fox's* masts were badly wounded, and her wheel shattered in such a manner that the ship would not answer her helm.[47] An incident during this action affords an interesting glimpse at the tournament side of a naval battle during the period. In the midst of a warm exchange, McNeill noted that a burning gun wad lodged in the enemy's mizzen chains had started a fire. McNeill bellowed through his speaking trumpet across to the *Fox* telling the enemy of this situation, and gallantly he ordered cease fire until the flames were put out.[48]

Capture of the *Fox* brought disagreement between Manley and McNeill into the open. The *Boston,* as noted, was tardy in coming to action, but McNeill was prompt in reaching for the laurel wreath. He sent Mr. Browne, his first lieutenant, on board the *Fox* to command the prize. This was too much for Manley who had sustained the brunt of the battle. The Commodore ordered McNeill to withdraw Browne which he was finally obliged to do "for the sake of peace."[49]

McNeill now urged Manley to turn southward for Charleston, South Carolina, there to clean ship and join Captain Nicholas Biddle in the frigate *Randolph* for a West Indian cruise. Manley at first agreed, as McNeill relates it, "but in a few days alter'd his Mind and his Course . . . Nevertheless I follow'd him as the Jackall does the Lyon, without Grumbling except in my Gizard."[50] A near accident on the night of June 27 caused another flare-up. In the darkness the *Hancock* changed course and barely missed a collision with *Boston.* McNeill claimed that Manley had not shown the proper signal, and he noted in the ship's log, "I wrote him a letter at noon and gave him my mind freely on his misconduct which nettled the Commodore very much."⁵¹ Manley replied immediately tossing blame back on McNeill for not knowing the signals. "You," he rebuffed the *Boston's* captain, "commonly keep a considerable distance astern. I should think . . . that we can Command our Ships to keep within hail of each other or so near as that we can hear the Bells strike as for the Fox she keeps so nigh that I can distinguish her Bell in the Cabin every Night as well as I can my own . . . " He offered to let the *Boston* go ahead, for "I will be bound to keep Compy with you" — a jab at McNeill's seamanship. And he closed his retort on a doleful but amusing note: "am afraid I cannot wait on you next Sunday on Account of my Lameness for I am now laying upon my beem ends & what is worse than that I cannot drink neither, Punch Wine nor Grog."⁵²

Soon after this exchange Manley, whose infirmity made him "very Anctious to get home" ordered the squadron to stand for Massachusetts. July 6, in the forenoon, a coal laden old sloop was captured and taken in tow by *Hancock*. Late the same afternoon *Fox* signaled the flagship that two sail appeared to be in chase astern. They were the British ship *Rainbow*, 44, and the 18 gun brig *Victor* under Commodore Sir George Collier. Apparently Manley did not view the situation with any concern for he continued towing the sloop through the night, obliging *Boston* and *Fox* to shorten sail to keep company. By sunup the next morning a narrow five or six miles separated the antagonists, and a third enemy, the *Flora* frigate of 32 guns, was now bearing down. Manley burned the coal sloop and prepared to engage.

Flora, the headmost Britisher, was the first to exchange shot with *Boston*, the rear American ship. Manley mistaking the *Rainbow*, now coming up fast, for a line-of-battle ship with 64 or more guns decided it best "to try his heels." The Americans scattered, *Hancock* to the southward, *Fox* run to the eastward, *Boston* pressed on sail and kept the wind to the northward. Commodore Collier, in the *Rainbow*, took out after Manley's *Hancock* which an English officer who had been held prisoner in Boston recognized. The *Hancock* could have easily outsailed the *Rainbow,* but Manley for some unexplained reason shifted weight forward putting his vessel down by the head and out of trim. At about four o'clock in the morning of July 8 the *Rainbow* was close enough to open with her bow-chaser and several broadsides of grape and round. By eight-thirty Manley was ordered to strike if he expected quarter. He made a last effort to run ahead and the Englishman poured in another broadside, when, as Collier reported, Manley "struck the Rebel Colours to his Majesty's ship, after a Chace of upwards of 39 hours." Before this the *Flora* had run the *Fox* to earth, and taken her after a hot action. Captain Brisbane of the *Flora* stated that, "The Ship that we afterwards learned to be the Boston was, at the time the Fox struck, as far to wind-ward as we could but discover the head of her Topsails out of the Water." McNeill escaped and sought sanctuary in the mouh of the Sheepscott River on the Maine coast.[53]

Upon coming on board the *Rainbow,* prisoner Manley damned McNeill for not assisting him, and himself for not resisting when he discovered that he had surrendered not to a ship-of-the-line but to a vessel hardly superior in force to the *Hancock.* Collier was delighted at taking Manley, "esteeming him more capable of doing mischief to the King's subjects than General Lee was."[54] Manley was carried to Halifax where his capture was happily acclaimed as being "of the utmost bad consequence to the rebels he being the chief executive officer of their navy, in whom the Congress place all their confidence, and who is the only man of real courage they have at sea."[55] Manley was transferred from Halifax to New York where he was closely confined on board a prison ship until exchanged the next year. The *Hancock,* one of the finest ships built in America during the Revolution, was taken into the Royal Navy, and, her original name being anathema, was renamed *Iris.* As HBM *Iris* she reappeared off the American coast to the discomfort of her former owners.

McNeill soon found that he had entered a trap as well as a haven. Enemy cruisers in pairs or greater strength paraded off the coast waiting for him to come out. *Boston* was brought up the stream as far as the Wiscasset settlement. While thus hemmed in "Sheepgut" River, McNeill's pen poured forth his troubles and self-justification to his wife Mary, the Marine Committee, John Langdon, and to his friend Captain Thomas Thompson of the *Raleigh,* among others.[56]

Sixteen English prisoners who were in the *Boston,* seven of them officers from the *Fox,* were sent overland under guard for Massachusetts by McNeill. For the 18th century seaman a prisoner was more than an enemy deprived of the chance to fire a cannon or wield a cutlass, he was insurance for his captor. Should the tide of war run the other way, an ever present likelihood, and he, the captor, should find himself a prisoner, his time in a prison ship or jail could be shortened by exchange with the enemy he had been lucky enough to take earlier. It is no wonder then that McNeill complained with unrestrained indignation to the Falmouth Committee of Safety when he heard that two of his prisoners had been "Negligently left behind" in that town.

> Were our poor Countryman who unfortunately fall into the hands of the Enemy no better guarded or let run at loose in this manner we might entertain some hopes of their being able to find their way once more to their own home, but alas the contrary is too well known. Many of them have been contrain'd to take arms against their Country, all who refuse so to do have been close confin'd and treated with such cruelty as would Shock the heart of a Barbarian untill they can be redeem'd by Exchange, suffer they must. It is not then great cruelty in us to neglect redeeming our own people knowing full well what hard measures they have while in the hands of the foe, what mistaken pitty that is which only extends to our Enemys when they fall into our hands, and neglects our own people who meet such cruel Treatment among them. This is but poor encouragement for men to enter into the Service of their Country, who tho they may take and convey home Prisoners enough to redeem themselves in case of their being

taken, yet have only this Melancholy reflection for their Comfort, Namely That their indolent, faithless Countrymen, suffer such to Slip through their fingers while they poor Souls are sure to perish in a Prison unless they be redeem'd.[37]

Captain Thompson, still at Portsmouth undermanned and lacking some guns, wrote to McNeill congratulating him on his "safe arrival" in Maine, and forwarding a ludicrous suggestion — "If you can engage more men than you want should be glad to have them."[38] The unhappy captain of the *Boston* responded, "Sixty men short of what I brought out, the Scurvy taking every day."[39]

Taking advantage of a temporary lapse in the British vigil off the river's mouth, the *Boston* sneaked out, ran along the shore, and ducked into Casco Bay about August 1, 1777. From Falmouth, McNeill reported to the Marine Committee that four Royal frigates were off the harbor, and that he did not know when he would reach Boston, but "by care and good conduct" he hoped to save his vessel "for a more fortunate cruise than has been our last." All of Manley's "errors" were restated for the Committee's benefit, then McNeill ended with a prayer, "May God strengthen the Hands of the Congress and save our Country by his Mighty Power, joined with their honest Endeavours, for Sure I am that they have but indifferent prospects from the ability of many of us Employ'd under them" -- we may be sure that McNeill did not include McNeill in this group.[60]

The presence of a numerous enemy and Manley were not the sole causes of gastric disturbances in McNeill's "gizard," for friction had infested the *Boston*'s wardroom, and dangerous dissension existed among the officers. Richard Palmes, Captain of Marines, seems to have been a leading troublemaker. On August 10 McNeill placed Palmes under arrest for unofficer-like behavior and repeated breach of orders, with the warning; "At your Perril break your Arrest, in which case I shall treat you as you deserve." The next day he issued another order to Palmes; "You may thank your own folly and impertinence for what has now befallen you. I dispise your insinuations of Cruelty, as indeed I do Every thing Else you can say of me con-sisitent with truth. You may go to the house of Office as offten as Nature calls, provided you return immediately to your berth and keep your 'Tounge Still as you pass and repass."[61]

This distasteful affair was unfolding as the Captain and all hands should have been pulling together for the safety of the ship. The *Boston* took another leap-frog jump down the coast from Casco Bay to Portsmouth where she remained several days before making the final dash on August 21 to skulk into Boston harbor from whence McNeill had departed with great hope three months before. At least the frigate had been saved to serve another day.

For McNeill, troubles were far from over and his reception in Boston was not cordial. He was aware at once that opinion held him responsible for the loss of the *Hancock* and capture of the popular John Manley. McNeill, in a lengthy letter to the Marine Committee, now pulled out all the stops in his villification of the imprisoned Manley.

> I hold it criminal to asperse the character of any man, much more the Absent, and in some cases Scarcely Justifiable to Speak all the Truth, for which reasons were I not under a Necessity I should now say very little of Capt. Manley, but inasmuch as I find my self involved in a chain of difficultys by his blunders and misconduct, I must in justice to my self say, That he is totally unequal to the Command with which he has been intrusted, he being ignorant, Obstinate, Over-bearing, and Tyranical beyound discription, a man under whose command none can live with pleasure but such creatures as himself, and those also must be of his own makeing.[62]

McNeill's differences with his officers continued to mount. James Warren of the Eastern Navy Board told John Adams in a letter dated September 7, 1777, of a "great mis-understanding between the Captain and his officers who it is said will not again go to sea with him, and who say he never will again man his ship." The *Boston's* officers openly avowed that had McNeill obeyed Manley's orders, not only the *Fox* but the *Rainbow* and *Flora* would have been taken. Warren concluded that "There was certainly great blame somewhere" but "I won't pretend to say where."[63] The situation worsened when McNeill withheld the officers' prize money for refusal to turn in their cruise journals to him as prescribed.

The defiant Marine officer Palmes, who had cast his commission into the fire on board ship, was still under arrest and had to be dealt with. McNeill characterized him as a composition of "the Fool and Knave," but had he showed signs of behaving properly, the captain, with his hands full of other matters, was inclined to return him to duty. Palmes was granted liberty but seems to have been irreconcilable, and McNeill was forced to ask the Eastern Navy Board to bring him to trial charged with "misaplication of the Ships Stores, Neglect of duty, disobedience of orders, and attempts to excite Murmuring and Mutiny among the Ships Company."[64]

While under arrest Palmes went from Boston to Providence to present himself and his case before two Eastern Navy Board members, Messrs. Vernon and Deshon. He convinced these gentlemen so thoroughly that they not only tried to get Palmes his prize share through the intercession of General Warren, but transferred him on the spot from the *Boston* to the *Warren*.[65] This grossly unjust and unreasonable action on the part of the naval officials in behalf of a man who was a prisoner-at-large awaiting trial for serious offenses almost defies explanation. Could Vernon and Deshon have been totally unaware that by this extraordinary step they were guilty of destroying discipline and the authority of a commanding officer — two absolutes without which any good military organization is an impossibility? A stunned Captain McNeill turned to higher authority, the Marine Committee.

Never was a man taken from under Arrest and preffer'd to any other Employment without first undergoing a Court Martial. Nor is it possible that ever good order should Exist in armys, or fleets without taking care to punnish cashier, or repremand, such as shall on due trial be found guilty of such offences. If precedents of this kind be permitted once to take place, farewell Discipline and good Order, farewell Honour, and honesty. The Service will then become a recepticall for unclean birds who will hereby be Encouraged to take Shelter there, and all men of good principals will totally forsake it.[66]

In another baffling decision, the Marine Committee, brushing aside McNeill's complaint, sustained the Eastern Navy Board's action, and here the matter officially dropped.[67]

Conditioned by the recent unsavory experience, and never a man to stifle an opinion, McNeill gave one on Marine officers on board a Continental frigate.

I must now beg leave to give my Opinion respecting Marine officers for such Ships as ours, so much hampered for want of room. I think in conscience a Subeltern is Enough, three Marine officers takes up so much room to accomodate them that we are pinch'd beyound measure to afford it. Then they have Little or no duty to do, are allways in the way and apt to disagree with the Sea officers so that it takes much trouble to mannage them, then they run away with so much of the prize money from Officers who are really usefull, that 'tis painfull to hear the murmerings it Occasions. Might it not be proper to Lessen their number down to one on board the frigates and give what the other two did Enjoy between the Chaplin and Surg'n.[68]

Captain McNeill had a most unique faculty for keeping the caldron boiling. An altercation between a peace officer and one of the *Boston's* crew placed McNeill squarely in a hassle with the civil authorities. While the *Boston* was undergoing thorough cleaning and being refitted alongside John Hancock's pier, her guns and stores were offloaded to the wharf. After several attempts at sabotage by plugging up the cannon vents had been detected, McNeill posted a guard over the stowage area. It was this sentry who had the run-in with a constable. Because the seaman was carrying out his orders, McNeill refused to allow his ship to be boarded or to give the man up. Here McNeill demonstrated one quality of a good naval officer; loyalty and an abiding interest in the welfare of his men. This facet of McNeill's character stands out again and again as one examines his surviving written words.

The heavy complaints against McNeill filtering down to the Marine Committee, plus his own intemperate language about Washington's favorite, Manley, led the Committee on November 12, 1777, to suggest to the Eastern Navy Board the advisability of suspending him "till his conduct respecting his last Cruize is properly enquired into."[69] Since a proper court could not be held without Manley, and he a British prisoner, the hearing was deferred until Manley's release the following year. In the meantime, with McNeill under suspension, the *Boston* frigate would get a new captain from New England, but she would not leave port again in 1777.[70]

At Portsmouth the problem of getting cannon for the *Raleigh* frigate, Captain Thomas Thompson, was rendered particularly difficult because there was no foundry capable of casting guns in New Hampshire.[71] John Langdon tried Massachusetts and Rhode Island for cannon where not only were costs excessive, but local needs got first call on the output of the furnaces. On April 29, 1777, the Marine Committee, despairing of filling the *Raleigh's* needs in America, ordered Thompson to sail partially armed for Brest, France, there to complete his suit of cannon. At the same time the Committee cautioned the Captain not to "lavish away Money" and reminded him that "Expedition and vigilence are excellent qualities in a Sea Officer. Frugality is an absolutely necessary one in all men that are connected with the American Revenue."[72]

The *Raleigh* lingered on in port shorthanded for several more months, and, according to British intelligence, with only six or eight of her 32 gun allowance.[73] She was joined, probably early in August, by the *Alfred* which had just been extensively altered at Boston under the direction of Captain Elisha Hinman.[74]   It was almost mid-August when the two Continental ships departed the Piscataqua River and took the sea for France under sealed orders received some weeks earlier.[75]   Although Thompson's ship did not have a full set of guns when getting underway, she certainly mounted enough to fight with as subsequent events will show.[76]   An interesting last minute instruction from the Marine Committee reached New Hampshire after Thompson and Hinman had sailed — "you are to take particular notice that whilst on the Coast of France or in a french Port, you are as much as you conveniently can to keep your Guns covered and concealed and to make as little warlike appearance as possible."[77]

Three days out a small schooner from New York for Halifax was taken.   She was in ballast except for 20 barrels of flour, and the captors found over four thousand dollars in counterfeit Congressional and State of Massachusetts money, which, reported Thompson, "I shall commit to the flames after preserving samples."   The schooner not deemed worth sending in was burned at sea.   On September 2 a snow was taken, and from her master, Captain Hooper, it was learned that on the day before he had straggled from the Windward Island fleet which was under convoy of four British warships — the *Camel*, Commodore the Honorable William C. Finch, *Weazel*, *Druid*, and *Grasshopper*.[78]   Thompson sent the prize snow off for a United States port, but not until he had possessed himself of the convoy's sailing orders and the British commodore's signals from on board.   The next morning the Americans raised the enemy fleet from the mastheads, and by sunset were near enough to discern their number at about 60 sail bearing east by north with the wind west.

Thompson, senior captain, hailed and told Hinman of his intention to run into the enemy fleet at sunrise.   He ordered the *Alfred* to stay close under *Raleigh's* stern until they were alongside the English commodore, then they would open a joint attack.   Over the night the wind shifted to north, and the fleet hauled up close to the wind, so that by daylight of September 4 the Americans found themselves to leeward, distance two or three leagues. The *Raleigh* soon closed but the *Alfred*, "extremely tender-sided" and unable to carry maximum sail, fell further astern and to leeward. Thompson could not take in any sail for fear of being detected, but he did keep his sails shaking in the wind until it was evident that the *Alfred* could not come up. "I determined," said Thompson, "to stand into the fleet and take my chances alone."

Courageously the *Raleigh* hauled into the enemy's midst. Using the captured signals, Thompson gave orders to the merchantmen so that they thought the *Raleigh* some British frigate which had joined. With ports down and cannon housed, Thompson maneuvered alongside to within pistol shot of the *Druid*, 14 gun sloop-of-war, "then we up sails out guns, hoisted Continental colours and bid them strike to the thirteen United States; sudden surprise threw them into confusion, and their sails flew all aback; upon which we complemented them with a gun for each State (a whole broadside into their hull)." On board the *Druid* surprise was complete. The first broadside fatally wounded her captain and killed the sailing master instantly. She could offer but feeble resistance. A sudden squall initially shrouded both ships, and when it lifted the merchant ships were seen scattering in all directions over the ocean surface like frightened chickens in a barnyard. According to Thompson's account of the engagement, the *Raleigh* lay alongside the *Druid* for 45 minutes pouring in 12 broadsides, and a constant fire of musketry from the tops. The British flag, *Camel*, about five miles distant when the firing opened, tacked with the other escort vessels and stood for the *Raleigh*. Thompson, in danger of being surrounded, reluctantly broke off the attack and ran down to the *Alfred* which was also cleared for action. The Englishmen continued to chase until nightfall when they turned into the fleet. For three more days Thompson and Hinman hounded the convoy, but Commodore Finch kept his flock around him tightly and refused to be enticed out to fight. The Continental vessels reset their course for France.[79]

Thompson's object had been to sink the *Druid* if he could not capture her, and undoubtedly he would have succeeded if he had not been driven off by the approach of the other English ships. When he left the *Druid* she seemed to Thompson to be water-logged and in a most shattered condition. This she was indeed, her rigging was cut to ribbons, and she was well holed below the water line. The sloop had six killed, five later died of wounds, and 21 wounded, to the *Raleigh's* loss of one boy killed and another wounded. *Druid* did not sink, however, but made repairs and reached Spithead, England, on October 3, 1777.[80]

Captain Thompson's lunge into a well covered enemy fleet was a romantic and bold act carried off with much elan. His rhetoric matched the deed -- "*I am determined never to war against the merchants where I have an opportunity of waring against the King*" (underscoring is Thompson's).[81] Well said, but here is a prime illustration of naval immaturity. The Continental ships sailed with definite instructions "to avoid large ships of war but we hope you will take some Prizes from the Enemy and carry them in with you"[82] Thompson's failure to understand that capture of merchant vessels and cargoes was most assuredly "waring against the King" as exchanging shot in a square set-to with a vessel of force cost him a once in a life time chance. He allowed a rich fleet of 60 vessels to slip from his grasp without taking one prize when it was easily within his power to cut out a number of the merchants. In contrast, the British commodore displayed naval know-how and stability. We can almost feel with him the angry emotion to accept the challenge to battle from these insolent rebel "privateers." Nevertheless, Finch, a trained and disciplined naval officer, who saw clearly that his duty was to insure safe passage for the merchant ships, refused to be drawn off. This one episode pointed up another naval lesson. Just as the Mc-Neill-Manley cruise illuminated the disastrous consequences of lack of teamwork between commanding officers, the *Raleigh-Alfred* cruise showed the folly of teaming ships of vastly different sailing qualities as consorts.

On October 7 *Raleigh* and *Alfred* came to anchor in the harbor at Lorient, France. They brought with them two prizes, Jamaicamen laden with sugar and rum, seized sometime after the Continental ships gave over dogging the Windward Island Fleet.[83] Thompson notified the American Commissioners at Paris and placed the ships under their direction. Arrangements were made to furnish the vessels with provisions and whatever was wanted. In the case of the *Raleigh,* cannon had priority and Congress' share of the prize money took care of the cost.[84] Chronically short of men and on the lookout for trained mariners of any nationality, both captains sent out recruiting officers to drum up men along the French waterfront.

Thompson and Hinman went to Paris where they presented themselves to Franklin and the other two commissioners for further cruising orders. The captains remained in the French capital for more than a month and apparently had a most delightful stay. Hinman, in later years, often spoke of dining with the Commissioners, and of "the most beautiful ladies he ever met," Marie Antoinette and the Marchioness de Lafayette.[85]

The Commissioners were anxious to see the *Raleigh* and *Alfred* off on their homeward voyage as the time was not propitious for a cruise in European waters. Word had not as yet reached Paris of Burgoyne's surrender at Saratoga, and ticklish negotiations were underway with the all important French alliance in the balance. Versailles was officially disturbed by the receipt of strong complaints not only from England but likewise from neutrals over the seizure of their vessels by Amer-

icans operating from French ports.   At all costs Franklin
wanted to avoid further obvious incident.   Accordingly on
November 25, 1777, Franklin and Deane signed orders for
Thompson and Hinman to return to Lorient and put their
ships in readiness for sea.   The exact course to be followed was
left to Thompson's discretion, but it was suggested that "one
or more of the India ships returning may be intercepted, that
part of the West India homeward-bound ships may be expected
about this time, as well as transports returning from New York
and elsewhere in America, and that by cruising in the proper
latitudes you may meet with them; that the British factories
and commerce on the African coast at this time lie without
any force sufficient to protect them, and that by running
along that coast you may greatly annoy and distress the enemy
in that quarter and afterwards go for the West Indies."   They
were cautioned "to avoid giving any offense to the flags of
neutral powers, and to show them proper marks of respect and
friendship."   The Commissioners, likely having heard the
distressing news of the Manley-McNeill debacle, expressed
happiness over the harmony and confidence which they observed existing between Thompson and Hinman.[86]   *Raleigh* and
Alfred sailed together at the end of December; only one would
reach America safely.

Earlier in 1777 several Continental armed vessels based
on French ports proved unusually effective agents for tight-
ening the tension between England and France.   Attacks on
British commerce in home waters by rebel ships being nourished
and protected in the harbors of a neutral neighbor brought
forth a storm of British diplomatic protest.   One of the public
cruisers, the *Lexington*, was commanded by a New England
captain, and to the movements of this 16 gun brig attention
is now directed.

Lexington, ex-merchantman *Wild Duck*, was a veteran
in the Continental service and one of the first Marine Committee vessels to get to sea in 1776.   Captain John Barry placed

the *Lexington* in commission and cruised her against the enemy with marked success. Barry was followed in the *Lexington* by William Hallock of Maryland. Returning from the West Indies in December 1776, *Lexington* was taken by an enemy frigate. A small British prize crew was placed in the brig together with a considerable number of her own men who were left on board after Captain Hallock and the other officers were removed. Seizing an opportunity, the Americans recaptured the *Lexington* and sailed her into Baltimore.[87] On February 5, 1777, Congress approved the Marine Committee's recommendation that Henry Johnson be appointed to command of the *Lexington*.[88]

Captain Johnson was at loose ends in Baltimore, having escaped from a British prison and but recently returned to America. He was a native of Massachusetts, a prosperous merchant, and may have been residing at Falmouth, Maine, at the opening of the Revolution.[89] Johnson had not been in the Continental service until this time but was known through his reputation as a privateer. Very early in the war he was enriching himself at the expense of the enemy as master of the Massachusetts sloop *Yankee*. Unfortunately for Johnson success proved his undoing. In July 1776 manning prizes had so drastically thinned his own crew that the prisoners were able to rise and take over the *Yankee*.[90]

Johnson and his vessel were brought to Dover and then up the Thames to London. Before transfer to a regular place of confinement, the American captives were held on their own ship. An appeal in behalf of the *Yankee* men signed "Humanitas" and addressed to the Lord Mayor of London luridly paints the unenviable lot of captured sailors.

> They are twenty-five in number, and all inhumanly shut close down, like wild beasts, in a small stinking apartment in the hold of a sloop, about seventy tons burden, without a breadth of air, in this sultry season, but what they receive through a small grating over head, the openings in which are not more than two inches square in any part, and through which the sun beats intensely hot all day; only two or

three being permitted to come on deck at a time; and then they are
exposed in the open sun, which is reflected from the decks and water
like a burning glass.

I do not at all exaggerate, my Lord: I speak the truth; and the
resemblance that this barbarity bears to the memorable black-hole at
Calcutta . . . strikes every one at the sight All England ought to know
that the same game is now acting upon the Thames on board this
privateer.

The putrid streams issuing from the hole are so hot and offensive
that one cannot, without the utmost danger, breathe over it; and I
should not be at all surprised if it should cause a plague to spread.
The miserable wretches below look like persons in a hot bath, panting,
sweating, and fainting for want of air; and the Surgeon declares that
they must all soon perish in that situation, especially as they are almost
all in a sickly state with bilious disorders.[91]

The writer asks relief especially for Captain Johnson and
the doctor, "men of character, of good families in New England," the latter of whom "after the battle of Lexington, April
10, [*sic.*] 1775, for many days voluntarily and generously, without fee or reward, employed himself in dressing the King's
wounded soldiers."[92] One may conjecture that "Humanitas"
was Johnson's brother who had not seen the captain for three
years, and found when he went to visit him that "they were not
permitted to talk together one minute in private."[93]

Johnson and his crew were removed to a British warship.
A brief newspaper announcement dated Newburyport, December 5, 1776, stated: "The friends of Captain Johnson, late commander of the Yankee privateer, are hereby informed, from
good authority, that he has escaped from London to France."[94]
An escape from English confinement does not appear to have
been too difficult if some money could be placed in the proper
hands.

As already noted, Johnson was back in Maryland just as
the Marine Committee was casting about for a captain to take
the *Lexington*. Within three weeks of receiving a naval commission, Johnson had the brig at sea carrying dispatches and
blank naval commissions for the use of the American Commis-

sioners in France. "The British Emissaries in France," warned
the Committee of Secret Correspondence, "are very inquisitive
about all Vessels and Persons coming from America, and therefore you will be very cautious of talking with any Person concerning the place from whence you came, where you are going,
or what is your business."⁹⁵ Pausing in passage long enough
to make two prizes, the *Lexington* entered Bordeaux on April
3, 1777, and the captain departed at once for Paris.

Mr. Van Zandt, alias George Lupton, a British agent operating within the official family of the American Commissioners, promptly informed William Eden in the British foreign
office of Johnson's arrival.

> And now for a piece of news, the noted Yankey, Capt Johnson who
> was taken sometime last summer and brought into London, but after-
> wards made his escape from onboard the man of war in which he was
> confined is arrived here, he brought dispatches from the Congress
> and this day delivered them to Mr. Deane in my presence and while
> we were at dinner, he left Baltimore 28th Feby last, the Congress
> was at that place at that time, he arrived at Bordeaux where his Ship
> is at present. She is called the Lexington, mounts 16 four pounders,
> is a remarkable fast sailing Ship; She has about 60 men on board,
> on his passage he took two prizes, the one an empty Transport which
> he set fire to at Sea, after taking everything that was valuable from
> onboard, the Scoundrel says she lighted him along very pritely for the
> best part of a night, and at last went to the bottom, the other was a
> Scotch Brig bound from some port in London to Jamaica loaded with
> Herring & Coals this vessel, he brought into port with him, tis
> thought she will sell for near one thousand pounds Sterling, this
> Captain is the most conceited Chap I ever met with, and I am much
> mistaken if his own imprudence don't bring him into your hands once
> more, from whom I am convinced he'll not make his escape to very
> easily . . . ⁹⁶

The Commissioners laid out for Johnson their plan for a
bold attack on the Irish linen ships out of Dublin. *Lexington*
was to cruise with two other Continental ships, the *Reprisal*
commanded by the Marylander Lambert Wickes and the *Dolphin*, Captain Samuel Nicholson, younger brother of the

Navy's senior captain. Johnson returned to his ship with orders to join Wickes and Nicholson at Nantes. Coming out of Bordeaux, the *Lexington* was chased by HBM *Foudroyant* but managed to elude the lumbering 80 gun ship-of-the-line.[97]

Under date of May 23, 1777, Wickes, senior of the three captains, issued sailing orders. If at all possible the vessels were to avoid parting from each other. Captures were to be sent into French or Spanish ports, but to maintain the masquerade of neutrality, "The Prize Master must not report or enter her as a prize, but as an American vessel from a port that will be most likely to gain Credit according to the Cargo she may have on board." The names of "reliable" merchants in the several ports who could act as prize agents were included in Wickes' instructions. An interesting arrangement was suggested for handling prisoners — "if you meet a Dutch, French, Dean, Sweed or Spanish vessel, when you have a number of prisoners on board, I think you would do well to put them on board any of those Vessels, giving as much Provisions and Water as will serve them into Port."[98]

The American squadron was windbound at Nantes for several days before getting out on May 28. They outran the waiting *Foudroyant* and set a course to the northwest. The Linen Fleet was missed, but the Americans continued to cruise for a month in the Irish Sea and the English Channel taking 14 prizes within a five day span, a total of 18 prizes in all, right in the enemy's backyard. Off Ushant on June 27, with a large enemy ship in close chase, the squadron was compelled to separate; the *Reprisal* and *Dolphin* got into St. Malo, and *Lexington* to Morlaix.[99]

In Wickes' report to the Commissioners of this first foray into English waters by Continental naval vessels he had only the highest praise for Johnson; "As I had not the pleasure of knowing Captain Johnston before I could not give him a Caracter sufficient to his Merritt; & Now beg leave to Recommend him as a Very brave Active Officer & worthy your

Action between the Continental brig LEXINGTON and the British
cutter ALERT.
Courtesy of Charles D. Childs.

Honours utmost Attention."[100] Silas Deane writing for Franklin and himself responded with a letter to Johnson dated July 25, 1777. "We are sensible of your Spirit, and gallant Behavior as an Officer, and of your attachment to your Country as an American, and shall with pleasure do justice to your Character in Our Letters to the Congress, who we doubt not will pay attention to your Merits." Johnson was alerted to stand by for orders, and because the recent cruise with Wickes and Nicholson had evoked such political and diplomatic thunder, he was constrained to keep his sentiments to himself.[101]

With British Ambassador Lord Stormont voicing his government's indignation at a still officially uncommitted French Court, the American Commissioners found it discreet to send the Continental vessels back across the Atlantic. On September 16 Johnson acknowledged receipt of his orders delivered with packets of dispatches and letters for delivery in America, and he advised the Commissioners that "tomorrow morning shall sail God willing."[102] It was intended to have the Lexington join Reprisal, but not effecting a rendezvous, each sailed independently to disaster.[103]

Two days out of Morlaix for Boston, the Lexington encountered a fast sailing Royal cutter, the Alert, 10 guns, Lieutenant John Bazely. The enemy commander reports the ensuing action:

> I gave chace at five in the morning and came up with him at half past Seven, had a close Engagement till ten when he bore up and made sail, as soon as I got my Rigging to rights, again gave chace and came up with him, at half past one, renewed the Action till half past two, when he Struck. I have been so fortunate as to have had only two men Killed and three wounded, one of which is since Dead with my Mast, Rigging and Sails Much Cutt and Damaged.
>
> The loss on the Rebels side, are seven men Killed, and eleven wounded, in the former are Master and Lieutenant of Marines, in the Latter first Lieutenant and Gunner with her rigging Mast and Sails much damaged.[104]

Before surrendering, Johnson threw the dispatches he was carrying overboard in a weighted bag. Any of several factors may have accounted for the *Lexington* being taken by an enemy ship of inferior force. Richard Dale, a *Lexington* officer, stated that she was short of ammunition, and still another suggestion was that Johnson's French seamen would not stand their guns. The *Alert* was a new cutter with a copper sheathed bottom making her very fast. In addition, although *Alert* mounted fewer cannon than her American adversary, they were ten pounders compared to 2 six pounders and 14 fours in the *Lexington*.[105] Johnson's spirited record allows only the conclusion that he fought his ship to her fullest capability. Heavier shot and superior speed seem to have spelt the difference.

Word of the *Lexington's* loss reaching Paris carried also the erroneous report that Captain Johnson was killed in the battle.[106] Johnson was alive, a prisoner in England for the second time. Again he made his escape, this time from Mill Prison. He was back in New England by July 24, 1778, on which date the Marine Committee requested the Eastern Navy Board to hold a court of inquiry on Johnson's conduct relative to loss of his command.[107] Duty in the *Lexington* was Captain Johnson's only service in the Continental Navy. For the remainder of the war he resumed privateering ventures both as owner and master, frequently stalking prey in his familiar hunting grounds around the British Isles.

In the course of 1777 the Continental Naval career of one more New England captain ended, and for another it began. Elihsa Warner, commanding the *Fly,* was at Philadelphia remanning and repairing after locking horns with an enemy ship off New Jersey the previous fall.[108] The *Fly* was ready to resume service in April, and Warner received Marine Committee orders on the 18th to proceed down the river to the protection of the Cape May Channel, "for the purpose of securing a Communication & passage between this City and the Sea and to protect and assist all American Vessels inward or outward bound as well as to oppose the enemy all in their power."[109] After this date Warner's actions became totally obscure. It may be presumed that he complied with his orders and that *Fly* patrolled the Delaware Bay entrance. When the British occupied Philadelphia in September 1777 and Admiral Howe's fleet arrived in the Delaware, we know that the *Fly* escaped the destruction which was the fate of all Continental vessels trapped in the river above the city. Perhaps at the approach of Howe's force, Warner fled southward thus evading the *cul de sac*. Command of the *Fly* passed to a Maryland captain, James Robinson, on a date unknown.[110] It is reasonable to assume that it was near the end of the year, and at Warner's own request springing from his desire to return to New England. After being away from home and family for 18 months, he asked for and was granted a 60 day leave by the Navy Board. In a letter dated at Providence, January 16, 1778, addressed to Congress (then sitting at Bordentown, New Jersey), Warner expressed his readiness to come south at the end of the leave period, but he asked permission to remain in Rhode Island until appointed to a vessel, preferably one sailing from a New England port.[111] The Journals of the Continental Congress note simply that Warner's letter was read on February 24, 1778.[112] And this is the last we hear of Elisha Warner, lieutenant in the *Andrew Doria*, commander of the *Fly*, and captain number 24, bottom man on the seniority list.[113]

Samuel Chew was appointed a naval captain on June 17, 1777, to command the 10 gun brigantine *Resistance*.[114] Chew was a seasoned seafarer whom it is said was born in Virginia and migrated to Connecticut with a brother.[115] He is referred to at times as being of New Haven, and yet again from New London. Before the war he was well-known to, and employed as a ship master by, the New London merchant, and later naval agent, Nathaniel Shaw, Jr. As early as August 1776 Shaw sponsored Chew for command of an armed schooner carried in by Hopkins' fleet, and which it was contemplated to take into Continental service.[116] However, Shaw found the schooner defective and sold the prize rather than retain her for the public use. Eight months later, that is in April or May 1777, Shaw purchased a brigantine without seeking any further authority or consulting the Marine Committee. His delayed action displeased the Committee and brought forth from them a strong letter of censure. Nevertheless, they decided to take the vessel, call her the *Resistance,* and name Captain Samuel Chew to command her because "we think the Public service will be benefited thereby."[117]   Blank commissions were sent to John Deshon, Connecticut member of the Eastern Navy Board, with authority to appoint the lieutenants and other inferior officers for the brigantine.[118]

The *Resistance* was in the process of conversion and outfitting under Shaw's supervision at New London during the summer and fall months.   Shaw called on the naval agents at Providence and Boston to supply articles which could not be had in Connecticut, and Chew journeyed north to make the request personally.[119]

It was probably the beginning of December 1777 when the *Resistance* set sail under general orders to cruise on the most likely stations to intercept enemy merchant or transport ships.   Chew was quickly rewarded with a valuable prize which arrived safely in Boston.   She was a ship from Scotland bound to the West Indies with a cargo valued at about £7,000, some in Welsh cotton which could be well used for Navy blankets.[120]   While expressing his pleasure at Chew's good fortune, Shaw also showed his keen disappointment that the prize was not sent into New London since it was he who had advanced money to purchase and ready the *Resistance.*[121]   Chew kept the sea as the year closed; we shall follow along with him in the next chapter.

This junior Yankee captain's success at the end of 1777 was a ray of encouragement in a generally dismal period for the fortunes of New England naval officers.   The anticipated striking force of the six frigates had failed to materialize.   Two remained blockaded at Providence, and another was river-bound in Connecticut. Of the three that sailed, one, the *Hancock,* was captured and added to the enemy's already overwhelming naval arsenal. *Cabot,* of the older vessels, suffered the same fate. Although the British frigate *Fox* struck (she was shortly retaken) and the *Druid* was soundly pounded by Captain Thompson in the *Raleigh,* not one vessel of the Royal Navy passed into American hands during the year.

The strength of enemy naval forces in American waters naturally varied and can only be estimated. The Earl of Sandwich, First Lord of the Admiralty, told the House of Lords in an address before Parliament in November 1777 that there were in America 93 warships including six ships-of-the-line.[122] In the meaning of "America" Sandwich included the West Indian and Newfoundland stations as well as the coast of the United States. There were, however, something over 70 vessels ranging from 64 guns down to 10's actively employed on the North American station.[123]

What results the New Englanders achieved against British commerce amounted to less than the preceding year. A total of 11 enemy transports and merchants were captured by New England-commanded Continental ships. In addition 18 vessels were taken during the joint cruise in which Captain Johnson of the *Lexington* took part. At least seven of the prizes were not considered worth sending in and were destroyed at sea. The smaller Continental vessels *Resistance,* Captain Chew, *Providence,* Rathbun, and *Lexington,* Henry Johnson (before being taken) had the most success.

The meaning of British sea power was once again painfully demonstrated as the brothers Howe joined to reduce Philadelphia and destroy Continental shipping in the Delaware. On the American asset side stands the stunning victory at Saratoga, bringing France to the brink of alliance and full partnership in the war.

CHAPTER V

A YEAR OF MIXED BLESSINGS — 1778

I hope we shall make a figure with the navy here notwithstanding the obstacles arising from the Scanty State of our Finances.

JAMES WARREN

Although 1777 proved disappointing, it had not been disastrous for the American cause at sea. Most of the Continental Navy continued intact, and some new or converted vessels were being added to offset losses. The Eastern Navy Board was authorized to give cruising orders, appoint officers, and was otherwise exercising regional supervision over naval affairs in New England. Shortage of seamen and the enemy blockade persisted, but prospects were not wholly unbright that 1778 would see the previous year's hopes come to fruition. This optimism was bolstered by the bright vista of a French fleet operating off the American coast ere long.

As 1778 opened several New England captains were without commands, and three more were British prisoners. Five ships under New Englanders were in home ports from Connecticut north to Boston, while four were out on active duty. It is with the latter group that the narrative for this chapter begins.

In January, Captain Rathbun, who had been at Georgetown, South Carolina, with the sloop *Providence* since the previous November, departed for a daring exploit to the Bahamas.

Rathbun had been with Commodore Hopkins in 1776 when New Providence was easily taken. He now decided to try the same thing with his one 12 gun ship.

The *Providence* was scarcely under sail when she was chased by three enemy craft. To lighten his ship and increase speed, Rathbun cast much of his water and other stores over the side, but the Britishers continued to gain. With night coming on rapidly Rathbun gave up running and attempted a ruse. As soon as darkness closed, all sails on the *Providence* were taken in, and the ship was completely darkened as she lay to. Within a few hours the enemy passed by under full sail and continued on without seeing the American. As soon as they were a safe distance off, Rathbun spread his canvas and set course for Abaco where the sloop came to anchor after a passage without further incident.

The *Providence* replenished at Abaco two days while the crew went to work making a scaling ladder for use in assaulting the New Providence forts. Then with guns housed and most of his crew below deck to allay suspicion, Rathbun sailed into Nassau harbor on the night of 27 January. Shortly before midnight a 25 man landing party was put in the boats, and muffled oars pulled toward shore. The improvised scaling ladder was brought into play, the surprised sentinels overcome, and the islanders awoke the next morning to find the American thirteen stripes flying over Fort Nassau.

Once the menacing guns of the fort were pointed out to the English commander of a 16 gun ship in port, he surrendered without resistance to four American sailors. Meanwhile Rathbun moored the *Providence* abreast of the town with springs on her cables to bring both sides to bear should trouble develop. The inhabitants were dissuaded from hostility when bluffed into believing that Rathbun's sloop was but one of a strong American force awaiting at Abaco. A large brig loaded with indigo was captured and added to the prize ship already mentioned. Two American vessels and some prisoners were released.

For two days Rathbun occupied the forts and held the townspeople at bay. Small arms, ammunition, and hundreds of pounds of gunpowder found in the forts were removed to the ship. The American tars found time enough to savor a delectable dinner of Bahama turtle before their captain had the *Providence* and the prizes ready for sea. Prior to embarking the landing party and casting off, Rathbun ordered the fort's guns spiked and all sponges and rammers broken. "We soon got over the bar," noted Lieutenant Trevett in his journal, "having accomplished every purpose we went there fore. We took a ship and a brig released two schooners and 30 American prisoners, and dismantled the forts, without any blood being shed." On the strength of this New Providence adventure alone, John Peck Rathbun must be ranked as one of the most resourceful, skillfully audacious, and successful captains in the Continental Navy.[1]

Making New Bedford, Massachusetts, late in February, Rathbun received congratulations from the Marine Committee.[2] Almost immediately thereafter Rathbun and his officers found themselves embroiled with the Eastern Navy Board over their refusal to turn over libeling of the prizes to the Continental Agent as prescribed by law. The dispute reached such proportions that the agent requested authority to call on the militia for aid in forcibly seizing the goods. Rathbun's contention that the Continent was not entitled to share in the prizes, elicited from Agent Leonard Jarvis the observation that, "there does not appear to me to be that Disposition to do Justice to the States that I could wish in Officers of the Navy."[3] It seems that when the legal procedure for handling prizes made by Continental vessels was fully explained to Captain Rathbun the matter was amicably settled.

While the work of extensively rebuilding the *Providence's* stern and quarters was undertaken by New Bedford ship carpenters, Rathbun returned to his home. He was still in Boston at the end of April when he acted as a courier to carry two thousand dollars in naval funds from William Story, Clerk of the Eastern Navy Board, to William Vernon at Providence.[4] From Rhode Island, Rathbun journeyed to New Bedford to rejoin his now ready ship. In mid-May instructions were delivered to Rathbun not to leave port until orders were received from the Committee of Foreign Affairs. Although the captain was not told why he was detained, it was because the Marine Committee had decided to send the *Providence* to France with important dispatches from Congress.[5] Whether the plan changed before orders to this effect were actually written cannot now be determined, however, Rathbun did not go to France.

It is noteworthy that in the face of seaman scarcity, Continental captains with reputations for being "prize takers" did not have excessive difficulties enlisting crews. The *Providence* was out again late in July or the first week in August cruising to the east of Nova Scotia. On August 7 about ten leagues from Louisbourg, the American sloop fell in with an enemy convoy of 30 armed transports standing for Halifax. Exhibiting characteristic spark, Rathbun took on one of the transports loaded with Highlander troops. The Britisher mounted 10 to 14 guns, and the engagement lasted from sunset to midnight before Rathbun quitted her without reaching a decision. The *Providence's* masts had been so wounded, that she had to take refuge in an inlet along the Nova Scotia coast, effect temporary repairs, and return to Boston, arriving on September 11, 1778.[6] There is no record of any prizes being made by Rathbun on this short cruise, but the *Providence* was soon on the prowl once more, having sailed about the 14th of November.[7]

Another of the New Englanders, Captain Samuel Chew, subsequent to making his first and quite rich capture in the closing days of 1777, turned the *Resistance* brigantine to milder latitudes. January 15 he put in at Port Royal, South Carolina, bringing in with him an enemy privateer sloop.[8] Pausing only long enough to arrange for selling the prize and to defoul his ship's bottom in a fresh water river, Chew was off cruising the West Indies.   On March 4 the *Resistance* became locked in desperate struggle with a British letter-of-marque mounting 20 guns.   Concluding that the only chance of taking his more powerful adversary was by boarding, Chew placed the *Resistance* alongside.   Just as this was accomplished and boarders called away, fire from the Britisher killed Captain Chew and three crew members.   The two vessels parted with victory going to neither.   *Resistance* put into Martinique for repairs, and was later carried to Boston by Lieutenant Leeds.[9]

The Marine Committee lamented the death of Chew, "a gallant sea officer," first of two "captains to the northward" killed in action while commanding Continental ships.[10] *Resistance* was offered by the Eastern Navy Board to Captain Daniel Waters who, when last heard from, had been captured with John Manley in the *Hancock*. Surviving the terrors of a British prison ship, Waters had returned to Massachusetts by the spring 1778. He declined command of the *Resistance*. Maybe Waters' refusal was based on a seaman's superstition about a dead man's ship, but more likely he felt himself entitled to something better than a 10 gun brigantine. The Marine Committee's reaction to Waters' stand was a sharp rebuke — "inform Captain Waters that should he again refuse such command as shall be offered him, we will consider the propriety of dismissing him from the service." The Committee did not wait for the Eastern Board to name another candidate, but determined themselves on William Burke for the *Resistance*.[11]

Captain Burke was a new name on the naval list. Like Manley and Waters, he was from Massachusetts, and like them he was employed at sea under General Washington's orders beginning in 1775. He was initially Manley's first lieutenant in the *Lee* and later commanded the *Warren* schooner. Captured in August 1776 by the British man-of-war *Liverpool,*

Burke was carried first to Halifax and transferred to a New York prison ship in October.[12] John Bradford, Naval Agent at Boston, recommended Burke to Washington as "a worthy, brave man," deserving of "a better fate."[13] In June 1777 his exchange was requested for an English officer of equal rank, but by Burke's own testimony, he did not regain freedom until the end of February 1778, and then only by escaping.[14]

Burke appeared at the temporary seat of government, York, Pennsylvania, in April 1778 to present a memorial in his own behalf before the Marine Committee and Congress. His petition for relief, strengthened with the magic name Washington and backed by Samuel Adams, received a favorable endorsement from the Marine Committee. After listening to the claim read on May 1, Congress granted Burke a captain's commission in the Continental Navy to rank from that date. Furthermore, he was voted back pay from the time of his appointment by the General to command the *Warren* schooner; another gesture clearly acknowledging the official status of Washington's "fleet."[15]

Burke hesitated before accepting command of the *Resistance*, but for reasons entirely different from those prompting Captain Waters to refuse the brigantine. Much bitterness existed against Burke among naval officers for his alleged conduct while a British captive. The feeling was strong enough to move sundry officers to protest to Congress against Burke's appointment.[16]

What actions on Burke's part caused this resentment can only be surmised. We know for certain that when taken, he spoke of his captors treating him with "great humanity," where "brutality" was the term usually applied.[17] Such an attitude on Burke's part may have paved the way for his confinement to be somewhat less severe than Manley's and Waters', his fellow prisoners. With this shadow cast over him, Burke reported on board his first, and what was to prove his only, Continental command.

As expected, France's treaty of alliance with the United States, concluded in February 1778, was quickly followed by war with her ancient cross-channel rival. A powerful French fleet under the Comte d'Estaing stood out of Toulon April 13 to contest British naval power on the American coast. Arriving off the Delaware Capes in July, d'Estaing sailed first to New York, but refusing to cross the bar at Sandy Hook to attack Admiral Howe within the harbor, continued north to Newport. After a projected joint land and sea assault against the enemy in Rhode Island aborted, and a furious storm extensively damaged his fleet, d'Estaing set course for Boston to refit. The French arrived in that harbor August 28.

Meanwhile about mid-August, the Eastern Navy Board at Boston, anticipating the arrival of d'Estaing, sent the *Resisiance* out as far as Cape Cod to look for the fleet and pilot them in. Burke missed the French, and stood to the southward where he was captured on the 28th by Admiral Howe's squadron sailing to intercept d'Estaing before the Frenchman reached Boston.[18] According to an enemy account, Burke readily disclosed the nature of his mission to the British admiral.[19]

The swiftness with which Burke lost the *Resistance* did nothing to improve his reputation. In notifying the Marine Committee of the loss, the Eastern Navy Board spoke critically of the captain. Yet, when Burke was paroled in October 1778 the account of his conduct was more satisfactory than had been expected, and the Eastern Navy Board revising their earlier opinion expressed the hope that what was previously said would not operate to Burke's disadvantage.[20] But it was of little moment since his brief tour in the Continental Navy was at an end. Although a court of inquiry in February 1779 acquitted him for surrendering the *Resistance,* Burke confined his sea duty to Massachusetts privateers for the remaining period of hostilities.[21]

In the preceding chapter, we left Captains Thompson and Hinman off the French coast, the *Raleigh* and *Alfred* having just departed for a return voyage to America via a circuitous course best calculated to take some prizes. A wine-laden sloop at anchor off the bar at Senegal, Africa, was captured before the Americans turned toward the Windward Islands.[22]

In latitude 16°31'N, longitude 55°40'W, at four bells in the morning watch on March 9, 1778, two sail were sighted from the masthead. Thompson hove to for the *Alfred* and spoke Captain Hinman, instructing him to join *Raleigh* and haul down to look over the strangers. Hinman was to investigate the sternmost ship unless it was discovered that she was the larger, then Thompon in the *Raleigh* would take over. By ten o'clock, when five or six miles separated the four vessels, it was clear to the Yankees that they had encountered enemy ships of force and not merchants. *Raleigh* and *Alfred*, retaining the weather gauge, held the same course as the Englishmen. Then, in Thompson's words:

> On seeing us haul the wind the headmost ship tack'd, then the other tack'd; by this we found that they were trying to work up and get our wakes; the Raleigh I found sailed nearly as well as they, but the Alfred dropped astern and to leeward withal — As the weathermost ship passed under the Alfred's lee, standing to southward on the third tack, Captain Hinman hoisted his colours and fired severl shot, which were returned under English colours; they were then two miles apart, and the other ship four miles to leeward of her consort, the Alfred was about three miles astern of us. I had determined to tack to the Southward and on seeing the firing I ordered the master to put the ship in stays immediately and to stand towards the Alfred that we might close together, when the weathership stood to the Northward again, which would have been a favorable opportunity to attack her if she chose to come up, as the other ship to leeward could not have fetch'd up to his assistance in less than two hours. The instant our helm was put a-lee (without waiting any signal from me) I saw the Alfred right before the wind, and set studdingsails and every other light sail she could set, it was then half past twelve, wind E.N.E. light breeze. I had not determin'd in my own mind what was best to be done, as I knew not their real force, but I imagined either was an overmatch for the Alfred; which I suppose Capt. Hinman discover'd being near them, and knowing the Alfreds best sailing was on one mast, thought that it was his only chance to escape; he might likewise

think the ships might pursue us, being the largest ship . . . I am sorry
he tried to effect his escape at that time as I plainly saw the leeward-
most ship bearing then S.W. would cut him off before he could pass
her or I could give him any assistance. As I saw the Alfred bear away
I did not go about just then, but ordered the courses to be hauled up,
thinking that would tempt the weathermost ship to stand on for us,
but found in a few minutes they were determin'd to act more cau-
tiously, as they both made towards the Alfred; I then ordered the
master to veer and make sail toward the Alfred, and run between her
and the other ship to take off her fire and give the Alfred an opportunity to escape, who I thought gained upon them, but in a few
minutes the two got up and began a furious fire, which was returned
by the Alfred as fast as they could; just as we had got our studding
sails hoisted we had the mortification to see the Alfred haul down her
colours; it was then one o'clock, the firing lasted about ten minutes;
we were then within three miles of the ships.[23]

The sea smooth and wind light, the British were able
to take possession of the *Alfred* quickly and turn on the *Raleigh*.
Thompson changed course to effect escape from what he evaluated as "certainly a superior force." He ordered lumber and
spare gear to be thrown over the side to lighten the ship, and
other weight, about 35 tons, shifted to improve sailing. Slowly
the *Raleigh* pulled ahead, and after 19 hours the enemy, giving over the chase, stood southward with the prize.

The "superior force" which captured *Alfred* and put the
Raleigh to inglorious flight was *Ariadne,* 20 guns, and *Ceres,*
16, ships of the Royal Navy. Opposed to this enemy armament
of 36 cannon, the Continental ships jointly mounted 56 guns.
Thompson, a brave experienced seaman but a rank amateur in
naval tactics, was incapable of meeting the situation and bringing his full strength into play. While Thompson hung back
first on one course and then another, grossly overestimating the
strength of his opponent, and completely undecided on a mode
of action, the Englishmen acted with the sureness of professional and longstanding experience in a regular navy. Correctly
judging that the Americans individually were more than a
match for either of their ships, the British captains engaged

jointly, cut out the *Alfred* and easily took her. They ignored Thompson's sideline efforts to distract them from their smoothly executed plan of attack. Once *Alfred* was disposed of, they both turned on *Raleigh,* and she got away only after a long run.

In his own defense, Thompson asserted that all his concern was for the *Alfred,* and that only after Hinman's sudden and unexpected surrender did he make sail to clear the area.[24] Hinman on the other hand claimed flatly that Thompson deserted him.[25] At this point the harmony which had heretofore existed between the captains came to an abrupt end. Had they thrown their combined weight of metal into action simultaneously, not only would the *Alfred* have been saved, but also the capture of the two British ships made not unlikely. Thompson, as the senior officer and squadron commodore, must share the major blame with a lack of naval training, discipline, and experience which was general in the Continental Navy.

Returning with the *Raleigh* into Boston harbor early in April, Thompson found that he was widely censured for not supporting the *Alfred.* William Story informed Vernon, "The doctr of the Alfred has been at the Board and gives a particular Accot of Capt Thompson's behaviour. he is Condemned by every One and they are Crying out why don't your board turn him out and hang him, &c &c I am Sorry the Service Suffers by the Misconduct of the officers in the navy."[26] Of course, "every One" did not condemn Thompson, he had his supporters. Ellery wrote from Congress, "I hope Capt. Thompson is not culpable. I entertain a high opinion of him."[27] Navy Board member James Warren caused Thompson's report to be printed in the press so that people could make a fairer judgement on "the reputation of a Gentleman, whose character till now, merited the esteem of the public."[28]

On May 8, 1778, the Marine Committee wrote to the Eastern Navy Board on "the disagreeable business of the Alfred's loss" as follows:

From various concurring informations as well as from Captain Thompson's letter to the Committee on the 7th of April last, the Committee are of the opinion that both the public Interest and the honour of Captain Thompson render it necessary that a Court of Enquiry should be held on his conduct But this Enquiry the Committee think cannot properly be made until Captain Hinman or some of his officers can be heard upon the Affairs and in the mean time it is not fit that the public should be deprived of the use of the Raleigh. It is therefore the desire of the Committee that you forthwith suspend Captain Thompson from the Command of that Frigate until a full and fair enquiry can be made into his Conduct.[29]

Captain Hinman and his officers, after surrendering the *Alfred,* were taken on board by his captors and later removed to the *Yarmouth* for passage to England and confinement in Forton prison. While in the 64 gun *Yarmouth* they heard the melancholy account of her recent battle with the American frigate *Randolph* which blew up during the engagement snuffing out the life of Nicholas Biddle, one of the most brilliant and promising captains in the Continental Navy.

Several stories revolving about the captain during his captivity in 1778, which undoubtedly the years have mellowed, have passed down through the Hinman family. One concerns his conversation with the British captain of the *Ariadne* immediately after being taken. Referring to Thompson, the Britisher inquired who "that damnd rascal was who ran away?"

"Sir, he is your countryman," replied Hinman.

"He is a rascal, come from where he may" was the Englishman's comment.

"Had I his ship, I would have taken you, Sir."

"That is loud talking, Capt Hinman."

After stating the force of the *Raleigh,* Hinman asked his captor if he had such a ship did he think he could have captured his own two vessels. The Royal Navy captain thought he could, to which Hinman added, "I think I could do as much as you."

"I believe you can," concluded the Britisher.

Upon arrival at Gosport, England, Hinman was brought before a Scotch magistrate for examination. The judge exploded, "How dare you fight His Majesty's ships, you rebel of His Majesty's Colonies?"

"I dare fight His Majesty himself if I met him on the high seas."

"Who are you, Sir?"

"Elisha Hinman, Sir."

"What's your occupation?"

"I command the *Alfred*, commissioned by the Government of the United States in North America."

"Where was you born?"

"In Woodbury, Sir."

"*And where* is Woodbury?"

"Ten miles from Darby, Sir."

As the story goes, the Scotchman roared approval of the Yankee humor and called for wine to toast this sharp-witted American captain.[30]

Since wars are transitory, and friendships and business associations more lasting, American naval prisoners in England were frequently able to call on prewar connections to aid escape. Hinman spent but a very brief time in Forton prison before he brought this system into play. One night after thoughtfully leaving some money for his wardroom officers and oiling the sentry's conscience with ten guineas, he walked out into the darkness. He trooped through the rain for ten miles until he found a safe night's lodging near London. The next morning Hinman got word to a Mr. Wren in the city. Wren sent his carriage for the Captain with instructions to feign intoxication as a masquerade for his bedraggled appearance. Hinman stayed on in Wren's house for three weeks while arrangements were made for a boat to carry the American escapee to France.[31] Leaving Elisha Hinman on the European continent for the time being, we pass across the Atlantic once again to focus attention on the movements of other New England captains in 1778.

"We . . . are exceedingly pleased to hear that the Warren, after having been so long cooped up in the Bay had got out to sea," enthused the Marine Committee over the good news from the north that during the first week of March Captain John B. Hopkins, commanding the *Warren* frigate, had left the Providence River and succeeded in running past the enemy blockade off Newport.[32]

Circumstances combined to aid the *Warren's* escape. The night was exceedingly dark with little wind until the critical moment of passing closest to the British force. It then came on to blow hard into the northwest speeding Hopkins on his way. The *Warren* was chased and did not come through without damage. Her mizzen yard was shot away, main yard wounded, and she was hulled several times; only one man was slightly wounded.[33] But she was free and could throw her weight into the fight.

Hopkins was under orders to gain New London if at all possible. The wind, however, was unfavorable and weather extremely severe. With many in the *Warren's* crew (about 170 men) not having as much as a change of clothing, Hopkins felt compelled to stand for a short cruise in warmer climate.

Off Bermuda, *Warren* made her first prize, a ship from Whitehaven bound for Philadelphia loaded with salt and dry goods. Hopkins took 120 bales of duck and some other articles (likely clothing for his men) on board his frigate. Soon after a snow from St. Eustatius for Ireland was taken. Both prizes were manned and ordered to any safe port in Massachusetts or New Hampshire. The *Warren* turned north once again and arrived in Boston, March 23. A newspaper dated in January 1778, which Hopkins took out of the captured ship, gave Massachusetts its latest news from England.[34]

For months the *Warren* lay "in a most destitute and forlorn Situation" wanting a crew. Captain Hopkins visited his Rhode Island home where he took a hand enlisting seamen.[35] The Marine Committee's proposal that *Warren* and other Continental frigates join Admiral d'Estaing before New York was not carried out. It seems probable that Hopkins was able to man the *Warren* for a short cruise in search of the Cork Fleet during August and September.[36] If this cruise, which concluded the frigate's movement and Hopkins' sea service for 1778, produced any notable results the facts have not been preserved.

After the sloop *Providence* led the way the previous year, and more recently the *Warren* escaped from Narragansett Bay, Hoysted Hacker with the ship *Columbus* was next to try. Expectations were none too bright that he would make it, and precautions taken accordingly. William Vernon wrote from Providence, "we have Landed all her Stores except 4 fowl Guns to keep off a Boat, wch brings the Ship to a light set of Ballast and much facilitate her Sailing, besides if she falls into the Enemies hands they will gain an Old Ship and Twenty five Men wch we think sufficient to run the Ship to N. London."[37] Upon reaching that Connecticut port, guns and stores, which were transported overland, would be put back in the *Columbus*. Only favorable wind and thick weather were awaited. Hacker made the attempt on the night of March 27, and to James Warren it seemed that he "took a poor time."[38]

By chance a merchant brig sailed the same evening as the *Columbus*. The brig was detected by an enemy patrol craft whose signal guns caused two frigates to get underway immediately. It was these British frigates which intercepted the Continental ship. Finding escape impossible, Hacker ran the *Columbus* hard aground near Point Judith. He and his men spent the night stripping the ship of her sails and most of her rigging. The following morning a boatload of English sailors was driven off by small arms fire from the beach, and salvage work continued until nightfall before the Americans abandoned the hull. She was then burnt by an enemy landing party. Incidentally, the merchant brig which unwittingly acted as informer got safely out to sea.[39]

The *Providence* frigate, Captain Abraham Whipple, was still to make the hazardous dash from her extended confinement in the Providence River. Whipple had long been inactive and his ship uselessly moored at her 1776 building site. To expedite getting her manned, the Eastern Navy Board, on its own authority, offered an additional money advance over and above what was allowed by Congress to every man entered on board.[40] By the end of March 1778 Whipple had shipped only 130 sailors, but he was determined to accept his undermanned condition and push out on the first good wind. He was ordered to France to load cannon and other supplies, but since he had to pass through a line of the enemy's ships, no dispatches or papers of any great consequence were entrusted to the *Providence*.[41]

On the 30th of April, at night, *Providence* with her crew now swelled to about 170 men came under sail in a brisk wind. She was discovered by the British frigate *Lark*, which, according to Whipple, had been fitted out for the purpose of taking him, and a severe running battle ensued. Whipple claimed to have disabled the *Lark* and to have sustained the fire of 11 other enemy ships before passing out of the Bay in a most shattered condition. Narrowly evading a British ship-of-the-line the first day at sea, the *Providence* continued on course. A passage of 26 days brought her to Nantes in company with a captured wine-laden brig.[42] There Whipple learned that the *Boston* frigate and sloop-of-war *Ranger* were already in French waters. John Paul Jones of the *Ranger*, never one to let his presence go long unnoticed by a senior officer, wrote Whipple congratulations on "his release from pergatory," and an unflagging devotion to the ladies stirred him to ask for news about "our agreeable widow or my little affair of the heart at Providence."[43]

The *Boston* had been brought to France by Samuel Tucker who succeeded to command of that frigate at Boston after Hector McNeill's suspension in November 1777.[44] Tucker, a

master mariner of Marblehead, Massachusetts, had followed
the sea since as an 11 year old boy he ran off to join the British
Navy and fight the French. Like Manley, Waters, and Burke,
he was one of that company of naval officers who began Revo-
lutionary War service under appointment from Washington.
The General named Tucker captain of the armed schooner
Franklin on January 20, 1776, and he moved to the *Hancock*
some months later.[45] It was to this early activity in Washing-
ton's "fleet" that Tucker owed his selection by Congress,
March 15, 1777, to be a captain in the Continental Navy.[46]
No vessel was available for him until McNeill's difficulties left
Boston without a commanding officer.

"The Boston hath on a pretious cargoe" was the way William Ellery informed a confidant that Tucker's ship had been
selected to carry John Adams to France where he was to replace Silas Deane. Under date of February 10, 1778, the Eastern Navy Board issued orders to Captain Tucker.

> Sir: Notwithstanding the general instructions given you, you are to
> consider the Honourable John Adams, Esq. (who takes passage in the
> Boston), as one of the commissioners, with the Honourable Benjamin
> Franklin and Arthur Lee, Esqs. and therefore any applications or
> orders received from him as valid as if received from either of
> the other two. You are to afford him on his passage every accommoda-
> tion in your power, and to consult him on all occasions with respect to
> your passage and general conduct, and the port you shall endeavor
> to get into, and on all occasions have regard to the importance of his
> security and safe arrival.[47]

Adams, then, was not merely a passenger but would
assume the role of "Commodore" or naval official afloat
authorized to give the captain orders. Traveling with Adams
were his son John Quincy and sons of Silas Deane and William
Vernon making the educational trip to Europe prescribed for
all young gentlemen. Thanks to keen observing by this "pretious cargoe" the details of an ocean crossing in a Revolutionary
warship, including the seasickness, boredom, nauseating food,
and smell of putrid water, have been saved for us.

After dining ashore with his distinguished charge Friday, February 13, Tucker accompanied him in the *Boston's* barge to the frigate which was lying out in the stream. Adams sized up Captain Tucker as "an able seaman, and a brave, active, vigilant officer, but I believe he has no great erudition. His library consists of Dyché's English Dictionary, Charlevoix's Paraguay, The Rights of the Christian Church Asserted vs. The Romish and other Priests who claim an Independent Power over it, the second volume of Chubb's Posthumous Works, one volume of the History of Charles Horton, Esq., and one volume of the Delicate Embarassments, a novel."[48] Nevertheless, Adams concluded, "I found him after a while as sociable as any Marblehead man."[49] From a Braintree man, this came close to a compliment.

Tucker weighed on February 15, came around to Marblehead harbor, and anchored about noon the same day. Adverse winds and heavy snow held the *Boston* there for two days. Since a goodly number of the crew were native to this coastal community, the ship swarmed with mothers, wives, and sisters begging leave for their men to come ashore if just for one hour. Tucker was forced to refuse most requests knowing full well that a sailor once ashore could decide to stay.

Four days out to sea, the *Boston,* being then in the "squally latitudes" (36° to 39° North), was struck by a storm of hurricane force. The wind raged in full fury for three days. "No man could keep upon his legs," recorded Adams, "and nothing could be kept in its place; an universal wreck of every thing in all parts of the ship, chests, casks, bottles, etc." If the hatches were kept closed the stifling air was suffocating, and if opened the sea water poured in until everything below decks was afloat; "Our little world is all wet and damp." Had the *Boston* foundered, two future presidents of the United States would have been lost.

In fair weather *Boston* flew along nicely at better than eight knots, covering about two hundred miles in a twenty-four hour period. Adams noted the same inattention to economy in the Navy as there was in the Army and was not the least hesitant about exercising his official prerogatives.

> I am constantly giving hints to the captain concerning order, economy, and regularity, and he seems to be sensible of the necessity of them, and exerts himself to introduce them. He has cleaned out the 'tween decks, ordered up the hammocks to be aired, and ordered up the sick, such as could bear it upon deck for sweet air. This ship would have bred the plague or the jail fever, if there had not been great exertions, since the storm, to wash, sweep, air, and purify clothes, cots, cabins, hammocks, and all other things, places, and persons. The captain, yesterday, went down into the cockpit and ordered up everybody from that sink of devastation and putrification; ordered up the hammocks, etc. This was in pursuance of the advice I gave him in the morning: "If you intend to have any reputation for economy, discipline, or anything that is good, look to your cockpit."

What Captain Tucker's inner reactions were to the statesman's "hints," we do not know, but can guess.

On March 11 Tucker requested and received permission from Adams to chase a vessel. Upon coming up she was found to be a 14 gun British letter of marque. The enemy opened fire, but seeing the *Boston's* broadside, thought better of it and lowered her colors at once. Many years later Adams would recall Tucker's words restraining his crew from firing: "Hold on, my men. I wish to save that egg without breaking the shell."[50]

The prize was the ship *Martha* out of London for New York. Her master said that the cargo of provisions and stores was insured by Lloyd's for 72,000 pounds sterling, but that it was actually worth ten thousand more. Tucker placed a prize crew on board the *Martha* and dispatched this rich catch for Boston.

Several days later an unfortunate accident occurred. First Lieutenant William Barron's leg was shattered by a gun burst. The leg was amputated, and Barron died after suffering great pain for more than a week. The lieutenant's body was committed to the deep in a chest weighted down with the fragments of the gun which had caused his death.

Adams' turbulent taste of life at sea ended on April 1, 1778, as the *Boston* glided past the Tower of Cordouan and came to anchor just below Bordeaux. Taking leave of Captain Tucker, Adams and his young charges started for Paris thankful for a safe, albeit a stormy voyage.[51]

Tucker stayed at Bordeaux for better than two months. French seamen were recruited while the ship was careened, thoroughly cleaned, and a new mainmast stepped in. The *Boston* was visited daily by throngs of sightseers. "One would think," Tucker wrote in the log, "they never saw a ship before, but it is all on account of its being a Boston frigate."[52]

By June 6 the *Boston* was ready for sea once again and sailed on a one month cruise off the British Isles and as far west as the Newfoundland Banks. On the 19th a Scotch brig, *John and Rebecca*, from Venice to London loaded with cream of tartar and raisins, was captured. This prize, the first of four made on the cruise, was sent to Boston where the cargo was certain of bringing a good price. The others Tucker ordered to Lorient, and he laid down a course for the same port.

Upon arrival at Lorient, Tucker sent his second lieutenant to Paris to advise the Commissioners of the results of his latest cruise and to receive their further orders for the ship's employment. The number of log entries noting resort to the "cat" give testimony that the *Boston* had a troublesome and mutinous crew at this time. A French general came on board and took out 47 French sailors and marines ignoring both the captain's loud objections and the evidence in the ship's book that they were not pressed but had signed on as volunteers. Tucker's protest letter to Paris drew a noncommittal reply from the Commissioners who understandably wanted to do nothing which would disturb our new ally.[53]

Having sold his three prizes, Tucker weighed anchor August 1 in compliance with the Commissioners' orders for Boston to join the *Providence,* Captain Whipple, at Nantes, a scant two days sailing distance from Lorient.[54] *Providence* came down the Loire River to Paimboeuf, the Yankee captains exchanged courtesy visits, and the ships complimented each other with 13 gun salutes. They then sailed in company and arrived at Brest on August 14 to meet the *Ranger.* "Thank God, there will be two frigates and a sloop of war belonging to the thirteen United States together, and I hope Heaven will send us success in the cruise, and that we all may return to America, plentifully loaded with his divine goodness."[55] These were Tucker's reverent musings on the possibilities offered by the combined strength for the three captains to be heavily blessed with "divine goodness," *i.e.* enemy ships and rich cargoes.

The *Ranger,* 18 gun sloop-of-war, was built at Portsmouth, New Hampshire, for the Continental service in 1777 and in December of that year, commanded by Captain John Paul Jones, she arrived in France. In the *Ranger,* Jones made daring forays around the British Isles, fought and took His Majesty's ship-of-war *Drake,* 20 guns. Jones sent his first lieutenant, Thomas Simpson to the *Drake* as prize master. On May 6, 1778, Jones placed Simpson under arrest for disobedience of orders — by this action and the results which followed the lieutenant becomes subject to inclusion in this study.

Simpson was from Portsmouth, New Hampshire, and a brother-in-law of John Langdon; two circumstances which may account for his selection as the *Ranger's* first lieutenant.[56] He shipped on the sloop in that station with the understanding that when Jones was transferred to a larger vessel in Europe, command of the *Ranger* would go to him.[57] Simpson was extremely popular with the men, and the opposite was true of Jones. Fearing that Simpson's presence as a prisoner on board the *Ranger* would excite the crew to insubordination, Jones had him confined on a French ship, from where he was further transferred to a prison ashore.[58]

Simpson himself as well as the ship's officers and men flooded the American Commissioners with letters and certificates denouncing Captain Jones. One such petition signed by the "Jovial Tars" asked the release of "our first Lieutenant who is now confined innocently, *as we think,* in a lousy, dirty french Gaol."[59] The Commissioners wrote to Jones on June 3 that it was their desire to see Simpson released on his parole to go to Nantes for passage to America and trial by court martial; a decision arrived at not by "any decided opinion concerning his guilt or innocence," but that "his confinement in a prison on shore, appears to us to carry in it a degree of severity which cannot be justified by reason or law."[60] Jones complied and notified the Commissioners that he was going even further.

> At the time when I took Lieutenant Simpson's parole I did not expect to have been so long absent from America; but as circumstances have now rendered the time of my return less certain, I am willing to let the dispute between us drop forever by giving up that parole, which will entitle him to the command of the *Ranger*. I bear no malice; and if I have done him an injury, this will be making him all the present satisfaction in my power. If, on the contrary, he has injured me, I will trust to himself for an acknowledgement.[61]

This letter makes it clear that Jones released Simpson from any formal obligation. The Commissioners acted on this basis and issued a captain's commission for Simpson. They gave him the *Ranger;* a command to which Jones himself said Simpson was entitled.

By August 15 Jones, now at Brest and disturbed by prevalent rumors that he had been turned out of his ship and out of the naval service, had a change of heart. He sent messages to the Commissioners and Captain Whipple, senior naval officer present, again requesting that Simpson be brought to trial, and pointing out that there was now a sufficient number of Continental naval captains in France to constitute a court martial (regulations required that a court martial consist of at least three captains).[62] The Commissioners were agreeable but stipulated that Simpson remain in command of *Ranger* until a judgement was reached.[63] However, Captain Elisha Hinman, expecting upon his return to America to face a court of inquiry on the loss of the *Alfred*, declined to sit. This left only two eligibles, Whipple and Tucker, and no court was summoned.[64] Simpson had come off unscathed aided by friendly support from the naval captains present in Europe, all New Englanders, and John Adams, a sympathetic ear in Paris. The Marine Committee approved the Commissioners' decision and continued Simpson in command of *Ranger* until the sloop's capture in 1780.[65]

The Continental ships, Whipple as squadron commodore, sailed together from Brest on August 22, 1778, carrying ammunition, arms, copper, and clothing for America.[66] Three prizes, a snow and two brigs from which the Americans replenished their rum supply, were taken on the westward passage.[67] Tucker was still having trouble with his crew and had to transfer two mutinous fellows on board the Commodore. The squadron made Portsmouth, New Hampshire, on October 16. Six days later Whipple and Tucker hove up and bore away for Boston while Simpson remained in his home port for the rest of the year repairing and cleaning down the *Ranger*.[68]

Captain Elisha Hinman returned from France as a passenger in the *Providence*. He immediately notified Henry Laurens, President of Congress, of his arrival and availability to stand trial. Since Hinman's court of inquiry was not held until early the next year, however, the findings shall be examined in the succeeding chapter.[69] In matter of time we have now arrived at the point of introducing Silas Talbot, a Rhode Island army officer whose colorful reputation built upon daring naval exploits against the enemy led in 1779 to a captain's commission in the Continental Navy.

Talbot, the ninth of fourteen children, was born in Bristol County, Massachusetts Bay, but he early settled in Providence

CAPTAIN SILAS TALBOT

Courtesy Naval History Division, U. S. Navy Department.

and must be considered a Rhode Islander. He had embraced the sea since he first shipped as a cabin boy on a coastal voyage to the southern colonies. In the tense months before Revolution flared, Talbot was in the group of Providence young men secretly shouldering muskets to drill by candle light in a sugar-house loft. On June 28, 1775, Talbot was commissioned captain in one of the Rhode Island regiments of foot and participated with Washington's force in the siege of Boston. When Commodore Hopkins appealed to Washington for soldiers to man his sickness-decimated fleet and bring the ships around to Providence from New London in April 1776, Talbot could not resist the urge to get back to his familiar element and volunteered for the service.

Captain Talbot rejoined Washington around New York and took command of a fire ship for the purpose of destroying one or more of Admiral Howe's fleet in the Hudson River. A heroic but unsuccessful attempt was made against the 64 gun ship *Asia*. Talbot was severely burned, and for his bravery was promoted to major. During 1777 Talbot, wounded in the defense of Philadelphia, was granted leave to return to his family. While in Providence he placed himself under the command of Major General John Sullivan then preparing a joint attack with d'Estaing's fleet against the British on Rhode Island.

When the French left Narragansett Bay the English stationed an 8 gun schooner manned by a crew of 45 in the eastern passage between the island and the main. She was called the *Pigot* in honor of the commander in the area, General Sir Robert Pigot, and very effectively shut off the channel to Providence. The idea of boarding and taking the schooner by surprise was just the kind of adventure which had great appeal for Talbot the army major with the heart and predilections of a sailor. After some convincing, General Sullivan decided to let him have a go at it. A small coastal sloop named the *Hawk* carrying 2 three pounders was obtained, and sixty soldiers from the different regiments volunteered.

By the end of October 1778 Talbot was ready. The *Hawk* went down the river in short stages as the wind allowed. On the night of the 28th Talbot took in all sails, and with bare poles *Hawk* drifted through Fogland Ferry without alerting the shore batteries. Sails were now set as the American stood directly for *Pigot*. The Englishmen topside hailed and then opened small arms fire which Talbot declined to answer. The two ships came together, and the *Hawk's* jib boom tore through and held in the schooner's fore shrouds. At that moment Talbot's soldiers opened with such a volley of musketry that all the enemy sailors on deck were driven below. All that is, according to Talbot's report, with the exception of the schooner's captain, Lieutenant Dunlop of the Royal Navy, who "behaved with the greatest resolution, and Defended the Sides of his Vessel in his Shirt and Drawers for some time without a single soul of his Crew to assist him."[70] The Americans ran out on the jib boom, boarded and carried the *Pigot* without a man on either side being killed. Talbot sailed his prize into Stonington, Connecticut, where he landed his prisoners and marched them back to Providence.[71]

For this well-planned and brilliantly executed attack on a King's ship, Talbot received wide acclaim. Rhode Island presented him with a sword, and from Congress he received promotion to lieutenant colonel and personal congratulations from President Henry Laurens.[72] The British remembered Talbot also, labeling him as "one of the greatest archrebels in nature."[73]

Completion or near readiness of newly-built ships and others purchased under Congressional authority were counted on to offset losses at sea during 1778. One vessel obtained in New England with the amusing name *Industrious Bee* was fitted as an 18 gun brigantine, and rechristened, as more befitting a fighting ship, the *General Gates*.[74] Selection of commanders for vessels of this size was left to the Eastern Navy Board. Upon the high recommendation of John Bradford, Boston prize agent, the Board appointed John Skimmer.[75]

Skimmer added one more to that growing group of Massachusetts officers who entered the Continental Navy via the road of early sea service under Washington. Skimmer commanded the schooner *Franklin* in 1776 and *Lee* the next year.[76]

During the summer of 1778 the *General Gates* left Boston on her first cruise. Included in the crew was John Skimmer, Jr. son of the captain, carried on the ship's muster as "Boy," rating ½ share in prize money distribution.[77] A brig was captured in short order and sent to Boston where she arrived at the end of July with her cargo of fish which was much wanted for the use of the Army and the French fleet.[78] Two more prizes were taken, a schooner and a letter of marque brig called the *Montague*. In the engagement with the latter vessel, Captain Skimmer was killed; the second and last New England Continental Naval captain to give his life in active combat against the enemy.

Skimmer left a widow and 11 young children. John Bradford, who as we have seen was instrumental in procuring a naval commission for Skimmer, prepared a memorial to Congress asking assistance for the late captain's family. The matter was referred to the Marine Committee, which, after being satisfied that Skimmer was a "brave and worthy officer" who "lost his life in a severe engagement with the enemy," recommended, and Congress approved, a payment of $400 annually in quarterly installments for three years to enable the widow to support her family.[79]

After the death of Skimmer the *General Gates* returned to Boston near the end of August bringing her prizes in with her.[80] For the second time the Eastern Navy Board offered a command vacated by death to Captain Daniel Waters. It will be remembered that Waters had declined the proffered command of the *Resistance* when Captain Chew was killed, and for his refusal was threatened with dismissal from the Navy.[81] This time he accepted public service and sailed for the

West Indies about mid-November in company with the *Providence* sloop, Captain Rathbun. The *General Gates* was at sea until after the first of the year.

An old 28 gun frigate named the *Queen of France,* to honor the ally on which so much depended, was purchased in France for the Continental Navy by the Commissioners. She sailed into Boston harbor from Europe carrying a cargo of clothing and stores in May 1778 under Captain John Green of Pennsylvania with French officers and men.[82] The Marine Committee gave permanent command of the frigate to Captain Joseph Olney whose previous Continental ship was the *Cabot* which he lost in 1777.[83] When the *Queen of France* arrived in America the French crew was paid off, and Olney was faced with the ever vexatious recruiting problem. Lack of seamen plus requisite outfitting combined to hold the frigate idle at her moorings for the rest of 1778.

During this year another frigate of 32 guns was being built on the Thames River at Norwich, Connecticut, with the help of Mohegan Indian labor and "tory timber" from confiscated loyalist holdings.[84] At a time when the number of unemployed captains on the naval list far exceeded the available commands, Governor Trumbull urged appointment of a local favorite to the Norwich frigate.

> I take the liberty of addressing you at this time in commendation of Capt. Seth Harding of this State not of myself only, but at the desire of my Council of Safety. This gentleman has from the commencement of the War been employed in the service of this State as Commander of an armed vessel, in which character he has distinguished himself on several occasions, principally in the Spring of 1776 in Boston. This action was particularly gallant and has seldom been equal nor perhaps has any one man during the war, with so small a command as a Brig of 16 guns, taken such a number of prisoners as he did on that day only ... and I would propose him to your Honbl Board to be appointed to the command of the Frigate now building at Norwich which is so far as to require the speedy appointment of a Captain. As much merit and service may be pleaded in favour of Captain Harding as of any gentleman, and there is no one who can man the ship more

expeditiously than him, from the opinion which the seamen in general entertain of him. I would likewise mention that of the many appointments in the Navy hitherto, this State has never nominated one.[85]

On April 20 the Marine Committee replied to the Governor, and as nicely as possible told him that the choice of a commanding officer was none of his business.

> We have the honor of acknowledging your letter of the 2d inst. and very unhappy in not being able to comply with the request of your Excellency and your Council of safety. The gallant conduct of Captain Harding entitles him to notice, but when you Sir, and your Council of safety consider that by the destruction and Capture of several of our frigates their Captains are thrown out of actual service, you will easily perceive that it would be doing not only injustice to those officers some of whom at least are very valuable, but to the Continent to pass by them, and appoint to the command of the frigate at Norwich any Gentleman who hath not had a Command in the Continental Navy let his merit be ever so great. It would particularly disappoint the expectations of Captain Hinman who hath wrote to us on the subject should we honor Captain Harding with Command of that frigate. Indeed it is not with us to appoint it is our duty only to nominate and recommend.

The Committee then went on refreshing Trumbull's memory on the subject of officer nominations from Connecticut.

> We beg leave to answer the last paragraph in your Excellency's letter to observe, that it is not the practice of States to recommend Navy Officers, and that Captain Saltonstall was nominated to Congress by the Marine Committee in consequence of recommendations from the Delegates of your States.[86]

Trumbull was not the least bit impressed by the Committee's implied intention to recommend Connecticut officer Elisha Hinman. Working through the state's delegation in Congress he persisted in his design. Early in September 1778 the Governor sent Harding to Philadelphia presumably on the assumption that he could press his case before the Marine Committee and influential Congressmen. Captain Hinman had not as yet returned from English imprisonment.

September 24, Harding, sounding very sure of himself, addressed a letter to President Laurens stating that he was ready to leave Philadelphia the minute he received his commission, and urging the legislature to get on with his "business."[87] The very next day, after the letter was read on the floor, Congress resolved that "the new frigate building at Norwich, in Connecticut, and now nearly ready to be launched, be named the *Confederacy*." Congress then proceeded to the election of a captain, "and the ballots being taken, Captain Harding was elected."[88] A personal and political triumph for Governor Trumbull over Marine Committee objection and just treatment for the older captains was accomplished.

The fact that Seth Harding's commission was granted through influence and pressure from persons in high position was, as we know, more the usual than the extraordinary, and in no way detracts from his suitability for the command. By training and wartime experience he was as qualified as any man to captain the *Confederacy*.

Harding was a long-time resident of Norwich, the place where his ship was on the stocks. He was born in 1734 on Cape Cod in Massachusetts Bay Colony, and removed to Connecticut with a young daughter after the death of his wife. As master of Connecticut ships he prospered in the Nova Scotia and West Indian trade. Four years before the Revolution Harding settled in Liverpool, Nova Scotia, where he owned a profitable salmon fishery and entered politics as a representative from his district in the provincial General Assembly. In full sympathy with the colonial cause, he found his position in Nova Scotia untenable and returned to Norwich soon after the war opened. Governor Trumbull and the Committee of Safety appointed Harding a captain and gave him command of a brig in the Connecticut State Navy. He operated with marked success against British shipping in Massachusetts Bay, Long Island Sound, and against Tory activities between Connecticut and Long Island.

The *Confederacy* was launched November 8, 1778, and towed down the Thames to be completed at New London.[59] Procurement of cannon in adequate quantity was a big problem. The Eastern Navy Board persuaded General Sullivan to part with the guns out of the captured British schooner *Pigot* to fill out the *Confederacy's* suit.[90] Recruiting was very slow, Governor Trumbull's assertion that Harding could expeditiously man the ship to the contrary.[91]

The original Connecticut frigate, *Trumbull*, Captain Dudley Saltonstall, in defiance of effort and money spent attempting to pass her over the bar, clung to the river-prison where she had been confined since built in 1776. In March 1778 when tides were running high, Saltonstall was furnished with extra men and four thousand dollars.[92] Deshon of the Eastern Navy Board went to Connecticut and remained there for some months determined that "she must be intirely stript of her Yards and Top Mast, and all her Story even to a Swept Hole that if possible to bring her to 9 or 10 feet Water."[93]

The Marine Committee, without informing the Eastern Navy Board of their action, asked Governor Trumbull and the Connecticut Council to see what could be done about getting the frigate out. Calling on state officials clearly reflected Marine Committee displeasure with Saltonstall and the Navy Board's failure. The Board was very annoyed, and it may be imagined that they were little placated by the Committee's explanation — "With regard to the Trumbull, the Governor & Council of Connecticut were desired to assist in getting her out of the River because you were not then assembled at Boston, and not from any the most distant Idea of your incompetency to the business."[94] Meanwhile the subject of the "business" stayed put.

Deshon supervised another try in October, but the *Trumbull* grounded on the bar, lay there a whole tide, and had to be hauled back into the river again. In a move likely dictated by awareness that even if the ship could be brought out in this advanced season of the year she could not be manned and put into service, the Marine Committee requested that further attempts be laid aside for the present.[95]　So the stubborn *Trumbull* remained where she always had been.

While Saltonstall was denied active sea duty in 1778, he was called upon to don his naval uniform and perform different service as a senior Continental officer.　June 1778 was the month of courts martial with Captain Saltonstall presiding. "Capt Manley is now on Tryall at a Court Martial," wrote James Warren and John Deshon on June 10 to Vernon, "Thursday is appointed for the determination of this Court. Capt McNeills comes on Friday next.　he conducts in the present Similar to what he did in the former Court of Enquiry, which is to Create as much Charge and perplexity as possible. Capt Thompson's Tryall comes on immediately after McNeills and after him H Harkers Court of Enquiry concerning the loss of the Columbus."[96]　The courts convened on board the *Raleigh*.

After many months' confinement on board a British prison ship in New York harbor, John Manley returned to Massachusetts in April 1778 to stand trial for the loss of the *Hancock* frigate.　His earlier reputation, Washington's high opinion of him, and public sympathy for the sufferings of a prisoner were aligned in his favor.　On June 13 the Court rendered its opinion.

> No part of the Charge is supported against Capt Manley except that he was deficient in establishing a proper System of Signals previous to the Ships Sailing and during the Cruise and also of Imprudence on 30th of May 1777 in laying by for a large Ship of the Enemy to come down upon him before he had tryed her Sailing.　That the Court have the fullest reason to Attribute this Conduct rather to Inexperience than any Censurable Motive.　The Court are further of Opinion that Capt Manley did all that lay in his power to save the Hancock and that he did not in any Instance during the Cruise discover any want of Courage but on the contrary great Zeal for the good of the service he was Engaged in.　The Court therefore Acquit him of every part of the Charge and beg leave to recommend him to Congress as a Spirited and brave Officer.[97]

There can be no argument with the court's finding that Manley was inexperienced in the naval tactics demanded of a commodore engaging enemy warships. But Manley was an experienced sea captain who lost his ship through two critical personal errors for which he certainly should have been held responsible. In the first place, by unwisely shifting his weight he threw the *Hancock* out of trim allowing the slower Britisher to overtake him, and secondly, he exaggerated the force of his antagonist and gave up without a fight. The court chose to ignore these factors.

Although completely exonerated, there was no public vessel which could be offered to Captain Manley. He engaged in privateering, and it was not until 1782, near the end of the war, that he again took the quarter deck of a Continental ship.

The decision reached on Manley allowed but one verdict in the case of Hector McNeill, late captain of the *Boston,* who already stood suspended. If Manley was innocent then McNeill had to be blamed. His brother officers sitting in judgement found him guilty of failing to support the *Hancock,* and he was dismissed from the naval service.

The court's decision was a stunning blow to McNeill who held himself "Exceedingly Agrieved," and "thereby rob'd of his reputation and exposed to perpetuall infamy." A friend of long standing, John Paul Jones, freely offered condolences, but his aid did not go beyond sympathy. McNeill went to Philadelphia and remained many months in a futile effort to have the court martial decision reversed. The Marine Committee did recommend to Congress in January 1779 that "the Sentence of the Court Martial against Capt. McNeill be not carried into execution." Congress never acted on the suggestion, and the dismissal stood.⁹⁸

From the evidence available to us of the *Boston-Hancock* affair, it is clear that McNeill deserted his superior officer in the face of the enemy and ran. That this may or may not have been a mistake in judgement does not alter the fact, and his removal from the Navy seems justified. After McNeill's return to Boston from Philadelphia he plunged into privateering both as an investor and ship master.

Next to be called to account for not properly assisting his consort was Captain Thomas Thompson. Like McNeill, Thompson was popularly condemned and under Marine Committee suspension. An unusual aspect of Thompson being brought to trial at this time was that the chief prosecution witness, Elisha Hinman captain of the captured *Alfred,* was still in Europe. There seem to be two probable explanations for this. Thompson may have demanded his trial on the chance of being cleared before Hinman's damning testimony could be heard. Or, the Eastern Navy Board believing that sufficient evidence was at hand from the *Alfred's* surgeon and others, and anxious to have Thompson off their necks, ordered the court to proceed.

Thompson was found guilty as charged and cashiered from the Continental Navy. He did not take the verdict easily; charges went off in all directions against Hinman and appeals forwarded to Congress for the case to be reopened.[99] The court martial proceedings were ordered to lie on the Congressional table for consideration in August, and Hinman, upon arrival in America, heard that Thompson was recommended for another command.[100] Ultimately the findings were sustained, and Thompson's naval career was over although he clung to the hope that he would be vindicated when Hinman was tried. At home in Portsmouth Thompson's reputation seems to have suffered not at all. He was soon active as owner and bonder of New Hampshire privateer ships, and later was commissioned a colonel of artillery in the state militia.[101]

The final captain to come before the bar in this series of reckonings was Hoysted Hacker for the loss of the *Columbus* when chased ashore at Point Judith. Since the *Columbus* was stripped of her guns before attempting the perilous run of the blockade, the old converted merchant hull was considered but "a trifling Loss."[102] Hacker had held off the enemy until most of the ship's rigging and any other material of value had been removed. He was given a clean bill of health by the court of inquiry, and was free to sail and lose a Continental ship another day.

In summary then we find that 1778 was the terminal year for the Continental service of five more New England captains. Skimmer and Chew gave their lives; two others, Thompson and McNeill, were broken by court martial, and Burke's brief career ended abruptly in a British prison. Tucker, Simpson, and Harding were new names added to the captains' roll during the year, and Lieutenant Colonel Talbot gained renown and army advancement for his daring descents on British naval vessels.

New Englanders commanding public ships captured 18 merchant prizes and one schooner of the Royal Navy. In turn they lost three ships-o-war: the *Resistance,* and two from Commodore Hopkins' original 1776 fleet, *Alfred* and *Columbus.* More than offsetting these losses four new vessels, *Ranger, Queen of France, General Gates,* and *Confederacy,* were given to northern captains.

Whipple's and John B. Hopkins' Rhode Island frigates, heretofore bottled up at Providence, were able to escape through the British cordon and begin their active careers. The *Providence,* Whipple, went to European waters and successfully operated with *Boston* and *Ranger...* The *Boston,* after a dismal maiden cruise with McNeill at the helm in 1777, redeemed herself by carrying John Adams to France and taking some prizes of value. Captain John Peck Rathbun continued on his winning and picturesque way highlighted by the New Providence attack.

Numerically, British naval power in North America seems to have remained at substantially the same level as the previous year.[103] Now, however, they were facing a first rate sea power, France. The threat of a French fleet appearing off the American coast weighed in the British decision to evacuate Philadelphia and fall back on New York although Admiral d'Estaing's timidity before New York and failure to relieve Newport were disappointing.

To meet the needs of the French ships a further strain was placed on the Continent's meager naval material and money resources which were already aggravated by a spiraling inflation and currency depreciation. While the French squadron was refitting at Boston, prior to departing for the West Indies winter cruising ground, the Eastern Navy Board advanced about £35,000.[104] The strong ally, that "pivot on which everything turned," naturally took priority over the Continental vessels.

For the Continental Navy in general, and the New England captains and their ships in particular, 1778 may be called the peak strength year just before marked withering set in.

The Eastern Navy Board's final report of the year to Philadelphia, written Christmas Day, included the following arrival news: "*General Arnold* packet ninety days from Bordeaux. John Ayres, Esq. Commander died at Bordeaux."[105] This closing note is of interest only because of the mention of John Ayres whose name appears on the Continental Naval captains' list although no record of the date or circumstances surrounding the appointment has been found.

Ayres was from Massachusetts, and early in 1776 under a commission from Washington he commanded the *Lynch* schooner and cruised with Commodore Manley.[106] At the end of that year he was in the service of the Massachusetts Board of War reconnoitering a British fleet reported off Block Island.[107] Subsequently, Ayres seems to have done some privateering and to have been employed from time to time by the naval authorities to take charge of cartels and packets. He never was in command of a Continental warship.

CHAPTER VI

SUCCESSES AT SEA AND TERROR AT PENOBSCOT

1779

The moral courage and lofty sentiments that come in time, to teach the trained officer to believe any misfortune preferable to professional disgrace, were not always to be expected.

J. FENIMORE COOPER

"THERE REMAINS in this harbor Six Ships," advised the Eastern Navy Board on the general state of the Navy in New England as 1778 was coming to a close. A singular circumstance rendered it impossible for the Board to predict when any or all of them would be ready to sail. "We mean the manning of the ships this alone delays them every Ship here might sail in fourteen days if they could be manned it is not easy to describe to you the difficulty we are under on this account and the losses the Continent sustains by the Conduct of the Privateers who are always seducing by every art the Men from the public Service after they have received the bounty and clothing and become largely in debt these men they secreet and send privately to some out ports where they go and take them in and elude the search of our officers."

The Board urged an embargo on privateering until the Continental vessels could be manned.[1] This might well have been a practical solution, but calling halt to a lucrative business would have aroused such a howl that Congress would not have adopted the proposal even if seriously considered.

The six ships in Boston were the frigates *Alliance, Deane, Queen of France, Warren, Providence* and *Boston*. If one adds to these the *Ranger* at Portsmouth, *Confederacy* and *Trumbull* in Connecticut, and the sloops *Providence* and *General Gates* at sea, we have practically a complete roster of the Continental Navy at the beginning of 1779.

Captain Olney had his ship in a more advanced state of readiness than any of the other New England commanders. The *Queen of France* had most of her wood, water, and provisions on board, and 136 officers and men. She had dropped down from the city into Nantasket Road to await the completion of her gun carriages and some other last minute work. Whipple, Tucker, and John B. Hopkins had their vessels alongside Boston wharves all graved but in various stages of fitting and ballasting. *Warren*, damaged in the head by a ship drifting on her in a storm, was being repaired, and the *Providence* was fitting a new foremast. The *Warren* had no men, *Boston* "a few," and *Providence* had eleven.[2]

Officers from each of the ships were out in town beating the recruiting drums. Enlistment appeals, like the following, appeared in the newspapers.

> The Continental Frigate Warren, John B. Hopkins, Esq., Commander will sail on a Cruise in Six Days from the above Date; all that are willing to enter as Marines, Seamen, or Landsmen (Friends of the Independent States) are desired to repair on Board.[3]

Manning was painfully slow. In early February *Boston* and *Warren* had about 70 men each and *Providence* only 30. Simpson with the *Ranger* up in New Hampshire was doing no better. In Connecticut Captain Harding was finding such trouble getting a crew together for the new frigate *Confederacy* that he impressed French sailors as they arrived at New London in a cartel vessel from New York. He was soon obliged to release them when the French authorities strenuously objected.[4]

The cost of everything was exorbitant and most items were in critically short supply; "rice, butter, and cheese is not to be procured at any price." Flour, a shipboard staple for which New England depended on the millers of Baltimore, was wanted in great quantities and was not available. The seaman's elixir, rum, was equally hard to come by. General Gates contributed 50 hogsheads for naval use from the Army's rum reserve.[5]

Most serious of all to the Eastern Navy Board was the lack of money; "the moving cause & spring of all things which we have been destitute of this four or five weeks."[6] The Board was harried from all sides by naval agents, ship-builders, laborers, merchants, officers, and seamen, demanding cash for services, goods, and wages. A stream of pleas for money went unheeded by the Marine Committee, or brought forth drops when a flow was needed. Of course, the Committee could give only what Congress granted, and faced with a dwindling treasury, Congress was able to grant little. The individual members of the Eastern Navy Board borrowed some 20 thousand dollars on personal notes to continue naval business.[7]

On January 11 the "lucky sloop" *Providence*, Captain Rathbun, arrived at New Bedford from a cruise which began the previous November in company with the *General Gates,* Daniel Waters.[8] *Providence* was in a leaky condition caused by copper sheathing ripping off her bottom in extremely foul weather.

Rathbun had continued his remarkable series of successes against British trade. Plying the well-traveled shipping lanes, he took five prizes heavily laden with such wanted items as flour and rum. The first capture, a Quebec schooner bound for New York, was made in concert with the *General Gates* before the two Continental sloops parted in a gale. Another of the prizes was originally taken by an American privateer off Barbadoes, retaken by a British ship, and finally retaken once again by Rathbun. In due course all prizes arrived safely in New England ports.[9]

The Eastern Navy Board sent congratulations to Rathbun, and from Philadelphia William Ellery wrote: "Capt Rathbun's Success hath given me a great Satisfaction not only on account of the public benefit derived from it, but because I procured him his appointment . . . if among his takings he should take any snuff and reserve a bottle for me he will much oblige."[10]

While the *Providence* was repairing at New Bedford before going out again, Rathbun requested detachment from his command to remain ashore temporarily because of poor health. To replace him the Eastern Navy Board appointed the omnipresent Captain Hoysted Hacker. "A man," commented Ellery, "of whom I have not the highest opinion."[11] This was Hacker's second tour in command of the *Providence* sloop.

The Eastern Navy Board, reporting the change of command to the Marine Committee, brought forth Rathbun as a "very Active Spirited Officer" who had "sailed a long time in a Small Sloop & by his Spirit and Success has made a great deal of money to the Continent." The Board proposed that a larger ship be built for Rathbun. At the same time they called to the Committee's attention Captain Dudley Saltonstall, one of the first officers in the Navy, who had long suffered inaction and financial loss because of the *Trumbull* not being able to get out of the Connecticut River. The Committee replied that they were aware of the disadvantages under which Saltonstall had labored and would shortly consider his case.[12]

Captain Elisha Hinman had still to be called to account for surrendering the *Alfred* in March 1778.[13] The court martial convened February 12, 1779, in the great cabin of the *Providence* frigate with Abraham Whipple presiding. Hinman was charged by Thomas Thompson, who had already been stripped of his naval commission, of disobedience of orders, neglect of duty, and unprecedented conduct. After "duly and maturely" considering all the evidence produced before them, the court "fully and clearly" arrived at the opinion that Hinman was not guilty of any part of the charges, and did "acquit the said Elisha Hinman with the highest honor, approving the whole of his conduct on the 9th of March 1778, he having behaved himself according to the strictest rules of naval discipline and agreeable in all respects to the 27th Article of the Rules and Regulations of the Continental Navy."[14]

Thompson publicly attacked the court's decision in the Boston newspaper *Continental Journal and Weekly Advertiser*. He pointed out alleged irregularities during the trial, and observed that Hinman had come home with the president and a majority of the court members (Hinman had returned from France in the frigate *Providence* commanded by Whipple), "and they must be prejudiced in his Favour, by hearing his account of the matter to often on the passage." For the record, Thompson caused to be printed in the press the dissenting opinion of one court member, Captain Henry Johnson, who believed Hinman to be clearly guilty.[15]

Although acquitted with the "highest honor," Hinman was joined to the ranks of unemployed naval captains. Unfortunately no Continental command was offered to Hinman, and he followed the usual pattern into privateering for the remaining war years except for his service in connection with the frigate *Trumbull* which shall be considered later.[16]

Withdrawal of the enemy from Philadelphia and his concentration on reducing the southern states brought swarms of New York-based privateers south. Virginia and Maryland were especially alarmed since few merchant vessels sailing out of or into Chesapeake Bay escaped. This was the major cause of the flour shortage in New England already alluded to. A Baltimore merchants' committee, asserting that their interests had been neglected, petitioned Congress for naval protection of their trade. The appeal reached understanding ears in Congress and in the Marine Committee now presided over by a Virginian, Richard Henry Lee. Widespread dissatisfaction also existed in official circles over the New Englanders' tendency to consider the Continental Navy as a local defense force, and the Yankee "homing instinct" which caused them to send all prizes into northern ports no matter where captured. Lee assured the Maryland merchants that help was on the way, and "the main Object of their Cruize is the protection of the Southern Trade particularly that of the Delaware and Chesapeake."[17]

At the same time as demands were being made for the vessels in New England to come south, Connecticut's Governor Trumbull was asking the Eastern Navy Board for authority to join the same ships with several state craft in an expedition to rid Long Island Sound of enemy cruisers. The Navy Board was inclined to accede to Trumbull's wishes, but the Marine Committee had no mind to brook further detours in getting the ships cruising off the southern coast.[18] To placate Trumbull, the Committee detailed Captain Harding of the *Confederacy* to operate under his direction for a period not exceeding ten days before turning south.[19]

Captain Joseph Olney of the *Queen of France* was issued Marine Committee orders under date of February 10, 1779, to "sweep in the first place this coast from the Southward of Cape May to the Bar of Charles Town, and afterwards to Cruize in such Latitudes and Longitudes which are best calculated to give the greatest aid and protection to the Trade of Delaware, Chesapeake, and Charles Town, and as often as circumstances and the safety of your Ships will admit of it, you are to enter the mouths of Delaware & Chesapeake for the purpose of destroying the small armed Vessels from New York that lurk about the Capes to the certain destruction of almost every Merchantman that sails . . . . The great delay expence and trouble in manning the Ships for sea has induced this Committee to direct and Order you, to continue this Cruize as long as your Provisions and other circumstances will admit . . . you will return into the Port of Philadelphia or some convenient one in the Bay of Chesapeake."[20]

Simpson brought the *Ranger* around from Portsmouth ready for sea on February 25 and moored in Nantasket Road near the *Warren* and *Queen of France*.[21] The latter vessel was still in port and had been manned for some time. Arrival of some of Rathbun's prizes made Olney's crew most anxious to get underway. Initially the Eastern Navy Board had held the *Queen of France* awaiting approval to send her to New London per Trumbull's request. When Philadelphia vetoed this idea it was found upon inquiry, March 2, that Olney had never received the Marine Committee's orders of February 10. Since the *Queen of France* had been delayed this long the Navy Board thought it advisable to hold her several more days in anticipation that Captain John B. Hopkins would have about 160 officers and men in the *Warren* and be enabled to join Simpson and Olney.[22]

The three ships lay in the Road awaiting a wind until the morning of March 13 when they came to sail in company "to Chastice the Insolence of those Small Cruisers upon the Coasts of Virginia and the Carolinas."[23] Orders to all captains were exactly the same as those issued earlier to Olney. Inclusion of the *Warren* in the squadron made Hopkins the superior officer, and consequently commodore for the cruise.

In short order the wisdom of sailing several Continental ships together was demonstrated. On April 6 off Cape Henry, Virginia, an armed British schooner out of New York was captured. At four in the morning of the following day two fleets were sighted, one to leeward of ten sail and another to windward consisting of nine sail. Hopkins made a signal for all vessels to give chase to the windward fleet.

The Englishmen were a fleet of transports and store ships bound for Georgia from New York under convoy of the 20 gun ship *Jason*. By two o'clock on the same afternoon Hopkins' squadron had taken seven sail including the escort vessel. The transports carried no troops save several officers, but they were richly laden with dry goods and provisions for the army plus the complete accoutrements for a regiment of light dragoons which the British intended to raise among loyalists in the southern states.

After manning the prizes the aforementioned New England "homing" urge set in, and Hopkins ordered his squadron and the captives to stand for the northward. In this connection it should be kept in mind that his orders definitely directed him to cruise as long as provisions would permit, and then "return into the Port of Philadelphia or some convenient one in the Bay of Chesapeake." Hopkins said his decision was shaped by "intelligence of a large number of armed vessels, being off Chesapeake and Delaware Bays."[24]

Warren became separated from the rest of the fleet in a thick fog off the Georgian Banks on April 11 and came into Boston harbor alone on the 16th. The *Queen of France* and some of the prizes straggled in during the next several days, and *Ranger* took two of the captures with her to Portsmouth.

The immediate acclaim accorded Captain John B. Hopkins' good fortune was reminiscent of the exuberance aroused by his father's attack on New Providence in 1776. "We most Sincerely Congradulate the United States Upon this most important good news as we Conceive the Capture of this Fleet of Transports with Supplys for Cambells troops will prove fatal to the Army & Navy in Georgia," was the Eastern Navy Board's somewhat overzealous appraisal.[25] Temporarily the flour scarcity was eased by a quantity included in the captured lading. The Marine Committee with "much pleasure" sent personal congratulations to Hopkins; "your conduct with that of the other Commanders that were in Company with you has our intire approbation which we request you will communicate to them. We doubt not but you and they will use your utmost exertions in again preparing your vessel for the Sea and we have sanguine hopes from your Zeal and Activity that great Credit will result to our Navy from your proceedings."[26] But like his father, young Hopkins' place in the sun was exceedingly brief.

When the *Warren* dropped anchor in the Road, Hopkins sent Marine Captain Palmes up to Boston to report to the Navy Board.[27] Elated over the news of what had been accomplished, the Board nevertheless was quite aware that once tied up to a city pier the ship's company would storm ashore and scatter.

Palmes was instructed to return to the ship with directions for Hopkins to stay out in the stream and not come up. Palmes replied that it was too late for when he left her *Warren* was already under sail. Hopkins himself appeared before the Board the following day exclaiming that he could not get his officers and men to sail until the prize money was settled. It was their contention that they had signed on for a cruise, and it was over.[28] Thus a crew which took many months and extreme expense to muster was allowed to evaporate after a cruise of slightly over 30 days. The *Warren* would again lie idle, unmanned, and useless.

To prevent the same thing happening to the *Queen of France,* the Board dispatched an order to Olney to anchor in Nantasket Road, keep his officers and men on board, and submit a list of his needs which would be sent down to him so that his ship could resume cruising without delay. Olney ignored the directive and came right up to town. He allowed his crew ashore, and the *Queen of France* was shortly as deserted as the *Warren.*[29]

The reason for this reprehensible conduct on the part of Hopkins and Olney cleared somewhat when it was learned at the Navy Board that these commanders had, by threats and coercion, been designated as prize agents to represent their crews. This was a most unethical if not illegal step. It meant that Hopkins and Olney would not only receive a captain's share of the prizes but also an agent's commission on each man's entitlement. Although admitting that there was no positive proof, the Navy Board believed that the two captains were involved in an even more disreputable scheme.

It was estimated that a seaman's share in prizes taken by Hopkins' squadron would be about two thousand dollars. Sailors, always "fond of money in hand" and not inclined to wait out the lengthy litigation required for prize condemnation, were induced to sell their shares for three or four hundred dollars. The Navy Board suspected that Hopkins and Olney were buying up the discounted shares. Disgusted, the members wrote the Marine Committee — "We must inform you by Appearances and their Conduct that they are more attached to their own Interest & Emoluments then to the honor & benefit of the United States we may pronounce this without doing them any Injustice no men were ever more asiduous in Search of gain than those two Captains have been." Striking a responsive chord, the Navy Board asked the southern-controlled Marine Committee "to determine upon the Propriety of bringing those Ships & Prizes into the Port of Boston" when "they might have been anchored in Hampton road in a few hours." Some of the ship officers said the captures were actually made in sight of the Virginia coast.[30]

On May 3, 1779, the Navy Board further informed the Marine Committee that having "Contemplated with deliberation" they had suspended Captain Hopkins from command of the *Warren* as,

> he has been flagrantly guilty of Breech of orders . . . he has been guilty of great misconduct in Suffering his men to disperse on his return to this Port after a Cruise of only about five weeks when his Ship had been prepared at a great expense of time & money for a Cruise of near five months contrary to the Express orders of this Board . . . no one could Suppose the Cruise to be at an end by the fortunate Circumstances of their taking a number of prizes any more than if he had gone into the Delaware or Chesapeak agreeable to your orders to Capt. Olney and where we think he should have carried these prizes especially as he was within a few hours Sail of the Capes of Virginia . . . he has been guilty of great Inattention to his Business while he has been attending to matters of a private nature.

Anticipating a logical Marine Committee question, the Navy Board answered before asked.

> If you Enquire why we have made the destinction we do & why the other Captains are not Exposed to the same Censure we answer that Capt Hopkins was the Commanding Officer & therefore is answerable for the return of the Ships that he set the Example of Suffering his men to disperse against positive orders & when he had every offer of Assistance to proceed in a Short time on his Cruise.[31]

In fact Captain Simpson had written to the Navy Board explaining why he had gone to Portsmouth with the *Ranger*, and they had found his reasons satisfactory. The Board mentioned Saltonstall, Hinman, or Rathbun, all "very good officers," for Hopkins' place in the *Warren*.[32]

The Marine Committee sustained Hopkins' suspension and, in a further step, ordered that Olney be treated similarly. A court of inquiry was directed on the conduct of both commanders to be followed by a court martial if necessary.[33] Hopkins demanded a court martial for, as he phrased it, "Public Enquiry is the only Effectual Method of determining the Justice of Public Accusations."[34] However, a lack of sufficient officers at any one time to convene a court caused the Eastern Navy Board to defer trial until late September 1779. In the interim the Board received further complaints against both captains for not paying prize money to the seamen. Olney was also accused by one of his lieutenants of taking the cabin furniture of the *Queen of France* when he left the ship.[35]

Hopkins' hearing was held on board the frigate *Deane* at Boston, and although the proceedings have not come to light among the surviving records and papers there can be little doubt about the findings. Notice to stand by for trial was likewise posted to Olney, but there is no indication that one was ever held on him.[36]

At this stage of the Revolution when all things were in short supply except naval captains, suspension was tantamount to dismissal. Hopkins' and Olney's service in the Continental Navy was at an end. Both signed on as privateer masters in their native Rhode Island.[37] For command of the *Queen of France* the Marine Committee named John Peck Rathbun, and to the *Warren*, Dudley Saltonstall.[38] The unfolding future events proved the latter choice disastrously unfortunate.

The brig *General Gates*, Captain Daniel Waters, came into Boston harbor April 13, 1779. Waters, after parting from Rathbun at sea the previous December, had fruitlessly cruised in West Indian waters and put into St. Pierre, Martinique, to repair leaks. On his passage northward he fell in with a Massachusetts naval brig, and together they took an enemy privateer.[39] When a survey showed that the *General Gates* was not worth repairing she was sold out of the Continental Navy.[40] This left Waters without a public ship, and one more Continental captain slid back into privateering.

The same day that the *General Gates* arrived in port, the frigates *Providence*, Whipple, *Boston*, Tucker, and sloop *Providence*, now under Hoysted Hacker, sailed. They were sent out at the request of the Council of Massachusetts to sweep the Bay for ten days in search of small enemy cruisers reported as having left New York bent on ravishing the Massachusetts coast.[41] Whipple was to be back in Nantasket Road within several days to await an important assignment from the Marine Committee.[42] Tucker and Hacker, after scouring local waters, were directed to proceed to Delaware Bay to take on a supply of bread and put their ships under further instructions from the Marine Committee.[43]

No enemy was discovered in Massachusetts Bay, and the *Providence* frigate was again riding her anchor on April 22. Captain Whipple came ashore ill; perhaps the injury sustained several years earlier was troubling him. The Navy Board doubted that he would be able to take the ship out. Preparations were made to name another commander, but after examining Whipple, two physicians proclaimed the veteran mariner fit for sea duty.[44]

Leaving the Bay, Tucker headed for Philadelphia in compliance with his orders, but Hacker lingered in the New York area where those who had confidence in him, and the fates which guided him safely through the rocks and shoals of previous failures, were at last vindicated. Off Sandy Hook, May 7, the *Providence* sloop, after a sharp hour and a half action, took one of the few Royal Naval vessels captured by the Continental Navy. She was the 12 gun brig *Diligent* which had left New York for the Chesapeake as part of Commodore Collier's fleet and had straggled from the main body. Before the Englishman struck, Hacker had four men killed and ten wounded.[45]

Hacker carried the prize into New Bedford. Wishing to forestall repetition of the Hopkins-Olney affair, the Navy Board reminded Hacker that he had been fitted out to cruise for three or four months, and not to harbor any idea that quick success and return to port in a few days meant that the cruise was ended. To make certain that the sloop's crew would have no chance to jump ship, Hacker was at once ordered to operate briefly in Vineyard Sound together with the prize and in company with two Massachusetts privateers. Lest he have some apprehension about his prize being retaken, the Navy Board assured Hacker that in the event of that contingency she would be paid for by the Continent anyway since she had reached New Bedford safely and was being brought out again under the Board's direction.[46]

Providence and the *Diligent* were at Boston on June 10 after encountering only a few lumber sloops of no value in Vineyard Sound. The *Diligent,* a fine ship, was purchased into the Continental Navy at a very high price, over £26,000. Hacker was allowed the choice of switching his command to the *Diligent* or remaining in the *Providence.* He elected to stay with the "lucky sloop," and command of the *Diligent* was given to Lieutenant Philip Brown, first lieutenant in the *Providence* when the capture was made.[47]

Meanwhile Captain Tucker had brought the *Boston* into the Delaware; the first New England built and commanded frigate to arrive in that Bay. Toward the end of May he was joined by the new Connecticut frigate, *Confederacy,* Seth Harding. The *Confederacy* had been delayed at New London for many months beyond her expected date of sailing. Manning was the major reason for this, and it is little wonder when even Naval Agent Nathaniel Shaw was offering seamen family care and other inducements to fill up a privateer he owned rather than the Continental vessel. There was much official dissatisfaction with Harding for his dilatoriness in getting the frigate to sea. Deshon wrote to Joshua Huntington, building supervisor of the *Confederacy,* "For Goodness Sake let us stir our Stumps and Get this Ship out of Sight as Soon as posable."[48] The Marine Committee threatened to remove Harding from command and to call a court of inquiry to examine into his conduct.[49] This unpleasant prospect seems to have fired Harding, and he cast off from New London soon after the beginning of May 1779. He opened his sealed orders when clear of Montauk Point, Long Island, and set all sail to proceed to the Capes of Delaware as directed. The *Confederacy* rounded Cape Henlopen several weeks later and came up as far as Lewestown, where Harding awaited further instructions from Philadelphia to operate with the *Boston.*[50]

The Marine Committee intended that Tucker and Harding cruise off the coast between 35° and 40° North Latitude to meet American merchantmen from the West Indies, particularly Captain Read's *Baltimore* carrying Continental stores, and escort them safely into Delaware and Chesapeake ports through a nest of enemy privateers which had collected to intercept. Both frigates were to be back inside the Capes after three weeks.[51]

Carrying out the orders, *Boston* and *Confederacy* sailed in company the first week in June. On the 24th of the month they had the good fortune to fall in with the *Baltimore* and her consort, the *Retaliation,* which were shepherded safely into port. In addition, three prizes were made on the short cruise, the most significant of which was a 26 gun privateer ship.[52]

Returning to lower Delaware Bay, Tucker and Harding were met by Samuel Nicholson commanding the *Deane.* The Marine Committee, having a particular mission in view for the *Confederacy,* ordered Harding to proceed up the river as high as Chester.[53] We will leave Captain Harding here for the time being, coming back to him later in this chapter to follow *Confederacy* in her adventurous special assignment.

Tucker and Nicholson were ordered out together to go first to the Chesapeake and, if no British ships were found there, to cruise such stations considered best for intercepting enemy transports for New York and the homeward-bound West India ships. *Boston* and *Deane* were directed to keep the sea until September and then put into Boston port.[54]

This was a successful cruise netting eight prizes during July and August including the sloop of war *Thorn*. Several small privateers were sent into Philadelphia; a brig with 150 pipes of Madeira wine arrived at Cape Ann; and the Continental frigates brought the *Thorn* and the *Sandwich* into Boston with them on September 6. Another prize, the *Earl of Glencarron*, a Glasgow ship with a valuable dry goods cargo, was apparently retaken before she reached port.[55] On board this last ship mentioned was found a goodly quantity of paper and type for counterfeiting Continental money. It was the British intention to depress an already depreciated and discredited currency still further by circulating a flood of bogus bills. The reader may recall that this is the second time a prize ship cargo taken by a New England captain was found to be related to the counterfeiting scheme.[56] Captain Tucker, after a six months' absence from his native Massachusetts, learned that much had happened navalwise; some good and some which would require him to sit on a court martial.

When Rathbun replaced Olney in command of the *Queen of France* in June 1779, he took over his new duties with the same enthusiasm and energy which he had shown throughout his naval service. He was a popular successful captain, and within a few days after he reported on board he had the ship manned. Rathbun found great waste of all kinds in the *Queen's* stores, indicating that Olney had exercised little control or discipline.[57]

Captain Simpson stayed at Portsmouth with the *Ranger* from April, when he returned from the cruise with Hopkins and Olney, until June 13, 1779. Persistent urgings by the Eastern Navy Board failed to get him to Boston sooner. Shortly before leaving New Hampshire, Simpson wrote the Board that he wished to resign from the naval service. He expressed his resentment against both the Board and the Marine Committee for their treatment of Captains Hopkins and Olney.[58] Of course, Simpson had disobeyed his orders by returning to a northern port just as the other two had. But his reasons for so doing were found acceptable to the Board at the time. And again unlike Olney and Hopkins, there is no indication that Simpson was involved in any unsavory financial dealings with his crew.

In reply to Simpson's letter of resignation the Board, reiterating their good opinion of him as a man and an officer, suggested that he had been misinformed and should think it over. But if he persisted in his design, they felt he owed it to the Continent at least to bring the *Ranger* to Boston.[59] When Simpson arrived there he evidently gathered what was actually involved in Hopkins' and Olney's suspension, and he withdrew the resignation.

The frigate *Providence,* Captain Whipple, as noted, was held in port awaiting special assignment from the Marine Committee. However, when the newer and faster *Confederacy* arrived in the Delaware she was selected and the *Providence* released.[60] Thus, by mid-June 1779, Whipple, Rathbun, and Simpson had their ships ready to put to sea from Boston on a united cruise. Orders were written for Whipple, senior officer of the group, to proceed without delay and cruise to the south of the Newfoundland Banks for the purpose of intercepting enemy transports and merchants going and coming from New York, the West Indies, and Hudson's Bay. Whipple was allowed the discretion of returning to a convenient Continental port when provisions were nearly exhausted or replenishing in the West Indies to cruise on that ground during the winter season. The *Providence, Queen of France,* and *Ranger* took the wind on 17 June.[61]

While Whipple's squadron lay-to wrapped in a morning Newfoundland fog July 18, the sound of ships bells and an occasional signal gun were heard. As the overcast began to lift, the Americans found that they had stumbled into a Jamaica fleet of about 60 sail for London under convoy of a British 74 and several smaller vessels. The *Queen of France* was virtually alongside a large merchantman. Rathbun, past master at this business, playing the part of one of the escort ships, hailed the merchant skipper and requested him to come on board. When the Englishman stepped on the *Queen's* quarter deck he found himself a prisoner. A boarding party was sent back to the merchant and quietly took possession of her. Whipple and Simpson employed the same or similar tactics as the Americans remained in the fleet all day cutting out ten ships without raising an alarm.

Seven of the prizes arrived safely at Boston, one at Cape Ann, and two were retaken. The captured merchantmen were heavy with rum, sugar, ginger, pimento, and cotton, and in addition mounted a total of 113 guns. Ships and cargo were valued at one million dollars, making this by far the most lucrative catch of the entire war. Commodore Whipple returned his squadron to Boston on August 21, 1779, with all hands bountifully rewarded for two months at sea.[62]

At the time Whipple's squadron left on its cruise in June there remained at Boston three Continental ships: the *Warren* frigate, Saltonstall, sloop *Providence,* Hacker, and brig *Diligent,* Lieutenant Brown.

Saltonstall was in Connecticut with the barren *Trumbull* when ordered to replace John B. Hopkins in the *Warren.* Before going up to Boston he stayed on there for several weeks trying to recruit local seamen for his new vessel. The *Warren* manned with even more than usual slowness, reaffirming the Navy Board's belief that resentment stirred up by the deposed John B. Hopkins was at the bottom of the trouble.[63]

Trumbull was left without a commanding officer by Saltonstall's transfer. Efforts were once again renewed under Deshon's direction to get the frigate out of the river, and care of the ship was committed to Captain Elisha Hinman by the

Navy Board. Adopting a plan unspecified but "quite new," Hinman, with Deshon's cooperation, brought the *Trumbull* up to nine feet two inches of water. About August 12, 1779, she passed over the bar to be at last free of her river entrapment.[64] In a matter of two months Hinman had accomplished what Saltonstall had failed to do in two and a half years.

Praising Hinman's spirit, activity, and judgement, the Navy Board urged that he be given command of the *Trumbull*. The Board felt no doubt that this recommendation would be followed and assured Hinman accordingly. Hinman on his part began readying the frigate for sea and selecting warrant and petty officers. Since no word to the contrary was received from Philadelphia, the Navy Board naturally assumed that Hinman's nomination had been confirmed.[65] But much to the surprise and disappointment of the Board and Hinman, the Marine Committee disclosed on October 6 that Captain James Nicholson of Maryland had been appointed to command the *Trumbull*. In referring to the Board's recommendation for Hinman, the Marine Committee retorted that "we could not appoint him to the command of this Ship without breaking a general rule which we had before adopted viz of paying regard to Seniority in our appointments where merit is equal and to the Ships which our Captains have had. Captain Nicholson has had a ship and so has Captain Hinman but the former is the first Captain on the Navy List and we esteem him a Man of Merit, therefore he could not be passed by."[66] The seniority argument could not stand close scrutiny, *i.e.*, the selection of a new captain, Seth Harding, for the *Confederacy* over the heads of unemployed captains of long service. Nicholson, however, was a man of considerable influence which was early evidenced when he was placed first on the seniority list. Up to this point Nicholson's Continental Naval activity had been confined to running aground and abandoning the Baltimore built frigate *Virginia* to the enemy before she cleared Chesapeake Bay on her maiden cruise in 1778.[67]

The commander of the British troops at Halifax, Brigadier General McLean, acting under orders from Sir Henry Clinton, moved to establish a post on the Penobscot River in the Maine territory of Massachusetts. Ostensibly the project was designed to provide a settlement for that large group of loyalists which had fled to Nova Scotia at the outset of the Revolution. The more significant military aim was to provide a base from which British cruisers could easily prey upon Boston and Portsmouth commerce.

McLean embarked some 700 to 800 troops and sailed from Halifax escorted by three Royal Navy sloops-of-war. June 16, 1779, he put his troops and provisions ashore on Majabigwaduce Peninsula in the Penboscot River.[68] They began immediately clearing the wood and marking out a fort which was still being worked on more than a month later.[69]

Massachusetts had ceased to be a theatre in the land war, and her territory had been free of enemy troops since Howe pulled out of Boston in 1776. News of the Penobscot occupation was received with shock and widespread alarm. A loud cry went up against the "designing and artful wretches" now encamped on the State's eastern doorstep.[70] The legislature reacted quickly with a call for 1200 militiamen as an expeditionary force under Brigadier General Solomon Lovell to dislodge the enemy from Penobscot before he could be reinforced. Actually something under 900 of the militia were gathered, one fourth of them boys and old men unfit for service in the field.[71] Troops would move to Maine by water transport, and the operation plan included support of a naval force comprising state-owned and privateer vessels. In addition, the Council of Massachusetts asked that the three Continental vessels in Boston harbor, that is, the *Warren*, sloop *Providence*, and *Diligent*, be made available to join the expedition.

The Navy Board, pending approval from Philadelphia, tentatively agreed to order the ships on this service provided that the State would help man them, and that every assurance be given that the force mounted would make the combined

naval strength definitely superior to the enemy.[72]   The Marine
Committee endorsed the Board's conduct, but at the same
time emphasized that they should move with caution to safe-
guard the Continent's interests in a State's adventure.[73]   Captain Saltonstall of the *Warren,* senior ranking officer of the
three participating Continental commanders, was designated
Commodore for all naval elements.[74]

Saltonstall, as already pointed out, was having a most
difficult time mustering men for the *Warren* before the
Penobscot business was at hand. After the expedition was
decided upon, demands for seamen by the more attractive private armed vessels left Saltonstall with little hope of filling his
complement. However, so anxious was the State that the *Warren's* 32 guns be included in the naval armament that the
Council took the unusual step of ordering about 60 men impressed for service in the Continental frigate.[75]

As finally constituted the Penobscot fleet under Commodore Saltonstall consisted of the Continental Naval vessels *Warren,* sloop *Providence,* Hacker, *Diligent* brig, Lieutenant
Brown, three ships of the Massachusetts State Navy, one
belonging to New Hampshire, and 12 chartered Massachusetts
privateers. In all they carried 314 cannon of different weights.
Twenty-one transports and victualers were used. Two familiar
names, Captains Daniel Waters and William Burke of the Continental Navy, are encountered as commanders of private
armed vessels in the fleet.[76]

The Navy Board issued sailing directions on July 13,
1779, for Commodore Saltonstall to proceed with all the
ships under his direction to the appointed rendezvous at
Townshend, Maine, where the Continental sloop *Providence*
and several other vessels which had left Boston earlier would
join him. Saltonstall's orders included a directive "to consult measures and preserve the greatest harmony with the commander of the land forces, that the navy and army may cooperate and assist each other."[77] Winds detained the fleet in port
until the morning of July 19, when, the wind coming on fair,

they all sailed. The Navy Board voiced grave misgivings; "so much time has been taken up preparing for this Expedition that we doubt the success of it. The Enemy must be Stupid indeed if they do not reinforce that party with some additional Ships however the Temper of the People here & the pressing requisitions of the Government Admit of no deliberations."[78]

Saltonstall arrived at Townshend in due course finding the *Providence* already there. Hacker had taken an enemy sloop laden with rum and carried her into Casco Bay. Early on the morning of July 24 the Commodore signaled the entire force of armed ships and troop transports to get underway, and about 10 o'clock the same evening they came to anchor in Penobscot Bay.

The British were expecting them, for a secret operation was unheard of in the Revolution. General McLean erected secondary batteries on the peninsula and nearby Nautilus Island. His three warships formed a line to oppose the Americans should an attempt be made to force the harbor, and some transports were readied as fire ships.[79]

On the 25th opposing ships exchanged shots without effect, but the next day a party of about 150 marines landed and took the enemy battery on Nautilus Island. Captain Hoysted Hacker of the *Providence* supported the landing and was in overall command. American occupation of Nautilus Island compelled the enemy warships to remove deeper inside the harbor. General Lovell landed the main body of his troops and marines on the southwest side of Majabigwaduce under cover of naval gunfire on July 28. They gained the bluff some three or four hundred feet above the river, whereupon the enemy left his advanced posts and retreated within the main fort. Lovell was convinced that he did not have adequate strength to assault the bastion while the enemy retained additional fire power from the three naval vessels. Quick destruction or capture of these British warships was undoubtedly the key to success since the land forces were about evenly matched, and the enemy held the advantage of a strong entrenchment.

Saltonstall had overwhelming naval superiority, yet he refused to go in and attack. He persistently ignored the danger in delay and disregarded requests for action from his own naval officers and the General. On several occasions he was quoted as posing the totally irrational question, "What advantage would it be to go and take the enemy's shipping?"[80] Fruitless councils of war followed each other on the *Warren* while inactive days turned into weeks, and the enemy continued to strengthen his position. Finally Saltonstall agreed to move against the British ships provided Lovell would simultaneously attack the fort. The General refused this condition on August 6 with the argument that once the enemy ships were disposed of the fort must capitulate. At a naval council the next day the Commodore's position was sustained by a majority of the captains. Lovell then sent a belated request for a reinforcement of Continental troops. Wearied by the lack of "determined resolution," Captain Hoysted Hacker offered a plan of attack, but was voted down.[81]

In Boston an increasingly uneasy Navy Board had received no word from Saltonstall. Dispatches arrived on August 12 from General Lovell, but still nothing from Saltonstall. The Massachusetts Council showed the Navy Board the letters received from Penobscot including an account of the Commodore's behavior. The Board immediately penned him a sharp rebuke and positive order:

> We have for some time been at a loss to know why the enemy's ships have not been attacked . . . It is agreed on all hands that they are at all times in your power: if therefore your own security or the more advantageous operations of the army did not require it why should any business be delayed to another day that may as well be done this. Our apprehensions of your danger have ever been from a reinforcement to the enemy you can't expect to remain much longer without one. Whatever therefore is to be done should be done immediately both to prevent advantages to the enemy and delays if you are obliged to retire as we presume you would avoid having these ships in your rear while a reinforcement appears in front or the necessity of leaving them behind when you retired yourself. With these senti-

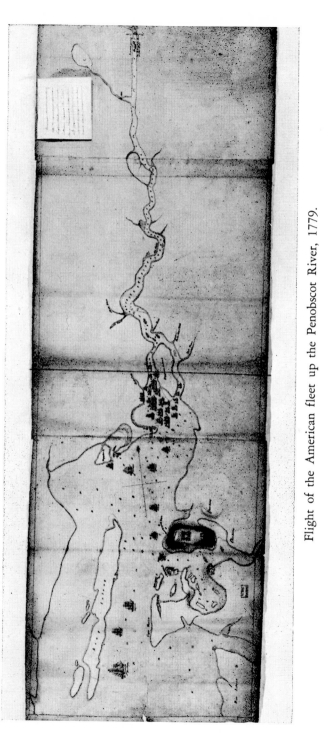

Flight of the American fleet up the Penobscot River, 1779.

Contemporary chart from the Map Division, Library of Congress.

ments we think it our duty to direct you to attack and take or destroy them without delay: in doing which no time is to be lost as a reinforcement are probably on their passage at this time. It is therefore our orders that as soon as you receive this, you take the most effectual measures for the capture or destruction of the enemy's ships and with the greatest dispatch the nature and situation of things will admit of.[82]

The Navy Board was correct, it was already too late. A strong British reinforcement was nearing Penobscot at the very moment they were sending this warning to Saltonstall.

Word of the American expedition to Penobscot was received in New York on July 28. A powerful naval squadron under Sir George Collier consisting of the 64 gun ship *Raisonable,* the *Blonde* and *Virginia,* both 32 gun frigates, one 28, two 20's, and a 14 gun sloop departed August 3 for Maine.[83] Collier's ships were sighted six days later near Martha's Vineyard, and on August 13 they appeared standing toward Penobscot Bay.[84]

The State ship *Active,* patrolling the Bay entrance, was first to detect Collier's force. Captain Hallet of that vessel ran in and reported to the Commodore. A boat was sent ashore to inform the General, and evacuation of troops and equipment to the transports was started. The ship captains reported on board the *Warren* for orders and found the Commodore overwhelmed by the crisis. Everything was in a state of panic and utter confusion. At a frantic council it was unanimously voted that the fleet would not stand and engage but would go up the Penobscot River.[85]

Early on August 14 Collier's fleet was coming within range. For a brief time a disposition to form a battle line and make a fight of it seemed to be evidenced. Then about noon Saltonstall signaled all ships to shift for themselves.[86] This opened a mad demoralized dash for the river by armed vessels and transports with the British in close pursuit. On both banks ships were being run ashore, fired, and the men scattering into the woods.

Saltonstall made no effort to cover the transports' rear, nor did he fire one stern chaser gun at the enemy while they played constantly on the Americans. It is reported that General Lovell went from ship to ship vainly pleading with the officers not to burn their craft. He and some of the more resolute sea captains urged that a line of ships be drawn across the narrows to bar the passage. Since the British ships had to come up the narrow river channel in single file, there is little doubt that this could have been accomplished with good results, but it was not attempted. The General came on board the *Warren* begging Saltonstall not to burn the frigate, but it was to no avail for the Commodore seemed consumed by panic. When Saltonstall asked what more he could do, a junior officer acidly replied that he had done nothing as yet.[87]

Some of the ships ascended the river to the fall line barrier before being destroyed. On August 16 the disaster was complete. Sailors, marines and militia were fleeing through the wilderness toward home. The entire American fleet was smoldering hulks with the exception of two vessels captured. The three Continental ships were counted among those blown up; an end particularly unsuited for the "lucky sloop" *Providence.*[88]

By the last week in August weary men from Penobscot were hourly plodding into Boston. Saltonstall arrived on the 31st, and Hacker was expected back in town the 2nd of September.[89] A joint committee of both houses of the Massachusetts legislature appointed a committee under the chairmanship of General Artemus Ward to investigate the fiasco which it was estimated cost the State 7 million dollars.[90]

Witness followed witness before the investigating committee giving essentially the same testimony. All agreed on Saltonstall's uniform backwardness, and that at the war councils he was "always preaching terror" of offensive action.[91] Each witness was asked his opinion whether or not the British ships could have easily been destroyed before arrival of the reinforcement, and all answered in the affirmative. The committee unanimously concluded that the principal reason for the failure at Penobscot appeared to be "want of Proper Spirit & Energy on the part of the Commodore." With the same unanimity General Lovell was cleared of any culpability.[92]

That Dudley Saltonstall was incompetent for the task which faced him at Penobscot, there is no doubt, and this was *a* principal reason for the unhappy spectacle. But there were other factors which contributed, and justice, if nothing more, demands their consideration.

The expedition was mounted with great haste and no appreciable planning. Troops provided were inadequate in number and quality. Only General Peleg Wadsworth, second in army command, seems to have touched on this point at the investigation hearings. Continental troops under General Gates were available in New England and could have been added to the militia. Massachusetts, however, did not request them at the outset nor did General Lovell until it was too late to do any good. There was no advance planning with regard to what steps would be taken should a British reinforcement appear on the scene. Thus when this happened utter confusion and panic took hold. For this Saltonstall was to blame, but equally so was General Lovell.

A closer examination of the investigation committee proceedings reveals the clear and concerted purpose of placing total blame on a Continental officer. There is no indication that Saltonstall testified in his own defense before the committee; perhaps he declined, but more likely he was not asked. All of the state naval officers, Massachusetts privateer captains, and principal militia officers were heard. There is no evidence that the other active Continental captain at Penobscot, Hoysted Hacker, told his story to the committee. Questioning was confined largely to naval failings which pointed directly at Saltonstall. Generals Lovell and Wadsworth and the state officers were all praised for their conduct. Colonel Paul Revere, commanding the artillery at Penobscot, stood accused before the committee of neglect of duty, refusal to obey General

Wadsworth's commands, and leaving with his men for Boston without orders. Revere came off with only a tame rebuke. On the particular charge of his quitting the field without orders, the committee reached the mystifying conclusion that the action "was not wholly justifiable."[93]

If, as it appears, Massachusetts seemed determined to whitewash local officers and place the entire responsibility on Saltonstall, the question may be asked, why? An answer appears in the record. On September 21, 1779, John Hancock, acting for the General Court of Massachusetts, wrote to John Jay, President of Congress, pointing out the State's problems resulting from the Penobscot affair. "We have therefore," said Hancock, "to request of Congress to pass such an order as shall enable this state to retain the six millions of dollars which were ordered to be raised in this state as a Continental Tax until such time as the expenditures of the Penobscot armament shall be liquidated and Congress shall order a reimbursement of that expense to be made this state." Hancock added the warning that unless the request was granted "it will be impossible for this state to furnish their quota of the Confederate Army for next campaign."[94] The Continent was being asked to foot the whole bill for a colossal Massachusetts mess.

The foregoing is in no way intended to mitigate Saltonstall's guilt, rather it is to shed some light on the course of events in Boston immediately after Penobscot and attempt to understand the reason.

Following publication of the investigation committee report, Saltonstall's court martial on board the frigate Deane, consuming the better part of October, was anticlimactic. He was dismissed from the Continental Navy after four years of service which commenced with the Alfred in Esek Hopkins' fleet, was followed by three inactive years with the entrapped Trumbull, and ended when the Warren frigate was burnt on the banks of the Penobscot River.[95] Saltonstall was master and bonder of a Connecticut privateer in 1781.[96]

Captain Hoysted Hacker faced a naval court of inquiry for his conduct at Penobscot and particularly loss of his command, the sloop *Providence*. At Saltonstall's war councils Hacker consistently voted for offensive action against the British ships, and it has already been noted that he prepared a plan of attack and submitted it to the Commodore. He was cleared with honor by the inquiry, and the Navy Board informed the Marine Committee: "Captain Hacker has by his behavior at Penobscot established his Character as a good officer & we wish to see him again employed."[97] There was no vessel for Hacker, but the Continental career of this most unusual officer was far from over. On November 4, 1779, he accepted assignment as first lieutenant in the frigate *Providence*, Captain Whipple.[98] Unquestionably the Navy Board was prompted to this move by Whipple's tenuous health. Should he fail while on a cruise, command of the ship could pass to an experienced Continental captain.

Before directing attention back into the Delaware to rejoin Captain Seth Harding and the *Confederacy* on her special assignment, we will delay long enough to see what happened during this year to the seagoing army officer, Lieutenant Colonel Silas Talbot. After winning acclaim and promotion for capturing the British schooner *Pigot* in October 1778, Talbot continued to fight his war on the sea rather than the land.

In the spring of 1779 a number of small British cruisers was raising particular havoc with Narragansett Bay and Long Island Sound shipping. Congress directed General Horatio Gates, commanding in the Eastern Department, to procure and arm some vessels for the protection of the coast. A small 12 six pounder sloop named the *Argo* belonging to New York loyalists was seized and placed under the command of Talbot.

The Colonel with a crew of about 60 made several very profitable cruises from Providence, New London, and Stonington during which the *Argo* was engaged in a number of sharp actions. In all he is reported to have taken 11 prizes and some 300 prisoners in the course of the summer and fall. The capture which must have been most satisfying to Talbot was made in August. She was the 14 gun privateer brig *King George* commanded by a much despised Rhode Island Tory, Stanton Hazard, who had been plundering his neighbors and old friends. After pouring in a quick broadside Talbot carried the privateer by boarding. He sent the *King George* into New London where the imprisonment of the infamous Hazard gave much pleasure to the local people.[99]

Understandably Talbot thought his record entitled him to a naval captain's commission and a more suitable command than the little *Argo*. He corresponded with members of Congress in this regard and told Henry Marchand, Rhode Island delegate, his intention to leave the Continental service if his desires were not met. Marchand cautioned Talbot to consider carefully before quitting a service in which he had won wide honor and rapid promotion.

Talbot's letters were placed before the Marine Committee, but Marchand vehemently warned, "We cannot create Men. — Nor will Our Circumstances permit us to build Ships for those Captains in the Navy who hang on us for Command who are already in our Pay, & who for want of Ships are eating the Bread of Idleness much against Their own as well as our Inclination."[100] Nevertheless, on motion by Henry Laurens, September 17, 1779, Congress resolved that, "in consideration of the distinguished merit of Lieutenant Colonel Talbot a Commission of Captain in the Navy of the United States be given him . . . and that the Marine Committee be directed to provide a proper Vessel for him as soon as possible."[101]

Officially a naval officer at last, Captain Talbot journeyed to Boston and conferred with the Navy Board. The Board had been negotiating to buy a fine 14 gun ship, the *Thorn*, recently taken prize by Captains Tucker and Nicholson, but was outbid by private interests. They had of necessity to inform Talbot that there was no Continental ship available for him. Talbot, by now a much discouraged new naval captain, returned to Providence and to the *Argo*. He remained with the sloop, and, when in the spring of 1780 she was turned back to private owners, Talbot stayed on board as master.[102] It is most unfortunate that an intrepid fighting officer like Talbot was not associated with the Continental Navy during the early years of the Revolution. We can only conjecture what could have been achieved had he commanded a frigate. Or had he been in Saltonstall's place at Penobscot the outcome might well have been very different.[103]

When we left Captain Seth Harding it was September 1779, and the *Confederacy* was in the Delaware River at Chester, Pennsylvania, awaiting directions from the Marine Committee. Orders came down from Philadelphia on the 17th of the month informing Harding that his ship had been designated to carry home his excellency M. Gerard, French Minister to the United States. Harding was directed to avoid "action with any vessel of equal or superior force" on the passage since the *Confederacy* was to be entirely for the accommodation of the Minister. The captain was to make for any port which Gerard thought proper and to otherwise "comply with his wishes."[104]

While preparing to receive the distinguished personage on board, Harding again tried impressment to fill out his crew when recruiting fell short. Boarding parties from the *Confederacy* seized men out of merchant ships passing up the Delaware. Harding thought he would be well at sea before the wrath of the Pennsylvania government could descend on him. He caught a dragon by the tail when an attempt was made to "encourage" sailors from the privately owned brig *Delaware* commanded by Captain John Barry. When it became clear that no mere merchant master was being dealt with, and that Barry had cleared for action to engage the *Confederacy* if necessary, he was allowed to continue to Philadelphia without interference.[105]

On October 17 Harding was informed that in addition to the French Minister he would have other distinguished passengers, John Jay and his family. Jay had been appointed ambassador to Spain. Previously Harding was instructed to comply with Gerard's wishes, now he was to be governed by orders from both the Frenchman and Jay.[100] The *Confederacy* weighed October 26, 1779.

Smooth seas and pleasant sailing were daily routine for the first 12 days. Between five and six o'clock in the morning of November 7 the *Confederacy* was making nine knots in a brisk breeze when suddenly the dawn's stillness was broken by the sickening crack of wrenching timber. In less than three minutes not a stick was standing. The frigate lost her three masts and bowsprit, and she lay a hulk violently rolling in the sea. When Harding recovered from the shock which undoubtedly overwhelmed him and everyone else on board, the injured men were removed below and all hands turned to clearing the wreckage. Every effort was bent to rig jury masts, for unless the ship could get some steerage way and the roll reduced she stood in imminent danger of foundering. Setting even small masts into place on the furiously tossing wreck proved no mean task, but toward evening Harding and his crew managed to bend on a little sail and get a sea anchor out to keep her head into the wind.

The next morning examination disclosed a greater misfortune than loss of the masts. The shank of the rudder had twisted and split. It was hanging freely and crashing into the stern of the ship with devastating effect. Below the split a ring-end bolt entered the rudder through which chains could be fixed to allow emergency steering in case of just such an accident. Harding managed to get a chain through the ring with considerable trouble only to see the bolt break and draw out under the strain. One other possibility existed. The *Confederacy's* rudder had been hung after the ship was launched, and to ease it into position an eye bolt was placed on each side of the rudder. Fortunately they had been left there. To each eye bolt a length of chain was now attached and crossed over the edge of the rudder in opposite directions. The chains fastened to heavy lines which passed through blocks at the end of spars run out of the cabin ports. From there the lines were led over other blocks through ports on the weather deck to the capstan. Although the strain on the ropes caused them to part frequently, this improvised device worked and some measure of control was achieved.

The cause of *Confederacy's* sudden disaster is undetermined. Several possible explanations may be considered. One or more of the masts could have been rotten wood, and giving way created a strain sufficient to bring them all down. But it is more likely that the rigging slacked off sufficiently to allow the masts enough whip-like motion to snap them as the ship rolled in a lively wind. This occasionally happened to vessels rigged in cold climate after they had spent some time in southern waters.

According to Captain Harding's navigation the *Confederacy* was dismasted and left practically rudderless in latitude 41°03'N, longitude 50°39'W, distant 1140 miles from Cape Henlopen. The frigate tossed and drifted with wind and current for near a fortnight before she had been repaired enough to set a course. Harding called a council of his officers on November 23 where it was unanimously decided that in her present condition *Confederacy* could not weather a gale, and therefore should seek milder latitudes at once by sailing for Martinique in the West Indies. In compliance with his orders, Harding submitted this opinion to Jay and Gerard for their final determination.

M. Gerard had consulted with two French naval officers, members of his company, on the subject. He was most anxious to be in Europe and informed Jay that he believed the ship should make for Cadiz, Spain. He argued that there was little difference in the distance between Cadiz and Martinique, and moreover between the ship and Cadiz lay the Azores and Canary Islands where they could run in if necessary. Further, calmer seas could be found going eastward as well as southward, and in a voyage to Cadiz there need be little fear of meeting an enemy. And, concluded Gerard, even though the *Con-federacy* should reach Martinique safely, he and Jay would probably be detained there until the following spring before they could get passage to Europe.

Jay, of course, had equally as much reason to be in Spain without a protracted delay. He was caught in an unpleasant situation between the Frenchman and Captain Harding and his officers. The political as well as the practical aspects of his decision called for careful consideration. Ship's officers, including the carpenter, more qualified to judge than Gerard or Jay, had said that they should not attempt to go to Europe. The rudder was giving infinite trouble, and water was entering the stern of the ship. Sails were rags, and the jury masts were not to be relied on. As regards a haven in the Canaries or Azores, they afforded neither repair facilities nor good harbor, and Jay could not bring himself to see the frigate and her crew left to their fate in those islands. He ordered Harding to go to Martinique, after which Gerard "ceased to observe that cordiality and frankness which had before attended his conduct toward me."

The crippled *Confederacy* limped south toward the West Indies. When ten or twelve days from a landfall, Gerard ventured that thought should be given to what side of the island of Martinique it would be most prudent to go. He preferred the north which was not exposed to enemy ships from St. Lucia. Harding properly remarked that it would be rash to make a decision until near or at the parting point, and then wind and other circumstances would dictate. This was the second time the French diplomat's recommendations had been rejected or at least not fully adopted. He was furious that his "observations should meet with so little attention; that he owed it to his conscience, and personal safety to mention and enforce them, and that he should represent the whole matter to his Court." As it turned out the northern passage proved

best and, according to Jay, credit for saving the ship by drag-
ging the Americans into accepting the northern coast was
claimed by Gerard.

Harding came to anchor at St. Pierre, Martinique, on
December 18, 1779, fifty-three harrowing days from the Capes
of the Delaware. He is deserving of high praise for his navigation and seamanship which made it possible to carry a critically damaged ship across 1400 miles of open sea. Credit is
likewise due John Jay for steadfastly standing behind the
professional judgement of the American sea officers. Contrary
to Gerard's gloomy prediction of lengthy delay in the West
Indies, the two diplomats were able to resume their passage to
Europe on board a French frigate within two weeks. Harding
stayed on at Martinique to refit the battered *Confederacy*.[107]

Following their fortunate cruise in August 1779, Captains
Whipple, Rathbun, and Simpson were back in New England
readying the ships to go out again. Simpson, as usual, selected
to go to Portsmouth rather than Boston. Whipple temporarily
went home to Providence to consult his own doctors and regain
his health. The rich prizes taken on the late cruise made sign-
ing on men less arduous than usual. By the end of October,
Providence and *Queen of France* together with the *Boston*,
Captain Tucker, were in Nantasket Road fully manned and
ready to proceed to sea. There they were shortly joined by
Simpson in the *Ranger* making a four-ship squadron needing
only orders to get underway. Three weeks passed while the
ships swung on their hooks with the tide, and crews became
impatient, quarrelsome and sickly.

On November 19 the four captains prepared a joint petition to the Navy Board requesting orders. The drain on provisions and the general hazards of holding completely manned
ships idle in port were pointed up.[108] The Board replied the
same day, but could offer nothing more than sympathetic
understanding until instructions were received from the Marine Committee. However, the Board voiced the prediction
that directions from Philadelphia would not be much longer in

coming. This surmise proved correct for the next day Commodore Whipple received his sealed orders together with the Navy Board's instructions to take the four ships under his command, and "to embrace the first fair wind, and without any kind of delay proceed to sea." Whipple was directed to open his orders "when five Leagues to the Southward of the Lighthouse." Should sickness or injury make it impossible for Whipple to exercise fleet command, it would pass to Hoysted Hacker.[109] We remember that following Penobscot, Hacker was without a ship, and he was now serving as first lieutenant in the *Providence*. Although filling a subordinate station, Hacker was a commissioned captain and senior officer of the squadron next to Whipple.

After sailing the prescribed distance south of the lighthouse on November 24, Commodore Whipple broke the seal and read that he was to take his ships immediately to Charleston, South Carolina, and "there persue the orders of the Commanding officer at that place"[110] Events on the passage to South Carolina will be considered as part of the Charleston story, and as such belong to the next chapter. *Providence, Queen of France, Boston,* and *Ranger* had departed New England waters for the last time.

During 1779 the Revolution broadened again when Spain entered the war against England in June. The major theatres of naval hostilities were in Europe and the West Indies, thus pushing the Continental Navy further into the backwater of the conflict. Admiral d'Estaing did not return to the American coast until September, and he left again in October after failing to force the enemy out of Savannah. Although not accomplishing its main objective, the presence of the French fleet off the coast, as Admiral Mahan points out, caused Sir Henry Clinton to order the evacuation of Rhode Island when he felt that he could not hold both that position and New York against a concerted attack.[111] The pressure of strong European enemies compelled the British to reduce their naval force in North American waters to about 60 vessels.[112]

The Continental Navy had an extremely active and rich year at sea in 1779. Ships cruised in squadron strength more than in any previous year, and the results were excellent. New England captains captured no less than 41 enemy ships including 11 taken by Colonel Talbot under army orders and the Royal Navy brig *Diligent* captured by Hacker. In turn three New England-commanded Continental vessels were lost at Penobscot and one, the brig *General Gates,* was surveyed as unfit for further naval service. These cannot be considered excessive losses, but unlike earlier years the reductions were not made up either by new construction or acquisitions. A critical lack of money and a growing conviction in Congress that the weight of the French and Spanish navies reduced the need for a Continental Navy account for this situation. No northern captains cruised in European waters this year.

The *Trumbull* frigate at last escaped from the Connecticut River through the efforts of Captain Hinman. She then immediately passed from our view as Captain James Nicholson of Maryland, backed by seniority and influence, stepped forward to take command. *Confederacy* under Seth Harding began her long delayed active career, and was shortly a dismasted wreck threatening to take the lives of an American and a French diplomat.

The naval services of five more New England captains came to a finish in 1779: Saltonstall, Olney, and John B. Hopkins by courts martial; Hinman and Waters for want of a ship to command. Silas Talbot switched from army lieutenant colonel to naval captain, but it was a paper transfer since there was no vessel for him.

CHAPTER VII

CHARLESTON — 1780

*We then bent our whole force and strained every
nerve for the defense of the town.*

COMMODORE ABRAHAM WHIPPLE

As 1780 OPENED only two Continental Naval vessels remained
in New England ports. The frigate *Deane* was at Boston, and
the *Trumbull* was not yet ready to sail from New London.
These ships were not under local captains but commanded by
the Nicholson brothers, Samuel and James. Captain Harding
was in the West Indies repairing the *Confederacy* after her
calamity, and Whipple had his four-ship squadron at Charleston, South Carolina.

Admiral d'Estaing's departure for Europe with the French
fleet in the fall of 1779 following failure to relieve Savannah
returned the sea uncontested to Sir Henry Clinton. Rather
than move back into Rhode Island, Clinton settled on an expedition to capture Charleston, the scene of his defeat in 1776
and a rebel privateer base against the West Indies. The South
Carolina Assembly's decision was to defend the city to the
last extremity, rather than to withdraw and harrass the British
from the back-country which previously had proven so effective. General Benjamin Lincoln, commanding the Continental
Army in the Southern Department, had retreated to Charleston following repulse of the joint American-French operations against Savannah. To hold the South Carolina capital,

Lincoln had about two thousand regular troops. Fear of the
smallpox and little taste for being trapped in a besieged town
slowed down the number of militia answering the call. Including those from North Carolina and Virginia, the militiamen
numbered somewhat less than the Continentals.[1] Four public
ships, as we have seen, were ordered south from Massachusetts
to strengthen Lincoln.

Whipple's squadron arrived off Charleston December 18,
1779, after a tempestuous 27 day passage from Nantasket
Road.   In a gale near Bermuda the *Providence* and *Ranger*
sprung their mizzenmasts, *Boston* her mainmast, and while the
Queen of France seems to have come through unscathed, Whipple said, "I believe if the gale had continued twelve hours
longer she would have foundered." On December 5 they fell
in with and captured a 12 gun privateer brigantine from St.
Augustine. The same day as the prize was taken, it was necessary to hold an inquest into a death growing out of a fight
between two flagship seamen.[2]

Whipple acquainted Governor Rutledge and General Lincoln of his presence and asked for pilots to take him over the
bar. Lack of wind held the ships out for several days longer,
and they came to anchor before the town on December 23.
Work was immediately started repairing or replacing the damaged masts. Captain Rathbun surveyed the *Queen of France,*
and found her in such poor condition that the Commodore
suspected she would be unable to go to sea again "without more
repair than she will be worth."[3]

Captain Simpson in the *Ranger,* accompanied by a swift
schooner, was ordered out on the 6th of January to render
assistance to a Spanish ship which had run on shore about 20
miles north of Charleston. Back in port five days later, Simpson reported to the Commodore that after doing all in his
power to help the Spaniard (what success he had is not indicated) he sent the schooner in chase of a sail to the eastward.
Lieutenant Page, commanding the schooner, spoke the chase
and was informed that she was a British troop transport for

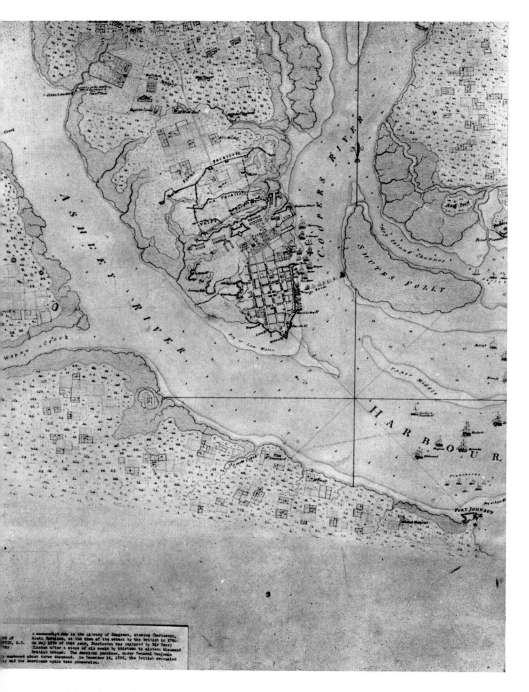

The siege of Charleston, South Carolina, by the British in 1780.

Manuscript chart from the Map Division, Library of Congress.

Georgia from New York. This vessel was not captured, but when pursued she made signals which led Simpson to conclude that she was part of a fleet from which she had separated. This intelligence, when passed on to the Governor and General by Whipple, caused considerable alarm.[4]

Lincoln directed Whipple to dispatch two Continental ships for a short cruise north and south of Charleston to scout out and give early warning of the enemy's approach. Whipple decided to go himself in the *Providence* with *Ranger* as her companion. They dropped down into Rebellion Road on 21 January and were there becalmed three days. Sunday morning the 23rd the weather was thick, and a brig was spotted outside feeling her way along. The Commodore ordered the pilot boat *Eagle* to look her over. By convincing the master that he was approaching Tybee, entrance to Savannah, the brig was decoyed into captivity. She carried 14 guns and New York loyalist troops. This brig, a new vessel, was bought into Continental service, named *General Lincoln,* and given to Captain Hacker to command. Whipple and Simpson were chased back into port by a couple of British 50's on January 29, but not before they had taken two sloops off Tybee lighthouse and gained information on the gathering enemy force in that area.[5] This proved to be the final sortie of Continental ships from Charleston. Hereafter all naval activity was aimed at direct defense of the harbor and town.

General Clinton with 7550 troops sailed from Sandy Hook the day after Christmas 1779. The British transports and victualers were escorted by Vice Admiral of the White Marriot Arbuthnot's powerful naval squadron consisting of five ships-of-the-line, each mounting 64 to 74 guns, six frigates of 32 to 50 guns, two 20's, and a 14. Included among the frigates were the former Continental vessels *Raleigh* and *Virginia.* Clinton's plan for the capture of Charleston called for a land siege combined with a strong naval assault from the seaward side.[6]

The British voyage south was as stormy as Whipple's had been. Several of the transports were lost, and an ordnance ship foundered. Almost all of the cavalry and work horses perished during the passage. It was the end of January before the scattered fleet began staggering into Tybee to regroup, repair, and provision.[7] With the freedom of movement which undisputed naval power assured him, Clinton made his initial move toward Charleston on February 10. The army landed on the coast at Edisto, 30 miles south of Charleston, and the next day occupied John's Island unopposed.[8]

In Charleston, meanwhile, the American sea and land commanders were actively working together in the closest harmony to prepare for the expected onslaught. Lincoln asked Whipple to remain on shore as much as possible "Consistant with the common good" so that they could be in constant communication with each other on the changing tactical situation. While the Commodore was exercising overall naval command from the beach, Captain Hacker took temporary charge of the *Providence* frigate.[9]

Governor Rutledge placed the State Navy comprising two ships, a brig, and galleys under Whipple. He further empowered the Commodore to impress all idle seamen into service, and granted him a warrant to search suspected houses with the right to force entry if necessary. Whipple very wisely delegated this assignment to the master of a State ship who would command more local cooperation than a Continental officer from the north.[10] Two French ships were also added to the defending naval armament.

To determine the feasibility of mooring the ships broadside to the channel entrance in a position to rake any vessel attempting to force a passage, Lincoln requested Whipple to have the inside of the bar and adjacent shoals sounded. Without delay the Commodore ordered Captains Hacker, Rathbun, Tucker and Simpson to accomplish this. The captains reported back on February 1 in unanimous agreement that such a disposition was impractical because "when an Easterly wind is blowing, and the flood making in (such an opportunity as the enemy must embrace for their purpose) there will be so great a swell, in five fathom hole as to render it impossible for a ship to ride, moored athwart, which will afford the Enemies ships, under full sail, the advantage of Passing us, should they affect that, the Continental ships cannot possibly get up to Fort Moultrie, as soon as the Enemies."[11]

The General was shaken by the captains' opinion since he conceived that Charleston's only possible salvation was in confining the enemy attack to the land. He acknowledged the risk of losing the ships if they should take station near the bar, nevertheless he was "fully convinced that the probable services, which they will render there, should the enemy attempt to come over the Bar, and the evils consequent on their getting into this Harbour that the attempt ought to be made, and that the measure thereby can be justified." Accordingly, he ordered Whipple to place the *Providence, Boston,* two state ships, and galleys in a position to command the channel entrance. Before executing this order, the State ships were replaced by the *Ranger,* Simpson.[12]

Whipple received permission from the Governor to demolish the lighthouse, all navigational ranges, and Fort Johnson; thereby denying any advantage to the enemy. Tucker and Simpson accomplished this defensive destruction with assistance from harbor pilots and Continental Marines.[13] It was now mid-February 1780.

Captain Rathbun was ordered to haul the decrepit *Queen of France* up into Ashley River opposite Wapoo Creek in such a position to ascend the mouth of the Creek. On the appearance of the enemy he would signal the alarm — a gun fired three times at one minute intervals. A constant row-guard along the shore line and inlets was likewise to be maintained. State ships and galleys were directed up the Ashley to take station at various distances from the *Queen of France,* and the entire defense in that area was placed under Rathbun. He was responsible for preventing Clinton's troops from crossing the river and attacking the town from that quarter.[14]

Complying with the General's orders of February 13, Simpson, Tucker, and Hacker had taken the Continental vessels down and moored off the bar. The Commodore and captains remained convinced that this was an error. Lincoln agreed to another thorough survey of the situation and directed Whipple himself to be present. On February 27 these findings, signed by Whipple, Hacker, Tucker, and Simpson, were forwarded to the General.

> At low water there is eleven feet in the Channel from the bar to five fathom hole, five fathom hole is three miles from the bar, where you'll have three fathoms at low water, they cannot be anchored untill they are at that distance from the bar, in the place where the ships can be anchored, the bar cannot be covered or annoyed.
>
> Off the North breaker head, where the ships can be anchored to moor them, that they may swing in safety; they will lay within one mile & an half of the shore. If any batteries are thrown up to act in conjunction with the ships, and the enemy's force, should be so much superior, as to cause a retreat to be necessary, it will be impossible for us to cover or take them off.
>
> Our opinion is that the ships can do the most effectual service for the defence and security of the Town to act in conjunction with Fort Moultrie, which we think will but answer the purpose of the ships being sent here, and consequently if so, the views of Congress. Our reasons are that the Channel is so narrow between the Fort, and the middle ground, that they may be moored so as to rake the Channel and prevent the enemy's troops being landed to annoy the Fort. The enemy we apprehend may be prevented from sounding and buoying the bar, by the Brig *Genl. Lincoln* and the State's Brig *Notre Dame,* and other small vessels, that may be occasionally employed for that purpose.[15]

Confronted with the same opinion for a second time, the General yielded to the judgement of his naval officers and allowed Whipple to station the ships as described above.[16] Thus, Lincoln conceded, we may well imagine with considerable reluctance and misgivings, that enemy ships would be able to pass over the bar. Hope must then rest on the combined fire power of Fort Moultrie and the Continental ships preventing the British from coming within range of the town.

As Clinton's army approached the south shore of Ashley River and brought artillery up, the situation of Rathbun's *Queen of France* and other ships in that river became untenable. Accordingly they hauled down to join the other defenders near Fort Moultrie. Whipple, now afloat in active command of *Providence*, released Hacker once again to the *General Lincoln* brig. With some of the small vessels, Hacker was sent to annoy the enemy at the bar and destroy any marker buoys he should set out. At the same time the other officers and men were striving to strengthen their defensive position by laying a chain obstruction across the channel from Fort Moultrie to the middle ground.[17]

In the midst of planning and executing a disposition of his force best calculated to ward off the powerful enemy already knocking at the door, Whipple likewise had to solve the day to day responsibilities of command. The men were in sorry need of trousers, and the pursers scoured the town rounding up material suitable for making this essential clothing article. A sailor in the *Boston* frigate found guilty by court martial of throwing a nine pound shot at the boatswain of that ship, petitioned the Commodore to have pity on "so miserable a wretch and remit the remainder of my stripes." The tar did not deny his guilt, but having already received a large dose of the "cat" he was convinced "that was the remainder of my punishment inflicted it would inevitably put a total period to my life." Lieutenant Adam Thaxter of the *Queen of France* informed Whipple that, "Doctor Jones who attends me have carried me through a regular course of Phisick, from which I find not much advantage, the cough which I have had for a long time has now fell upon my Lungs and I fear I will be of bad consequence." He asked to be relieved to return to New England "to live in the Country on a low diet . . . with the assistance of the Bark and Lime Water." Rum ran scarce, and Continental pursers recommended half rations. In lieu of the missing rum they suggested issuing two quarts of beer a day which "will be vastly better for health than drinking large quantities of bad water."[18] A letter from Philadelphia carried the Admiralty Board's reply to the Commodore's report on the poor condition of the *Queen of France.* The Admiralty proposed that if the *Queen* was no longer fit for a fighting ship she be loaded with as much rice as she could carry and proceed at once to the Delaware.[19] Whipple might be excused a faint smile at the irony of this suggestion at a time when the enemy fleet was already tightly blockading the port.

Vice Admiral Arbuthnot appeared off Charleston on March 4, 1780. He detached the heavy line-of-battleships for New York after determining that even at flood tide he would have to pass through too shallow water. The guns, provisions, and water were taken out of the heavy *Renown, Roebuck,* and *Romulus* to lighten them. We have Admiral Arbuthnot's testimony that Captain Hacker and his small group of brigs and galleys performed their assignment with some effect. After reporting to the Admiralty in London the measures taken to bring his ships higher out of the water, the Admiral added that he "lay in that situation on the open coast in the winter season of the year exposed to the insults of the enemy for sixteen days, before an opportunity offered of going into the harbour, which was effected without any accident, on the 20th of March, notwithstanding the enemy's galleys continually attempted to prevent our boats from sounding the channel."[20]

On March 20 the powerful British fleet passed over the bar and anchored inside the harbor. General Lincoln had previously given Whipple his belief that a splendid opportunity for striking the enemy would be presented just after he came in; that is, before Arbuthnot had time to replace the guns in his heaviest ships. The Commodore called a council of his commanders on board the flagship to consider what should now be done insofar as previous decisions had been based on the

assumption that the British would be unable to get such heavy
ships across the bar. All of the Continental captains were
present. The council reached the conclusion that the chain
obstruction thrown across the channel would not stop the
heavy ships Arbuthnot now had inside the harbor. And furthermore, should the British successfully run past the American
ships they could anchor to leeward in such a manner that the
enemy fire could not be avoided, nor could the friendly vessels
be protected by Fort Moultrie. Based on this analysis, Whipple,
with Lincoln's permission, shifted his entire force from the
bar and fort areas up Cooper River near Gadson's Wharf. A
line of ships was then sunk across the River from the town to
Shutes Folly. Some merchant ships, the State ships, and Rathbun's *Queen of France* were sacrificed to this purpose. *Chev-
aux-de-frise* were fixed on the decks of the sunken vessels,
and a boom composed of cables and chains connected to ships
masts protruding from the water was extended across; the
whole making a formidable barrier. Sunken galleys similarly
blocked Hog Island Channel.[21]

With this retreat up Cooper River above the line of block
ships the story of the American naval force during the siege of
Charleston comes to an end. The guns were taken out of the
ships and added to the shore batteries. Naval officers and seamen went ashore to become artillerymen. Clinton's troops,
gradually closing the ring, crossed to the north bank of Ashley
River. On April 9 the British fleet weighed and successfully
ran past Sullivan's Island under a withering fire from Fort
Moultrie. The Fort's small garrison surrendered May 5 in the
face of imminent combined assault from ship cannon and an
enemy landing force. Charleston was now invested by land
and sea; the beleaguered defenders capitulated May 10, 1780.[22]

Surrender terms required that all shipping afloat in the
harbor be handed over to the victors. The Continental Naval
ships *Ranger, Providence,* and *Boston* were taken into British

service. The *Providence* alone retained her original name, *Boston* was changed to the *Charleston,* and *Ranger* became *Halifax* in the Royal Navy.[23]

Loss of four ships at Charleston brought the Continental Navy close to extinction. The decision to defend the town from interior positions, thereby placing General Lincoln's out-numbered army under a state of siege, was a strategic error of the greatest magnitude. Also, at the point when it was finally decided that Whipple's naval force could not be placed near the bar in such a manner as to prevent the enemy from enter-ing the harbor, the ships should have been ordered out to sea immediately to avoid inevitable entrapment and loss. Charles-ton was a serious defeat for American arms, yet it was not the sorry spectacle of Penobscot repeated. The contrast between the two operations is vivid. At Charleston Lincoln and Whip-ple worked together to give the defense positive leadership and direction, whereas at Penobscot the military and naval com-manders fretted away a golden opportunity, vacillated, and argued their way to disaster. Saltonstall did nothing at Penob-scot, but Commodore Whipple and his captains acted with determination and zeal to defend Charleston with the means at their command. Superior force and freedom of movement finally decided the issue. Mistakes were made, but there was no dishonor at Charleston. Nevertheless we must agree with James Warren's summary — "It was indeed a misfortune that the ships were sent there."[24]

Five days following the surrender that is, May 15, Whip-ple, Hacker, Rathbun, Tucker, and Simpson, all now prisoners of war, addressed a joint plea to Admiral Arbuthnot asking paroles to return "to our friends and connexions in the New England States where we severally promise to remain inactive till a proper exchange shall have taken place."[25] Parole was granted, and the five Continental officers were shortly sailing north in a cartel vessel. They reached Chester, Pennsylvania, in the midst of a smallpox epidemic toward the end of June, and seemed to have remained there just long enough to make a futile request for money to the Board of Admiralty before continuing on to Boston where they arrived toward the end of June.[26]

Captains Rathbun, Tucker, and Simpson were quickly exchanged and lost little time before they were privateering. Whipple remained a prisoner on parole for more than two years until the Americans held a British naval officer of equivalent rank for which he could be exchanged. No courts of inquiry were called on the loss of the ships at Charleston since they were surrendered by the agreed terms of a higher military authority, General Lincoln. By now the Continental Navy was fast disappearing, and there was no possibility of new commands. The naval service of all these officers had come to a close. All, that is, with the exception of the remarkably durable Hoysted Hacker.[27]

After his fellow officers departed for the north, Captain Hacker remained in Philadelphia to appear before the Admiralty Board and offer to serve for the second time in a lieutenant's capacity. The Admiralty requested his exchange on June 28, and he was appointed first lieutenant of the frigate *Alliance*, Captain John Barry, September 5, 1780. Hacker sailed with Barry in the *Alliance* until June 1781 when he left the public service to go privateering.[28] Thus ended an uninterrupted naval career of over five and a half years which carried Hacker from New Providence with Commodore Hopkins, to Penobscot, to Charleston, and finally on board the *Alliance* under the courageous John Barry. If Hacker's service was not always brilliant or conspicuous, it was sustained in its action, and to him goes the distinction of taking one of the few British naval vessels captured by the Continental Navy.

The Charleston capitulation left only one New England captain in active command of a Continental vessel; that was Seth Harding of the frigate *Confederacy*. Since December 1779 Harding had his wrecked ship at Martinique repairing the splintered rudder and trying to obtain new masts. Although the local Continental Agent, William Bingham, promised to furnish Harding with what the ship needed, suitable spars proved extremely hard to come by. None was in store at the Fort Royal naval base, and those which could be purchased commercially were taken to refit a number of French warships which had also been dismasted.[29]

Harding was impatient with the delay and concerned that "the ships Bottom will undoubtedly sustain very great Injury by the worms." He was also beset with crew troubles which were the handmaidens of idleness. Sickness and desertions claimed their share, and French Admiral Picquet took all of Harding's French sailors, about 40 or 50 men. The *Confederacy's* Marine captain saw this as no loss, "a good riddance of Lubbers." One of Harding's young officers became involved in an *affaire d'amour* leading to a duel with a French lieutenant. English seamen in the crew, impressed out of captured merchant vessels, heartened by the sight of a British fleet off shore, mutinied and had to be put in irons.[30]

Just as soon as it would be possible for Harding to get in temporary masts and bend on sail, and provided no orders to the contrary were received, he intended to make for New England calling at the Dutch island of St. Eustatius enroute. Specifically, Harding wanted to take the *Confederacy* to Boston, and gave as his motive the opinion that "it is the best place on the Continent to Refit the Ship. As Sparrs of the best Quality. abound in great plenty. at that place," and the work could be accomplished "with much less expence to the Continent. than at Philadelphia, or at any other part of America."[31] However, the Admiralty Board had not forgotten how long it had taken initially to get the *Confederacy* out of New England waters. They sent Harding orders on February 28, 1780, directing him to touch at St. Eustatius, take in public stores, and then proceed directly to Philadelphia, "where the frigate will receive All necessary repairs."[32]

It was the end of March before the *Confederacy*, fitted with a jury rig of small masts, was again ready to take the sea. Harding had decided to join a large French fleet under the Comte de Guichen in an attack against the English bastion at St. Lucia. But, just as he was getting underway Agent Bingham delivered the orders to return to Philadelphia.[33] Had Harding been able to carry out his design of joining de Guichen's force, he would have achieved the historical distinction of being the sole Continental captain to take part in a British-French fleet engagement.

The *Confederacy* took in a large cargo of sugar and cocoa, and finally on Thursday morning, March 30, 1780, she slipped her mooring and set sail as escort to a merchant fleet of three brigs, a schooner and a sloop. Harding saluted St. Pierre and the French ships present with a departing 13 guns which were returned with 11.[34]

One day out several men came down with the dreaded smallpox. To prevent the disease from spreading throughout the ship, the poor wretches were isolated in the cutter swinging on the booms. The discovery that the maintopmast was badly sprung in two places compelled Harding to treat his makeshift rigging gingerly lest he find himself once again dismasted. Any number of tantalizing prospective prizes were allowed to pass unmolested because the *Confederacy* could not weather a strenuous chase. The frigate came under Cape Henlopen in squally weather on 25 April. Harding's personnel difficulties followed him in. Second lieutenant Thomas Vaughan took six men in the yawl to bring a pilot down from Lewestown, but once ashore Vaughan and the sailors kept going and never returned to the ship.[35]

The Admiralty Board's assured confidence that *Confederacy* would "receive All necessary repairs" at Philadelphia was easier of word than deed. As the spring turned to summer and then to fall the frigate lay alternately at Chester and Philadelphia, "Careening, Rigging, Manning, &c."[36] The naval

officials were destitute of money. The sorry plight to which
the Admiralty Board had been reduced is illustrated in the following plea sent to Congress on August 14, 1780:

> It is with great concern that we inform Congress that it is impossible
> to proceed with any celerity in fitting the Confederacy for sea. We
> have strained our Credit to the greatest stretch, and are Afraid that
> the Cable which is making for the Confederacy will not be delivered
> to us unless we can furnish Money to discharge part at least of the
> great debt which we owe to the Rope Maker, beside this we are
> indebted to others . . . To avoid Censure and hoping that Congress
> may be able to find out ways and means to fit out this fine frigate
> we trouble you with this melancholy picture.[37]

Continental naval officers and men were being paid in
depreciated paper currency while at the same time privateer
crews were receiving specie. Understandably this caused dis-
content and added nothing to the attractiveness of the public
service. Harding joined with Captain John Young of the
sloop *Saratoga* in pointing out to the Admiralty Board that
"the pay of the Officers & men in the Marine service of said
States which at the first establishment was Just & Generous
is now by Depreciation become so nearly reduced to nothing
as to be Considered by Seamen as no reward for Pass'd services,
or inducement to engage for the future. That the subsistance
Money allowed per Week to officers, whilst necessarily on
shore & in Port and refitting is depreciated to a sum below
the price of a single Nights Lodging."[38]

Out of Harding's and Young's appeal grew an Admiralty
Board resolution to Congress that pay and subsistence be paid
in specie or other money equivalent; that a twenty dollar
bounty be allowed every able seaman and ten dollars to each
ordinary seaman or landsman who would sign on for twelve
months; and that forty Continental dollars be considered as
equivalent to one dollar in specie. Congress accepted these
recommendations on July 11, 1780, but only as applied to
enlisted men. Since there were more than enough officers,
the legislators saw no need for, nor could the treasury afford,
any further encouragement in that direction.[39]

In October 1780 Harding stood trial and was relieved of any onus for the dismasting of the *Confederacy* the previous November.[40] John Jay's high opinion of Harding's conduct and ship-handling during the critical emergency aided the Captain's cause. But Harding was soon in hot water again with the state authorities over his favorite mode of "enlisting" men — impressment from vessels going up and down the Delaware. Philadelphia merchants put pressure on the Executive Council of Pennsylvania to take steps to stop this business. The Council President wrote a letter to Congress on November 30 advising that repeated complaints had been received against Captain Harding for impressing men, and that he was laying the matter before Congress "not with a view to hinder Captain Harding from pursuing his voyage, but that proper measures be taken to prevent such practices in future."[41] No formal action seems to have been taken against Harding. But when things became too warm the *Confederacy* dropped down the River to New Castle, Delaware, out of Pennsylvania's jurisdiction, and continued as before.[42]

Harding came close to being replaced in the *Confederacy* for a reason totally unrelated to impressment. James Nicholson, who had disappointed the Eastern Navy Board and Captain Elisha Hinman, by coming out of the south to take command of the Connecticut frigate *Trumbull,* was in Philadelphia while his ship was undergoing battle-damage repairs. After looking over the *Confederacy* and liking what he saw, Nicholson once again called forth his prerogative as number one naval captain and requested transfer to that vessel. "As the Senior officer in the American Service," he memorialized Congress, "I think myself justly entitled to one of the largest Ships in the Navy but instead of that I have one of the smallest." He complained that a junior officer, John Barry, had been appointed to the *Alliance* and Harding, "the Youngest in the Service," had the *Confederacy.* Nicholson considered his position injured by these appointments, and felt it would be particularly embarrassing if the ships were to fight a joint action, and the enemy found him commanding the weakest ship.[43]

The Admiralty Board was suffering constant embarrassments about Harding's press gang, so, it may be appreciated, that the Connecticut captain was not particularly popular with the members. They were in full sympathy with Nicholson's claim. However, it will be remembered that Harding was specifically named to command the *Confederacy* by Congress at the behest of Governor Trumbull, and they alone could remove him.[44] The Admiralty gave the legislators their opinion that Nicholson's claim was reasonable: "Was he now appointed to command the *Confederacy*, it would be of public utility, as under him she might be immediately manned." But Congress was unwilling to give this affront to old Governor Trumbull and dismissed the recommendation with a "not to be acted upon" endorsement.[45]

Sale of *Saratoga's* prize snow and her rum cargo brought the Admiralty Board unexpected money with which to push forward work on the *Confederacy*.[46] She was ready by December 1780 at which time Harding was able to muster near 260 willing and unwilling crewmen.[47] On the 18th of the month the *Confederacy* was joined by the *Saratoga* at Reedy Island in the Delaware. Harding had taken on board several French passengers for the West Indies where he was again headed with the *Saratoga* as escort to a merchant fleet. The convoy weighed on December 20, but Harding's pilot finding the weather bad came to anchor the same day while the *Saratoga* and the merchants continued out. Next afternoon Harding left Cape Henlopen astern and stood south in company with two brigs.[48]

Confederacy's new rigging was proving her a good sailer as she cut through the azure water. Marine Captain Hardy noted in his journal the final entry for 1780 — "the weather more moderate and pleasant . . . Latitude at Meredian by Obs. 29° 37' N."[49]

During 1780 the only prizes made by New England captains were those few seized by Whipple's squadron while en route to Charleston. The loss of four ships at Charleston was the heaviest single blow suffered by the Continental Navy in the course of the war, and wrote "closed" to the public service of Captains Whipple, Rathbun, Tucker, and Simpson. Of the 22 captains from New England whose Revolutionary naval careers have been followed in these pages, Seth Harding alone continued in active command as the Continental Navy dwindled to insignificance.

Near the end of the year England declared war on the Netherlands and promptly set about shutting off the flow of supplies to the United States from the Dutch Island of St. Eustatius. The scene of the European rivals' major naval operations in 1780 was West Indian waters rather than North Atlantic or the Mediterranean. Britain continued a strong force exceeding 50 vessels on the North American station based at New York.[50]

Disappointment in America arising from the failure of the French Navy to strike a decisive blow continued through 1780. In July Admiral de Ternay's fleet and a French army under Rochambeau arrived at Newport, Rhode Island, where they were soon blockaded by Admiral Arbuthnot coming north after his Charleston victory. Nevertheless, the stage was being set for the *coup de main* at Yorktown where, for a moment at least, control of the sea was wrested from the British, and the all-important victory was won. It seems unfortunate indeed that the Continental Navy was not able to play a part at Yorktown, crucial step toward American independence.

CHAPTER VIII

THE CURTAIN COMES DOWN, 1781-83

It is certain that the Revolution would have failed without its sailors. In spite of its short-comings, the record of the American marine during this critical period was an honorable one.

GARDNER ALLEN

The *Alliance, Confederacy, Deane, Trumbull,* and the sloop of war *Saratoga* were the whole of the Continental Navy as 1781 began, and when this sixth year of the war closed all but *Alliance* and *Deane* had disappeared from the naval register. Since *Confederacy* was the sole ship remaining under the command of a Yankee skipper, she is our particular concern.

Captain Seth Harding of the *Confederacy* spent the better part of New Year's Day 1781 futilely pursuing a sail which disappeared to the westward toward Bermuda. The sea was tumbling, but the weather was pleasant, and a gentle trade wind pushed the frigate along on a southeasterly course for Cap François (now Cap Haitien), Haiti.[1]

Noon on January 5 Harding gave chase to a vessel which was discovered distant 8 or 9 leagues. By nightfall he had closed the distance by half, and at 10 P.M. the *Confederacy* ranged alongside. The stranger answered Harding's hail that she was the brig *Elizabeth and Nancy*, Captain Byrne, in ballast from Nova Scotia bound for Turks Island in the Bahamas.

209

When Byrne was brought on board the *Confederacy* and discovered that his captors were American not British, he brought forth papers to show that his brig was American-owned from Salem, Massachusetts. He claimed to be en route Turks Island to take in a cargo of salt under the guise of an English trader. To carry out the deceit he had a forged set of British papers. Harding, hungry for a prize and suspicous of Byrne, carried the brig with him into Cap François where he arrived January 8, 1781.[2]

The *Elizabeth and Nancy* was libeled against in the French Admiralty Court, and the decision went to the captors. As it turned out, the prize was actually owned by a group of Salem merchants. In a lengthy memorial to Congress they petitioned for redress against Harding's "piracy" pointing out that the use of fraudulent papers to deceive the enemy was a regular practice, and furthermore that the French court could have no jurisdiction in the case.[3] A committee studied the petition and reported in essence that if the sentence of condemnation was valid there was no need for Congress to interpose, and if void the vessel could be recovered by legal processes and a damage suit brought against Harding by the owners. Since no tribunal existed in America for review or correction of decisions given by the French Admiralty, Congress ordered the petition dismissed.[4] We may be reasonably certain that George Crowninshield and the other owners carried their case to the French authorities. We have Harding's own word that he received no prize money.[5]

The *Confederacy* remained in harbor for three weeks as the crew enjoyed a pleasant liberty ashore in a scenic setting of magnificent beauty. February 1 Harding sailed on a short cruise with a French brig. Going out they saluted Samuel Nicholson and the *Deane* frigate on her way in.[6] *Saratoga* was already anchored at Cap François. Harding patrolled with the Frenchman for more than two weeks before returning to port after netting nothing.

The convoy which the three Continental ships were scheduled to escort to America was not as yet assembled, nor was the cargo of Continental supplies ready. In the interim, Harding, Nicholson, and Young, together with the privateer *Fair American* and the French brig, departed February 20 for a brief sweep through the Windward Passage. They were back within a week bringing with them a heavily laden merchant prize. It is said that she was from St. Kitts for Jamaica filled with some of Admiral Rodney's plunder from St. Eustatius.[7]

Harding took in a quantity of Continental Army clothing and loaded sugar, cotton, and indigo into the frigate's hold. On March 15, 1781, he sailed north with a giant fleet of 37 merchant ships convoyed by the three Continental vessels. One month later, April 14, as Harding herded his charges along near the Delaware Capes a large frigate was sighted bearing down. Neither the *Deane* nor *Saratoga* were in sight.[8] The merchantmen scattered for safety and *Confederacy* was cleared for action as a second ship was seen approaching. When the lead sail came within range she broke British colors and ran out a second tier of guns. She was the 44 gun frigate *Roebuck,* and her consort was the *Orpheus,* 32. Harding struck without resistance.[9]

The *Confederacy* was brought into New York harbor, Union Jack flying over the American bunting. "Among near 300 men on board her," wrote Tory journalist James Rivington, "were found a number of British seamen who had been forced into the enemy's service thro' the harshest treatment in their gaols, these with great alacrity immediately entered into that of their native country."[10] Another New York newspaper observed "that the Captain of the rebel frigate must escape every imputation derogatory to the conduct of an officer and a man of honour. We must allow even an enemy merit, when he is not found justly to have forfeited it."[11] After sale of her invoice, which was valued at some £50,000, the frigate was purchased into the Royal Navy under the slightly altered name *Confederate.*[12]

Captain Harding and his officers on parole landed home in New London from a cartel May 4, 1781.[13] The unfortunate tumultuous naval service of Governor Trumbull's favorite was finished. Beginning under a cloud, misfortune dogged Harding's path from the launching of the *Confederacy* until he was overwhelmed and compelled to surrender his command. The report circulated that a large portion of the *Confederacy's* sugar cargo was the personal propery of Harding and the crew rather than public stores. When confronted with the impropriety of his action, Harding retorted that "he Intended to leave the Service and was determined to make the Most of this cruise he could and then retire to Connecticut . . . to be Chose a delegate and take his Seat in Congress."[14]

Hard luck followed the sharp-nosed sailor into private life. He invested in a heretofore successful Connecticut privateer schooner *Young Cromwell,* but on her first voyage with Harding as part owner she was captured. Late in 1782 Harding sailed as master of a small 6 gun brigantine letter of marque and was prompty taken by a British man-of-war.[15]

There remains yet a final page to be written before the record of New England captains in the Continental Navy can be considered closed. Appropriately the last scene belongs to one of the very first Revolutionary sailors, John Manley of Marblehead.

Cleared in June 1778 of blame for losing the *Hancock* frigate, and having no public command in prospect, Manley turned to privateering. He had middling success, some hot action, and several harrowing experiences including two more stays in British jails. In the first instance he escaped with relative ease, but the second time he languished in old Mill Prison until exchanged at the very end of 1781. Once back in America, Manley again sought a Continental command.[16]

In the fall of 1781 Congress had dissolved the defunct Admiralty Board and handed the remnants of naval business to Robert Morris, Superintendent of Finance.[17] September 1782 Morris ordered Samuel Nicholson relieved of command of the

Hague and the frigate given to the senior officer in the eastern department. This was Captain Manley. The circumstances surrounding the appointment and shift of commanders are unknown. It is possible that Nicholson asked to be relieved, or he may have been removed for disciplinary reasons since the record shows he faced a court martial the following year.[18] Perhaps Manley took a leaf from James Nicholson's book and claimed the ship on the basis of seniority.

The *Hague* was the ex-*Deane* renamed after Silas Deane had fallen from official favor, and the Netherlands had received John Adams as the minister of an independent United States. Manley reported on board the very day he was appointed. *Hague* was fully dressed in multicolored flags, and a 13 gun salute honored the new captain while the crew in the tops roared approval. From the quarter deck Manley delivered a short prepared speech to "My good Lads and jolly Seamen" who had not forgotten the hero of Washington's "fleet."[19]

The date Manley departed Boston for a West Indian cruise is not known, but since his ship was ready and manned it is not likely he tarried long after assuming command. Even as the *Hague* came to sail, peace negotiations were underway, and the air was electric in anticipation of the war soon being over.

Manley's course took him to Martinique, habitual rendezvous for American cruisers. He is reported to have made several captures during the southern passage.[20] The day after Christmas 1782 *Hague,* in company with two privateers, cruised out of Martinique for the Leeward Islands.[21] About 300 miles to the eastward of Antigua in the early morning hours of 9 January the 44 gun enemy frigate *Dolphin* was encountered, and for the second time in his Continental service Manley decided "to show his heels." Four 74 gun ships-of-the-line teamed up with *Dolphin* in the ensuing 36 hour chase. Manley, all the while firing stern chasers at his pursuers, attempted to get the *Hague* under the French forts covering Baie Mahault on the eastern side of Guadeloupe and ran hard aground on a reef off

Grand Terre. There the frigate hung for two days while the enemy warships, in Manley's words, "were not very sparing of a heavy and brisk cannonade." The Britishers tried to warp in closer upon the *Hague,* but shoal water combined with cannon fire to keep them at a respectable distance. Lying immobile and subjected to incessant attack, Manley did not abandon his ship and take to the boats as several others had done, but worked his crew furiously to get the *Hague* off into deep water. He succeeded, and, aiming a few parting rounds at the frustrated enemy, came within the protective ring of French forts. The *Hague* sustained considerable injury in hull and rigging, but not a man was killed and only one slightly wounded.[22]

Manley was still at Guadeloupe on January 26, 1783, when he wrote to Boston informing that his damages had been repaired, and that he planned to depart the next day for Martinique to use the more extensive facilities at that place for "heaving down." The captain was still sensitive to the criticism from some quarters that he had surrendered the *Hancock* frigate too easily in 1777. Therefore, with the aforementioned letter to associates in Boston he enclosed a letter from the Viscount de Damas, Governor of Guadeloupe, praising Manley for his "good conduct, courage, and bravery" in the present incident. At Manley's request the French Governor's testimonial was printed in the Boston *Independent Chronicle.*[23]

Sometime in early January, before the *Hague* was driven aground, Manley captured a merchantman laden with provisions. She was the ship *Baille,* only six months old and mounting 20 six pounders. The Massachusetts Admiralty Court libeled *Baille* in behalf of Captain Manley in March 1783.[24] This was the last significant prize made during the war, and it was made by John Manley who in 1775, at the very outset of the conflict, took the first prize of any importance.[25]

A letter of February 5, 1783, from the Marquis de Lafayette announcing a general peace was laid before Congress and read on March 24. The immediate recall of all armed vessels cruising under commissions from the United States of America was directed.[26] The *Hague* arrived back in Boston the first week in May and, after clearing quarantine, was moored alongside Hancock's Wharf.[27] Stepping ashore Manley was handed Robert Morris' order for his arrest to answer a variety of charges brought against him by one of his officers. What prompted this action and whether or not a court was ever held is not now known. At the time of Manley's death in 1793 he was preparing memoirs which would have thrown some light on this last distasteful event had they ever appeared.[28] The *Hague* was decommissioned and sold at public auction October 2, 1783.[29] Two years later *Alliance,* the last ship, was similarly disposed of and the Continental Navy went out of existence.

*   *   *   *

We have now followed the efforts of the 22 known New England captains in the Continental Navy from the initial gun to the joyful ending of the struggle. It is deemed worth restating what has already been written in the preface, namely, that this group of men participated in the bulk of naval actions and commanded a greater number of public vessels by far than all the officers from other sections of the country combined. Since this was the fact, it would seem that conclusions reached about the New Englanders could validly be applied to the Continental Naval effort generally.

Each of the hardy New England men commissioned a naval captain was a seafarer with long experience afloat in command of merchant vessels. Shiphandling and navigation were second nature and did not have to be learned in the midst of war. In addition, some had the added advantage of earlier service in the British Navy or in privateers. Although nepotism and political favoritism played a heavy hand in the choice of naval captains, they were from the best and only possible element in the population from which sea officers could be drawn. They universally lacked a knowledge of naval tactics, the demands of warship command, and an ability to throw off parochialism where New England was concerned. Collectively they felt the want of naval spirit, tradition, and discipline which can only come with the years; advantages held and frequently demonstrated by the enemy. Some of the captains, Whipple, Rathbun, Hinman, for example, grew with their responsibilities and performed service worthy of a long-founded naval establishment. Others, of which Saltonstall and McNeill come to mind, failed to meet the test of either individual ship or squadron command. Nevertheless, no one can impugn the personal bravery of the "arch rebels" who sailed forth into the teeth, and frequently under the very nose, of the most powerful navy in the world.

That these 22 chose to fight their war on the sea, the element they knew best, is easily grasped. But the wonder is what stirred them to seek commissions and commands in the Continental Navy. Privateering offered larger prize shares, better and surer pay, plus freedom from the restrictions of Marine Committee, Navy Board, or naval regulations. Yet in no instance was a Continental vessel held in port for want of a captain, nor did any commander desert his ship for a private venture. On the contrary, as the war moved along and the number of captains outnumbered the public ships, all the strings were pulled as commands were eagerly courted. Again, when a captain was suspended or cashiered by court martial he did not accept the decision with indifference, but sparing not of expense or time went all out trying for Congressional reinstatement. Why was this so? Two explanations are immediately suggested; namely, that the captains preferred Continental ships because they were larger and heavier gunned than privateers, or if taken prisoner as members of a regular naval force they expected better treatment from the enemy. However, these answers will not suffice, for some of the privateers were newer, faster, and carried heavier metal than their Continental opposites. On the second count, preferential prisoner treatment, the British refused to recognize the existence of a

Continental Navy. They referred consistently to all American ships as "privateers" or "pirates" and consequently handled prisoners without distinction.

It must be remembered that in previous days the Yankee mariners who were to be the Revolutionary naval captains had sailed under the protection of the Royal Navy, and shared many a tankard with British naval officers in public houses from Glasgow to Trinidad. They were thoroughly imbued with the respect, prestige, and social position incident to naval uniform and rank. There is ample evidence in their actions and correspondence to justify the position that such considerations were an impelling factor to those merchant seamen who avidly aspired to a naval captain's commission. Witness the unrestrained political jockeying for position in October 1776 when the order of seniority among captains was being drawn up.

The uniform as an evident manifestation of position generated considerable interest. Captain Hector McNeill, early in 1777, wrote on this matter to Dudley Saltonstall, his senior, as follows:

> Sir. You will see by the Inclosed papers that a number of your Brother Officers have laid their inventions together in order to prevail with the Honble Congress to Establish a uniform for the American Navy. In doing this we have not nor do not desire to aim at the lead or the vain Superiority of dictating to our brethren to the Southward, we have also confined ourselves to such dress as the Local circumstances of our affairs will admit of, if you approve and second our requests to the Congress we shall esteem it a happiness, or if you can devise anything else more applicable to our present Situation we shall with pleasure acquiess therein. We have sent circular Letters to all Gentlemen Commanding in the Continental Service . . . [30]

Some months later Captain Elisha Hinman added this postscript in a letter to Saltonstall — "By Capt. Jones who is from Philadelphia understand that our Lappels is to be Red instead of Buff for our Coats."[31]

A time-honored British practice called for traders to haul down their pennants when in company with ships of war, and to lower certain sails as a sign of respect when passing a British warship on the high seas. Following suit, the American Congress by resolve of October 29, 1776, forbade privateer or merchant ships to wear pennants when in company with a public vessel without permission from the Continental officer commanding. If this ruling was not obeyed, the naval officer was authorized to board and take away the pennants from the offenders.[32] Here was another mark of distinction which the Continental captains jealously guarded and enforced. To illustrate, in Boston harbor, October 1779, just prior to departing for Charleston, Commodore Whipple circulated an order that "The Gentlemen commanding private armed ships of War or Merchantmen are desired to haul down their Pendants before to morrow 11 oClock AM. as it has given great uneasiness, to the Officers in general. And such persons not having obtained leave of me or any Captain the Continental Navy now in this Harbour . . . and in case this request is not complied with by the time pointed out, I will send my Boat and haul them down."[33] With equal pride Whipple and other captains when acting as squadron commodores, wore the broad pennant authorized for that station.

We arrive then at the general conclusion that the stature acquired, personal prestige, and the trappings of a naval officer combined with a genuine patriotism (at least in most) which saw public service as the greatest direct value to the common good must be assigned as prime reasons why the "Captains to the Northward" eagerly pursued careers in the Continental Navy.

The most sanguine patriot could not envision America raising a naval force strong enough to challenge the fleets of Great Britain. When Washington exclaimed: "In any operations, and under all circumstances, a decisive naval superiority is to be considered as a fundamental principle, and the basis upon which every hope of success must ultimately depend," he had reference to the French marine not the Continental Navy.[34] William Ellery stated in one sentence the only possible American offensive naval strategy—"Our great Aim should be to destroy the trade of Britain." While major naval actions against British sea power were reserved to the French and Spanish navies, commerce raiding was the operational objective for the Continental Navy, the State navies, and privateers — the three elements of America's sea warfare. Various plans were laid for Continental ships to operate with the French, but these always failed to materialize. Except for two notable instances the Continental Navy assiduously preyed on enemy trade and cross-ocean communications. The two deviations were at Penobscot and Charleston where the Continental forces were overwhelmed by superior enemy units and suffered disastrous losses while acting in support of Army operations.

How did the New England captains fare in this business of "destroying the trade of Britain?" The tally for all the war years, as close as can be determined, reveals that single Continental vessels under the command of New Englanders, or squadron action in which New England-commanded ships participated, resulted in the capture or destruction of 115 enemy merchantmen and several Royal Naval ships. Although unquestionably annoying and vexatious, particularly to the private owners and the English army awaiting supplies which never arrived, the figures are not staggering. Against a nation numbering her merchant fleet and warships in the thousands, these losses could not be classed "trade destroying." Privateers which outnumbered Continental vessels many times caused an amount of injury commensurate with this greater force. A count shows that privateer bonds issued to Massachusetts ships numbered 626, Connecticut 226, New Hampshire 43, and Rhode Island 15; a New England total of 910 privateers.[35] Hale states that in 1781 the privateer fleet of Salem, Massachusetts, alone consisted of 59 vessels mounting 746 guns, and carrying nearly 4,000 men.[36] Due to the irregular nature of privateering enterprise and incomplete records it is impossible to make anything approaching a definitive count of the prizes taken. However, Allen gives us some idea when he writes, "A very rough estimate based on the newspaper lists would indicate that the number of prizes taken and brought into port during the war by Massachusetts privateers and tried in the courts of the State was not far from twelve hundred."[37]

Compared with the number of captures made by privateers, those taken by Continental Naval ships were few indeed. We have seen throughout these pages how the public vessels were held idle in port months on end for want of crews while thousands of seamen, not sharing a concern for the common weal, were attracted to privateering. The Continental captains spent only a fraction of their time at sea, and at that they habitually had to resort to the press gang and the use of British prisoners to man the ships. A Congressional pronouncement against recruiting for privateers whenever naval vessels lacked men would have been of doubtful value for not only would the move have been most unpopular with influential merchants, but it would have been virtually unenforcible.

Following long and expensive inactivity, Continental men-of-war frequently put to sea only to be captured after one or two short cruises. While New Englanders were in command, 13 naval vessels were taken, destroyed, or run on shore to avoid capture by the British. If one excludes the shipping, some unfinished, destroyed at Philadelphia and New York to prevent it falling into the enemy's hands when they occupied those places, the New England captains suffered about 70% of the American naval losses during the war.

On the strictly military balance sheet of the war against British commerce, the Continental Navy cannot be considered as having weighed decisively in the ultimate outcome. The results achieved were not in keeping with the financial strain and the difficulties imposed on the Continent in building, manning, and administering a naval establishment. However, the Navy brought in supplies to sustain Washington's Army, convoyed merchant fleets, and filled another need, less tangible and not as subject to measurement, yet vital and one which privateers were incapable of performing. The Continental Navy did not represent private citizens or individual states, but it was an organ of the 13 United States, and in that capacity was a unifying factor. Ships of the Continental Navy were subject to a national jurisdiction, commanded by officers wearing a distinctive national uniform, and flew a national flag. Continental Naval captains gave and received the courtesy salutes customarily exchanged between sovereign nations. On the ocean, in West Indian and European ports, the Continental Navy was material proof, for all to view, that England's revolting American colonies were determined to be a free and independent country.

BIBLIOGRAPHY

A. MANUSCRIPT SOURCES

John S. Barnes Collection. New-York Historical Society. New York, New York.

Nicholas Cooke Papers. Rhode Island Historical Society. Providence, Rhode Island.

Early Records Section Files. Naval History Division. National Archives. Washington, D.C.

Simon Gratz Collection. Historical Society of Pennsylvania. Philadelphia, Pennsylvania.

Charles T. Harbeck Collection. Huntington Library. San Marino, California.

William Heath Papers and Miscellaneous Letters. Massachusetts Historical Society. Boston, Massachusetts.

"Inventory of the Continental Frigate Raleigh, Captain Thomas Thompson taken in January, 1778." *Josiah Fox Papers.* Peabody Museum. Salem, Massachusetts.

Journal of the Committee who built the ships Providence and Warren for the U. S. AD 1776. Rhode Island Historical Society. Providence, Rhode Island.

Journal kept by J. M. Connor, May-August, 1777, in Frigate Boston. Mariners Museum. Newport News, Virginia.

John and Woodbury Langdon Papers. New Hampshire Historical Society. Concord, New Hampshire.

Letter Book Navy Board Eastern Department, October 23, 1778 to October 29, 1779. New York Public Library. New York, New York.

Captain Hector McNeill's Log, May-July, 1777. Mariners Museum. Newport News, Virginia.

Papers of the Continental Congress. National Archives. Washington, D.C.

Papers Relating to the Penobscot Expedition, 1779. Transcripts from the Massachusetts Archives. New-York Historical Society. New York, New York.

Purviance Papers and Miscellaneous Letters. Maryland Historical Society. Baltimore, Maryland.

Nathaniel Shaw Papers. Yale University Library. New Haven, Connecticut.

Stevens, B. F., comp. *Facsimiles of Manuscripts in European Archives Relating to America* 1773-1783. London: Chiswick Press, 1898.

Silas Talbot Papers. Rhode Island Historical Society. Providence, Rhode Island.

The Adams Papers. Massachusetts Historical Society. Boston, Massachusetts.

Votes and Resolutions, September 2, 1777 *to January* 3, 1778 *and Letter Book, November* 3, 1779 *to February* 6, 1782, *Navy Board Eastern Department.* Library of Congress. Washington, D.C.

Abraham Whipple Papers. Rhode Island Historical Society. Providence, Rhode Island. There are also Whipple papers in the Detroit Public Library, Detroit, Michigan.

B. PRINTED SOURCES

Adams, John. *The Works of John Adams.* With notes by Charles Francis Adams. Boston: Little, Brown, 1865. vol. III.

Allen, Gardner W., [ed.]. *Captain Hector McNeill of the Continental Navy.* Contains McNeill letter book and papers. Boston: Massachusetts Historical Society, 1922. 108 pp.

Almon, J. *The Remembrancer; or Impartial Repository of Public Events.* London: Opposite Burlington House, 1775-1784. 17 vols.

Barnes, John S., ed. *Fanning's Narrative being the Memoirs of Nathaniel Fanning an Officer of the Revolutionary Navy* 1778-1783. New York: Naval History Society, 1912. 258 pp.

Beck, Alverda S., ed. *The Correspondence of Esek Hopkins Commander in Chief of the United States Navy.* Providence: Rhode Island Historical Society, 1933. 101 pp.

The Letter Book of Esek Hopkins Commander in Chief of the United States Navy. Providence: Rhode Island Historical Society, 1932. 151 pp.

Bigelow, John, ed. *The Complete Works of Benjamin Franklin.* New York: Putnam's, 1888. vol. VI.

Bolander, Louis H. "The Log of the Ranger," *United States Naval Institute Proceedings,* 62 (Feb. 1936). 201-211.

Burnett, Edmund C., ed. *Letters of Members of the Continental Congress,* Washington: Carnegie Institution of Washington, 1921-1936. 8 vols.

Correspondence of Silas Deane, 1774-1776. Hartford: Connecticut Historical Society, 1870. 239 pp.

The Deane Papers, 1774-1777. New York: New-York Historical Society, 1887. vol. I.

Fitzpatrick, John C., ed. *The Writings of George Washington from the Original Manuscript Sources* 1745-1799. Washington: Government Printing Office, 1931-1938. vol. 3 to vol. 26.

Force, Peter, ed. *American Archives.* Washington: M. St. Clair Clarke and Peter Force, 1837-1853. 4th ser., 6 vols. (Mar. 7, 1774 to Aug. 21, 1776); 5th ser., 3 vols. (May 3, 1776 to Dec. 31, 1776). No more published.

Ford, W. C., *et al,* eds. *Journals of the Continental Congress.* Washington: Government Printing Office, 1904-1937. 34 vols.

Johnston, Henry P., ed. *The Record of Connecticut Men in the Military and Naval Service During the War of the Revolution* 1775-1783. Hartford: Adjutant General of Connecticut, 1889. 779 pp.

Lincoln, Charles H., [ed.]. *Naval Records of the American Revolution* 1775-1788. Washington: Government Printing Office, 1906. 549 pp.

Lowrie, Walter and Walter S. Franklin, eds. *American State Papers.* Washington: Gales and Seaton, 1834. Class IX (Claims).

Massachusetts Soldiers and Sailors of the Revolutionary War. A compilation from the archives prepared by the Secretary of the Commonwealth. Boston: Wright and Potter, 1896. 17 vols.

Middlebrook, Louis F. *History of Maritime Connecticut* 1775-1783. Salem: Essex Institute, 1925. 2 vols.

Nash, Gilbert. *The Original Journal of General Solomon Lovell, Kept During the Penobscot Expedition,* 1779, *with a Sketch of His Life.* Boston: Weymouth Historical Society, 1881. 127 pp.

Neeser, Robert W., ed. *The Despatches of Molyneux Shuldham Vice Admiral of the Blue and Commander in Chief of His Britannic Majesty's Ships in North America, January-July,* 1776. New York: Naval History Society, 1913. 330 pp.

Paullin, Charles O. *Out-Letters of the Continental Marine Committee and Board of Admiralty August,* 1776 — *September,* 1780. New York: De Vinne Press, 1914. 2 vols.

Records and Papers of the New London County Historical Society. New London: New London County Historical Society, 1893. vol. I.

Rogers, Ernest F. *Connecticut's Naval Office at New London During the War of the American Revolution.* New London: New London County Historical Society, 1933. 358 pp.

Rolls and Lists of Connecticut Men in the Revolution. Hartford: Connecticut Historical Society, 1901. 375 pp.

Secret Journals of Acts and Proceedings of Congress. Boston: Thomas B. Wait, 1820-1821. 4 vols.

"Journal of Lieutenant John Trevett, USN." *Rhode Island Historical Magazine.* Newport: Newport Historical Publishing Company, 1885-1886. vols. 6 and 7.

"Papers of William Vernon and the Navy Board." *Publications of the Rhode Island Historical Society,* vol. VIII, no. 4. Providence: Rhode Island Historical Society, 1901. pp. 197-277.

Wharton, Francis, ed. *The Revolutionary Diplomatic Correspondence of the United States.* Washington: Government Printing Office, 1889. 6 vols.

C. NEWSPAPERS

Boston Gazette.
Columbian Centinel (Boston).
Continental Journal (Boston).
Evening Post (Boston).
Freeman's Journal, or New Hampshire Gazette (Portsmouth).
Independent Chronicle (Boston).
Newport Mercury.
New York Gazette.
Pennsylvania Gazette (Philadelphia).
Pennsylvania Packet (Philadelphia).
Providence Gazette.
Royal Gazette (New York).

D.   ARTICLES AND ADDRESSES

Allen, Gardner W. "States Navies and Privateers in the American Revolution." Paper read at meeting of Massachusetts Historical Society, Boston, Nov. 14, 1912. *Revolutionary War Miscellany, I,* (Compiled by Navy Department Library, Washington, D.C.).

Brewington, M. V. "The Design of Our First Frigates," *American Neptune,* VIII (Jan. 1948), pp. 11-25.

Clark, William Bell. "A Neglected Phase of Revolutionary History." An address delivered at the 162nd annual meeting of the State Society of the Cincinnati of Pennsylvania, Philadelphia, Oct. 4, 1945. Printed by the Society.

Eller, Ernest M. "Sea Power in the American Revolution," *United States Naval Institute Proceedings,* 62 (June 1936), pp. 777-789.

Foster, Joseph. "The Continental Frigate Raleigh," *Granite Monthly,* 60 (Nov. 1928), pp. 558-566.

Goodrich, Casper F. "The Naval Side of the Revolutionary War." Paper read before United States Naval Institute, Mar. 7, 1896. *Revolutionary War Miscellany,* I, (Compiled by Navy Department Library, Washington, D.C.).

Jewell, E. P. "A Curious Relic," *Granite Monthly,* 5 (1881-1882), pp. 64-68.

Morgan, William J. "The Stormy Career of Captain Hector McNeill, Continental Navy," *Military Affairs,* XVI (Fall, 1952) pp. 119-122.

Terwilliger, W. Bird. "William Goddard's Victory for the Freedom of the Press," *Maryland Historical Magazine,* XXXVI (June 1941) pp. 139-149.

E. SECONDARY WORKS

Allen, Gardner W. *A Naval History of the American Revolution.* Boston: Houghton Mifflin, 1913. 2 vols.
    Massachusetts Privateers of the Revolution. Cambridge: Harvard University Press, 1927. 355 pp.

Beatson, Robert. *Naval and Military Memoirs of Great Britain from* 1727 *to* 1783. London: Longman, Hurst, Rees, and Orme, 1804. 6 vols.

Brewster, Charles W. *Rambles About Portsmouth.* 2nd ser. Portsmouth, N.H.: Lewis W. Brewster, 1869. 375 pp.

C[alef], J[ohn]. *The Siege of Penobscot by the Rebels.* London: G. Kearsley, 1781. 44 pp.

Caulkins, Frances M. *History of New London, Connecticut from the First Survey of the Coast in* 1612 *to* 1860. New London: H. D. Utley, 1895. 696 pp.

Chapelle, Howard I. *The History of the American Sailing Navy, the Ships and their Development.* New York: Norton, 1949. Half tones, plans, and illustrations. 558 pp.

Clark, Thomas. *Naval History of the United States from the Commencement of the Revolutionary War to the Present Time.* Philadelphia: M. Carey, 1814. 2 vols.

Clark, William B. *Captain Dauntless, the Story of Nicholas Biddle of the Continental Navy.* Baton Rouge: Louisiana State University Press, 1949. 303 pp.
    The First Saratoga Being the Saga of John Young and His Sloop of War. Baton Rouge: Louisiana State University Press 1953. 199 pp.
    Gallant John Barry 1745-1803. New York: Macmillan, 1938. 530 pp.
    Lambert Wickes Sea Raider and Diplomat. New Haven: Yale University Press, 1932. 466 pp.

Ben Franklin's Privateers. Baton Rogue. Louisiana State University Press, 1956. 198 pp.

Clowes, William L. *The Royal Navy; a History from the Earliest Times to the Present.* London: Sampson Low, Marston and Co., 1899. vols. III and IV.

Cooper, J. Fenimore. *The History of the Navy of the United States of America.* Philadelphia: Thomas Cowperthwait and Co., 1841. 447 pp.

Dictionary of American Biography. Allen Johnson, ed. New York: Scribners, 1943-1944. 21 vols.

Emmons, George F. *The Navy of the United States, from the Commencement 1775 to 1853; with a Brief History of Each Vessels Service and Fate as Appears upon Record.* Washington: Gideon and Co., 1853. 209 pp.

Field, Edward. *Esek Hopkins Commander in Chief of the Continental Navy During the American Revolution 1775 to 1778.* Providence: Preston and Rounds Co., 1898. 280 pp.

Foster, Joseph. *The Soldier's Memorial.* Portsmouth, N.H.: n. pub., 1923. 351 pp.

French, Allen. *The First Year of the American Revolution.* Boston: Houghton Mifflin, 1934. 795 pp.

Frothingham, Richard, Jr. *History of the Siege of Boston and of the Battles of Lexington, Concord, and Bunker Hill.* Boston: Charles C. Little and James Brown, 1849. 420 pp.

Gammell, William. "Life of Samuel Ward," in Jared Sparks, ed. *The Library of American Biography.* Boston: C. C. Little and J. Brown Co., 1846. Vol. IX. pp. 231-358.

Goldsborough, Charles W. *The United States Naval Chronicle.* Washington City: James Wilson, 1824. 395 pp.

Greenwood, Isaac J. *Captain John Manley Second in Rank in the United States Navy 1776-1783.* Boston: C. E. Goodspeed and Co., 1915. 174 pp.

Hale, Edward E. "The Naval History of the American Revolution," in Justin Winsor, ed. *Narrative and Critical History of America.* Boston: Houghton Mifflin, 1888. vol. VI. pp. 563-604.

Hale, Edward E. and Edward E. Hale, Jr. *Franklin in France.* Boston: Roberts Brothers, 1887. 478 pp.

Harbeck, Charles T. *A Contribution to the Bibliography of the History of the United States Navy.* Cambridge: Riverside Press, 1906. 247 pp.

Herbert, Charles. *A Relic of the Revolution Containing a Full and Particular Account of the Sufferings and Privations of all of the American Prisoners Captured on the High Seas, and Carried into Plymouth, Eng-*

land, During the Revolution of 1776. Boston: Charles H. Peirce, 1847. 258 pp.

Hinman, R. R. *A Family Record of the Descendants of Serg't Edward Hinman, Who First Appeared at Stratford in Connecticut, About* 1650. New York: Case, Tiffany and Co., 1856. 81 pp.

Howard, James L. *Seth Harding Mariner.* New Haven: Yale University Press, 1930. 301 pp.

James, W. M. *The British Navy in Adversity; a Study of the War of American Independence.* London: Longmans, Green, 1926. 459 pp.

Knox, Dudley W. *A History of the United States Navy.* New York: Putnam's, 1948. 704 pp.

The Naval Genius of George Washington. Boston: Houghton Mifflin, 1932. 138 pp.

The Life and Surprising Adventures of Captain Talbot. London: Barnard and Sultzer, [1803]. 147 pp.

Lorenz, Lincoln. *John Paul Jones Fighter for Freedom and Glory.* Annapolis: United States Naval Institute, 1943. 846 pp.

Lossing, Benson J. *The Pictorial Field-Book of the Revolution.* New York: Harper, 1860. vol. II.

Maclay, Edgar Stanton. *A History of the United States Navy from* 1775 *to* 1901. New York: Appleton, 1901. vol. I.

A History of American Privateers. New York: Appleton, 1899. 519 pp.

Mahan, Alfred T. *The Influence of Sea Power upon History* 1660-1783. Boston; Little, Brown, 1890. 557 pp.

The Major Operations of the Navies in the War of American Independence. Boston: Little, Brown, 1913. 280 pp.

Mayo, Lawrence S. *John Langdon of New Hampshire.* Concord: Rumford Press, 1937. 303 pp.

Metcalf, Bryce. *Original Members and Other Officers Eligible to the Society of the Cincinnati* 1783-1938. Strasburg, Va.: Shenandoah Publishing House, 1938. 390 pp.

Neeser, Robert W. *Statistical and Chronological History of the United States Navy,* 1775-1907. New York: Macmillan, 1909. 2 vols.

Paullin, Charles O. *Diplomatic Negotiations of American Naval Officers,* 1778-1883. Baltimore: Johns Hopkins Press, 1912. 380 pp.

The Navy of the American Revolution. Cleveland: Burrows Brothers, 1906. 549 pp.

Ramsay, David. *The History of the Revolution in South Carolina.* Trenton: Isaac Collins, 1785. 2 vols.

Remick, Oliver P. *A Record of the Services of the Commissioned Officers and Enlisted Men of Kittery and Eliot, Maine, Who Served Their Country on Land and Sea in the American Revolution, from 1775 to 1783.* Boston: Alfred Mudge and Son, [1901]. 223 pp.

Saltonstall, Leverett. *Ancestry and Descendants of Sir Richard Saltonstall, First Associate of the Massachusetts Bay Colony and Patentee of Connecticut.* [Cambridge, Mass.]: Riverside Press, 1897. 265 pp.

[Sands, Robert C.]*Life and Correspondence of John Paul Jones.* New York: A. Chandler, 1830. 555 pp.

Schomberg, Isaac. *Naval Chronology.* London: T. Egerton, 1802. 5 vols.

Sheppard, John H. *The Life of Samuel Tucker.* Boston: Alfred Mudge and Son, 1868. 384 pp.

Sherburne, John H. *The Life and Character of John Paul Jones a Captain in the United States Navy.* New York: Adriance, Sherman and Co., 1851. 408 pp.

Sprout, Harold and Margaret. *The Rise of American Naval Power, 1776-1918.* Princeton: Princeton University Press, 1939. 398 pp.

Taylor, George. *Martyrs to the Revolution in the British Prison Ships in the Wallabout Bay.* New York: W. H. Arthur and Co., 1855. 44 pp.

Tuckerman, Henry T. *The Life of Silas Talbot a Commodore in the Navy of the United States.* New York: J. C. Riker, 1850. 137 pp.

Wilson, Thomas. *The Biography of the Principal American Military and Naval Heroes.* New York: John Low, 1819. 2 vols.

NOTES

CHAPTER I

[1]Robert Beatson, *Naval and Military Memoirs of Great Britain* (London: Longman, Hurst, Rees and Orme, 1804), IV, 85. A further description of action around the Boston harbor islands is found in Thomas Clark, *Naval History of the United States* (Philadelphia: M. Carey, 1814), I, 14-16.

[2]Peter Force, ed., *American Archives* (Washington: M. St. Clair Clarke and Peter Force, 1839), 4th ser., II, 608. Hereafter referenced as *Amer. Archives.*

[3]*Amer. Archives,* 4th ser., II, 988-990. For additional coverage of the Machias incident see Clark, *op. cit.,* 17-18; Allen French, *The First Year of the Revolution* (Boston: Houghton Mifflin, 1934), 360-361.

[4]John C. Fitzpatrick, ed., *The Writings of George Washington from the Original Manuscript Sources* 1745-1799 (Washington: Government Printing Office, 1931), III, 385-386 and 475-476.

[5]*Ibid.,* III, 415-416.

[6]*Amer. Archives,* 4th ser., III, 633-634.

[7]*Ibid.,* 4th ser., III, 688 and 683-684.

[8]Charles O. Paullin, *The Navy of the American Revolution* (Cleveland: Burrows Brothers, 1906), 518.

[9]Thirty-one British vessels totaling 3,645 tons were captured entering Boston harbor between 15 November 1775 and the evacuation of the town on 17 March 1776. Clark, *Naval History,* 21.

[10]*Amer. Archives,* 4th ser., IV, 256-257.

[11]Gardner W. Allen, *A Naval History of the American Revolution* (Boston: Houghton Mifflin, 1913) I, 68.

[12]Dudley W. Knox, *A History of the United States Navy* (New York: Putnam's, 1948), 10.

[13]George Cockings, "The American War" (London: 1781), as quoted by Isaac J. Greenwood, in *Captain John Manley Second in Rank in the United States Navy* 1776-1783 (Boston: C. E. Goodspeed, 1915), 25.

[14]Richard Frothingham, Jr., *History of the Siege of Boston and of the Battles of Lexington, Concord, and Bunker Hill* (Boston: Charles C. Little and James Brown, 1849), 270.

[15]Fitzpatrick, ed., *op. cit.,* IV, 284-285.

[16]Allen, *op. cit.,* I, 67-68; Greenwood, *op. cit.,* 17; Thomas Wilson, *The Biography of the Principal American Military and Naval Heroes* (New York: John Low, 1819), I, 104.

[17]Greenwood, *op. cit.,* 150.

[18]*Amer. Archives,* 4th ser., II, 1764.

[19]*Ibid.,* 4th ser., III, 231.

[20]Worthington C. Ford, ed., *Journals of the Continental Congress* (Washington: Government Printing Office, 1905), II, 240. Hereafter reference as *Journals of Cont. Cong.*

[21]Paullin, *op. cit.,* 81.

[22]*Journals of Cont. Cong.,* III, 485-486.

[23]William Gammell, "Life of Samuel Ward" in Jared Sparks, ed., *Library of American Biography* (Boston: C. C. Little and J. Brown, 1846), 2nd ser., IX, 316.

[24]John Adams, *The Works of John Adams,* notes by Charles Francis Adams (Boston: Little, Brown, 1865), III, 7-8.

[25]*Journals of Cont. Cong.,* III, 277 n.

[26]*Ibid.,* III, 278-279.

[27]Complying with the orders of Congress, Washington sent two of his own schooners, the *Lynch,* Captain Broughton, and the *Franklin,* Captain Selman, northward to the Gulf of St. Lawrence in search of the munitions ships. The English vessels were not captured.

[28]*Journals of Cont. Cong.,* III, 293-294.

[29]*Ibid.,* III, 311-312.

[30]*Ibid.,* III, 425-426.

CHAPTER II

[1]Adams, *Works,* III, 11.

[2]*Ibid.,* III, 12.

[3]*Ibid.,* III, 12.

[4]William B. Clark, *Gallant John Barry* 1745-1803 (New York: Macmillan, 1938), 67; Force, *Amer. Archives,* 4th ser., III, 1354.

[5]Adams, *op. cit.,* III, 12.

[6]Howard I. Chapelle, *The History of the American Sailing Navy, the Ships and their Development* (New York: Norton, 1949), 53 and 534.

[7]Captain John Barry, a resident of Philadelphia, had a brilliant career in both the Continental Navy and the U. S. Navy formed under the Constitution. Joshua Humphreys was the master designer of the first ships of the U. S. Navy including the historic frigates *Constitution, Constellation* and *United States.*

[8]*Journals of Cont. Cong.,* III, 1775.

[9]Fitzpatrick, ed., *Writings of Washington,* IV, 73.

[10]*Journals of Cont. Cong.,* III, 371-375.

[11]*United States Navy Regulations,* 1948 are over 300 printed pages as compared to the 1775 regulations which can be printed on eight or nine pages. See Allen, *Naval History,* II, 686-695.

[12]Alverda S. Beck, ed., *The Correspondence of Esek Hopkins Commander in Chief of the United States Navy* (Providence: Rhode Island Historical Society, 1933), 22.

[13]*Journals of Cont. Cong.,* III, 316.

[14]*Ibid.,* III, 443. The Commander in Chief, although sometimes addressed as "Admiral," was most commonly referred to as the "Commodore"; we will adhere to the latter.

[15]Henry Knox to his wife as quoted by Edward Field, *Esek Hopkins Commander in Chief of the Continental Navy During the American Revolution 1775 to 1778* (Providence: Preston and Rounds, 1898), 134.

[16]Field, *op. cit.,* 7.

[17]For 20 years Esek Hopkins was a trustee of Rhode Island College, now Brown University.

[18]Field, *op. cit.,* 34.

[19]Charles O. Paullin, "Abraham Whipple," *Dictionary of American Biography,* XX (1943), 66.

[20]It is conceivable that the suggestion of a smile on Whipple's face may have been caused as he reflected on his unnatural appearance in the very formal uniform, complete with long glass, in which the artist, Edward Savage, posed his subject.

[21]Hopkins to Whipple, Jan. 5, 1773, MS, *Abraham Whipple Papers,* Rhode Island Historical Society, Providence, Rhode Island.

[22]Field, *op. cit.,* 68.

[23]Leonard W. Labaree, "Gurdon Saltonstall," *Dictionary of American Biography,* XVI (1943), 317.

[24]Field, *op. cit.,* 82n.-83n.

[25]William B. Clark, *Captain Dauntless, the Story of Nicholas Biddle of the Continental Navy* ([Baton Rouge]: Louisiana State University Press, 1949), 100.

[26]Lincoln Lorenz, *John Paul Jones Fighter for Freedom and Glory* (Annapolis: United States Naval Institute, 1943), 73.

[27]Adams, *Works,* III, 12.

[28]Clark, *Gallant John Barry,* 68.

[29]*Journals of Cont. Cong.,* III, 426.

[30]*Ibid.,* VI, 929.

[31]*Ibid.,* VII, 281.

[32]Membership of the Navy Board of the Eastern Department remained unchanged until Deshon resigned without replacement in May 1781. See Paullin, *Navy of the American Revolution,* 101.

[33]The Navy Boards' relation to the Marine Committee was analogous to that of the present Naval Districts to the Navy Department at Washington, D.C.

[34]Paullin, *Navy of the American Revolution,* 253. Paullin is the only historian to treat primarily of the administrative rather than the operational history of the Continental Navy. It is indeed fortunate that Paullin's work is authentic, fully documented, and completely reliable. I have drawn freely on Paullin for the administrative structure of the Navy. See also Clark, *Ben Franklin's Privateers.* (Baton Rouge: Louisiana University Press, 1956).

CHAPTER THREE

[1]Robert W. Neeser, ed., *The Despatches of Molyneux Shuldham Vice-Admiral of the Blue and Commander in Chief of His Britannic Majesty's Ships in North America January-July,* 1776 (New York: Naval History Society, 1913), 275. Lieutenant Josiah together with the *Andrew Doria* journal fell into British hands when a captured transport in which Josiah was prize master was retaken.

[2]*Ibid.,* 120.

[3]See page 6.

[4]*Journals of Cont. Cong.,* III, 396.

[5]Adams, *Works,* III, 12.

[6]Clark, *Captain Dauntless,* 100.

[7]Clark, *Gallant John Barry,* 68; Beck, ed., *Hopkins Correspondence,* 47.

[8]Information obtained in correspondence with Mr. Clarkson A. Collins, III, Librarian of the Rhode Island Historical Society, Providence, Rhode Island.

[9]Neeser, ed. *op. cit.,* 124.

[10]Beck, ed., *Hopkins Correspondence,* 23-25.

[11]Field, *Esek Hopkins,* 95-97.

[12]Beck, ed., *op. cit.,* 27 and 30.

[13]*Ibid.,* 12.

[14]*Ibid.,* 32.

[15]*Journals of Cont. Cong.,* IV, 60.

[16]Hacker was promoted to captain on October 10, 1776, upon the recommendation of Commodore Hopkins. Hacker's first name invoked a multitude of spellings. On the first officer appointments he was called Hersted, but Hoysted seems to be correct.

[17]It is said that the three "insect" ships, *Hornet, Wasp* and *Fly* were named in the hope that they would carry a sting to the British.

[18]Hopkins to Captains, Feb. 14, 1776, MS, *Charles T. Harbeck Collection,* HR 183, Huntington Library, San Marino, California.

[19]See page 36.

[20]*The Letter Book of Esek Hopkins Commander in Chief of the United States Navy* 1775-1777, introduction and notes by Alverda S. Beck (Providence: Rhode Island Historical Society, 1932), 46-47 and 64-65. Hereafter referenced as *Hopkins Letter Book.*

[21]A number of naval historians set the date of sailing as February 17, presumably based on the date given by Hopkins in correspondence written during the spring and summer of 1776. However, the daily journal kept by Lieutenant Josiah of the *Andrew Doria* logs the sailing date as February 18. I am inclined to accept the contemporary journal against Hopkins' memory. Neeser, ed., *Shuldham Despatches,* 275.

[22]*Ibid.*

[23]For further accounts of the action ashore at New Providence consult Allen, *Naval History,* I, 97-100; Field, *op. cit.,* 113-118.

[24]Beck, ed., *Hopkins Correspondence,* 35.

[25]*Hopkins Letter Book,* 47. Hopkins' inventory lists 24 casks of powder taken by the Americans, the *Andrew Doria* journal records 20 casks, and the

English historian Robert Beatson, *Naval and Military Memoirs of Great Britain,* IV, 134, claims only 15 barrels were found. But regardless of the exact number of casks, the amount was small.

[26]The Commodore appointed Lieutenant Elisha Hinman of the *Cabot* to be master of this sloop. Hinman, a Connecticut man, was commissioned Captain in August 1776. We shall hear more of him.

[27]*Hopkins Letter Book,* 47. The *Hornet,* Captain William Stone, made a South Carolina port, and about April 1, 1776, was able to get back into Delaware Bay.

[28]Neeser, ed., *op. cit.,* 276.

[29]*Hopkins Letter Book,* 64. Hopkins does not disclose the source of his information.

[30]*Ibid.,* 45.

[31]Neeser, ed., *op. cit.,* 287.

[32]*Ibid.*

[33]*Amer. Archives,* 4th ser., V, 1156.

[34]Beatson, *op. cit.,* IV, 135.

[35]*Hopkins Letter Book,* 48.

[36]*Ibid.,* 46-51.

[37] *Amer. Archives,* 4th ser., V, 966.

[38]*Ibid.,* 4th ser., V, 1156.

[39]The British Fleet at Newport finding that rebel shore batteries made the place an uncomfortable anchorage departed for Halifax on April 7, 1776. This gave Hopkins an opportunity to run up to Providence on April 25. A false start was made six days earlier, but Captain Saltonstall ran the *Alfred* aground near Fisher's Island, and had to return to New London.

[40]*Papers of the Continental Congress,* 58, 259, MS, National Archives, Washington, D. C. Hereafter referenced as *Papers of Cont. Cong.*

[41]*Papers of Cont. Cong.,* 58, 263-265, MS.

[42]Beck, ed., *Hopkins Correspondence,* 45-47.

[43]*Journals of Cont. Cong.,* IV, 335-336 and 375.

[44]*Hopkins Letter Book,* 64.

[45]*Amer. Archives,* 4th ser., VI, 511. It was estimated that between four and five thousand seamen were serving in the Army in May 1776.

[46]*Hopkins Letter Book,* 52n. and 53.

[47]*Amer. Archives,* 4th ser., VI, 511. Tillinghast was naval agent at Providence.

[48]Edmund C. Burnett, ed., *Letters of Members of the Continental Congress* (Washington: Carnegie Institution of Washington, 1921), I, 489.

[49]*Amer. Archives,* 4th ser., VI, 886. This is the letter sent to Captain Saltonstall. Whipple's was the same and Hopkins' very similar.

[50]*Journals of Cont. Cong.,* V, 542-543.

[51]Adams, *Works,* III, 65.

[52]*Journals of Cont. Cong.,* V, 662.

[53]Field, *Esek Hopkins,* 235.

[54]*Journals of Cont. Cong.,* X, 13.

[55]Adams, *op. cit.,* III, 65.

[56]*Journals of Cont. Cong.,* V, 659.

[57]*Hopkins Letter Book,* 72.

[58]*Amer. Archives,* 4th ser., VI, 654-655.

[59]*Ibid.,* 4th ser., VI, 670.

[60]*Hopkins Letter Book,* 68.

[61]Clark, *Captain Dauntless,* 138; *Amer. Archives,* 5th ser., I, 1287.

[62]*Hopkins Letter Book,* 75.

[63]Charles O. Paullin, *Out-Letters of the Continental Marine Committee and Board of Admiralty August* 1776 — *September* 1780 (New York: De Vinne Press, 1914), I, 49. Hereafter referenced as *Marine Committee Out-Letters.*

[64]This was the Rhode Island attack and occupation force.

[65]*Marine Committee Out-Letters,* I, 50-51.

[66]*Ibid.,* I, 56-57.

[67]J. Fenimore Cooper, *The History of the Navy of the United States of America* (Philadelphia: Thomas Cowperthwait, 1841), 49.

[68]*Hopkins Letter Book,* 75 and 79-80.

[69]*Ibid.,* 87.

[70]John H. Sherburne, *The Life and Character of John Paul Jones a Captain in the United States Navy During the Revolutionary War* (New York: Adriance, Sherman, 1851), 26.

[71]*Amer. Archives,* 5th ser., II, 1277; *Hopkins Letter Book,* 91. The stranded *Hampden* was left in charge of Captain Joseph Olney whose naval service we shall follow in subsequent chapters.

[72]Lorenz, *John Paul Jones,* 90.

[73]Thomas Clark, *Naval History,* I, 42.

[74]"Subscribers" to Hacker, Nov. 14, 1776, as quoted by Lorenz, *op. cit.,* 91.

[75]Thomas Clark, *op. cit.,* I, 42.

[76]Jones to Hewes, Jan. 12, 1777, as quoted by Lorenz, *op. cit.,* 97.

[77]*Hopkins Letter Book,* 102.

[78]*Ibid.,* 52.

[79]*Ibid.,* 72.

[80]*Journals of Cont. Cong.,* V, 649.

[81]R. R. Hinman, *A Family Record of the Descendents of Serg't Edward Hinman, Who First Appeared at Stratford in Connecticut, about* 1650 (New York: Case, Tiffany, 1856), 816-821.

[82]*Hopkins Letter Book,* 57-58.

[83]Neeser, ed., *Shuldham Despatches,* 299.

[84]*Newport Mercury,* June 24, 1776; *Pennsylvania Packet* (Philadelphia), June 24, 1776.

[85]*Hopkins Letter Book,* 75.

[86]Frances M. Caulkins, *History of New London, Connecticut from the First Survey of the Coast in* 1612 *to* 1860 (New London: H. D. Utley, 1895), 511.

[87]Shaw to Hancock, July 31, 1776, MS *Nathaniel Shaw Papers;* Letter Book No. 5, Yale University Library, New Haven, Connecticut.

[88]*Hopkins Letter Book,* 76.

[89]*Amer. Archives,* 5th ser., I, 1004.

[90]*Marine Committee Out-Letters,* I, 27.

[91]*Westmoreland, Lowther, Esther, Watson* (Sept. 27, 1776), *Clarendon* (Oct. 2, 1776), *Georgiana* (Oct. 5, 1776). George F. Emmons, *The Navy of the United States from the Commencement 1775 to 1853* (Washington: Gideon, 1853), 40-41.

[92]*Amer. Archives,* 5th ser., III, 637.

[93]*Ibid.,* 5th ser., III, 422.

[94]*Ibid.,* 5th ser., III, 422-423.

[95]Louis F. Middlebrook, *History of Maritime Connecticut 1775-1783* (Salem: Essex Institute, 1925), II, 152. One prize, the *Clarendon,* with her cargo was valued at £10,731-14-14½.

[96]*Hopkins Letter Book,* 94.

[97]*Marine Committee Out-Letters,* I, 41.

[98]*Hopkins Letter Book,* 94.

[99]*Ibid.,* 76. Whipple had attempted to cruise in June but a brush with HBM *Cerberus* near Block Island cost him one man killed, and the *Columbus* was chased back into port.

[100]Whipple to Congress, June 10, 1786, MS, *Abraham Whipple Papers,* Rhode Island Historical Society, Providence, Rhode Island.

[101]*Amer. Archives,* 5th ser., II, 863.

[102]*Ibid.,* 5th ser., II, 595.

[103]*Hopkins Letter Book,* 89 and 96.

[104]*Ibid.,* 81-82.

[105]Two eminent naval historians, M. V. Brewington, "The Designs of Our First Frigates," *The American Neptune,* VIII (Jan. 1948), 11-25, and Howard I. Chapelle, *American Sailing Navy,* 52-114, present plausible but diametrically opposite points of view on the designer of these plans. Brewington holds them to be the work of Joshua Humphreys, and Chapelle states that they cannot be. A solution, if such be possible, is not germane to this work.

[106]Brewington, *op. cit.,* 14.

[107]Middlebrook *op. cit.,* II, 265; *Amer. Archives,* 5th ser., I, 1617.

[108]A confusing situation is presented by having two vessels named *Providence* in the Continental Navy at one time; the original 12 gun sloop and the new frigate.

[109]*Journal of the Committee who built the ships Providence and Warren for the U. S. AD 1776,* Rhode Island Historical Society. This most valuable manuscript preserves a day to day account of the building of the frigates and casts much light on the multitudinous problems involved. One interesting aspect is the appointment of inferior officers to the ships based on the number of seamen an officer candidate could recruit. Hereafter referenced as "Journal of Rhode Island Building Committee."

[110]*Ibid.,* May 27, 1776.

[111]*Journals of Cont. Cong.,* V, 422.

[112]"Journal of Rhode Island Building Committee," MS, Sept. 2, 1776.

[113]One Samuel Tomkins was originally appointed but did not serve. *Journals of Cont. Cong.,* V, 422.

[114]Brewington, *op. cit.,* 13.

[115]*Pennsylvania Gazette* (Philadelphia), June 19, 1776.

[116]Fitzpatrick, ed., *Writings of Washington,* IV, 284.

[117]*Journals of Cont. Cong.*, IV, 290.

[118]*Ibid.*, V, 444.

[119]Gardner W. Allen, (ed.), *Captain Hector McNeill of the Continental Navy* (Boston: Massachusetts Historical Society, 1922), 6. Contains McNeill letter book and papers.

[120]Burnett, ed., *Letters of Members*, I, 282.

[121]*Freeman's Journal, or New Hampshire Gazette* (Portsmouth), May 25, 1776.

[122]Oliver P. Remick, *A Record of the Services of the Commissioned Officers and Enlisted Men of Kittery and Eliot, Maine, Who Served Their Country on Land and Sea in the American Revolution, from 1775 to 1783* (Boston: Alfred Mudge, [1901]), 222.

[123]Marquis de Castelleaux as quoted by Joseph Foster, *The Soldiers Memorials* (Portsmouth: n. pub., 1923), 63.

[124]*Journals of Cont. Cong.*, V, 422. The *Langdon, Peabody, and Kittery Papers* in the manuscript collection of the New Hampshire Historical Society, Concord, New Hampshire, contain numerous references to Thompson's association with John Langdon.

[125]*Amer. Archives*, 5th ser., II, 181.

[126]*Journals of Cont. Cong.*, VI, 861. Names are spelt as they appeared on the list. For captains after this order was established, the date of commission determined rank standing.

[127]Hewes to Samuel Purviance, Jr., June 25, 1776, MS, *Purviance Papers*, Maryland Historical Society, Baltimore, Maryland.

[128]Lee to Purviance, Sept. 16, 1776 and Oct. 11, 1776, MSS, *Purviance Papers*, Maryland Historical Society.

[129]W. Bird Terwilliger, "William Goddard's Victory for the Freedom of the Press," *Maryland Historical Magazine* XXXVI (1941), 144.

[130]*Hopkins Letter Book*, 79.

[131]*Ibid.*, 91.

[132]*Ibid.*, 82.

[133]*Journals of Cont. Cong.*, VI, 913.

[134]Allen, *Naval History*, I, 180.

[135]*Boston Gazette*, Feb. 24, 1776, as quoted by Allen, *Naval History*, I, 180.

CHAPTER FOUR

[1]Cooper to Gerry, March 24, 1777, MS, *John S. Barnes Collection*, portfolio 316, New-York Historical Society, New York, New York.

[2]Allen, *Naval History*, I, 200.

[3]*Marine Committee Out-Letters*, I, 91.

[4]J. Almon, *The Remembrancer; or Impartial Repository of Public Events* (London: Opposite Burlington House, 1778), V, 135.

[5]Cooper, *History of the Navy*, 67.

[6]Allen, *Naval History*, I, 201.

[7]The *Hampden*, after a series of misfortunes, grounded and was lost in November 1777 while commanded by Lieutenant Ezekiel Burroughs.

[8]*Hopkins Letter Book*, 122.

9*Marine Committee Out-Letters,* I, 60 and 71.

10*Hopkins Letter Book,* 134-135.

11Beatson, *Naval and Military Memoirs of Great Britain,* IV, 188.

12*Hopkins Letter Book,* 122-123.

13Navy Board to Whipple, Oct. n. d., 1777 and John Deshon to Whipple, Oct. 28, 1777, MSS, *Abraham Whipple Papers,* Rhode Island Historical Society, Providence, Rhode Island.

14William L. Clowes, *The Royal Navy; A History from the Earliest Times to the Present* (London: Sampson, Low, Marston, 1899), IV, 109.

15Walter Lowrie and Walter S. Franklin, eds., *American State Papers* (Washington: Gales and Seaton, 1834), Class IX (Claims), 381-382.

16*Hopkins Letter Book,* 109.

17*Journals of Cont. Cong.,* VII, 284. Rathbun's name was subject to numerous spellings. Correspondence with his descendant, Mr. Russell Leigh Jackson, former director of the Essex Institute, Salem, Massachusetts and a muster role of the sloop *Providence* in the Rhode Island Historical Society decided the matter for me.

18*Hopkins Letter Book,* 136.

19"Journal of Lieutenant John Trevett, USN," *Rhode Island Historical Magazine, VI* (1885-86), 271-272. Hereafter referenced "Trevett's Journal."

20"Trevett's Journal," 274.

21*Ibid.,* 274-275.

22*Ibid.,* 276-277.

23See footnote No. 71, Chapter Three.

24Beck, ed., *Hopkins Correspondence,* 86.

25*Hopkins Letter Book,* 111.

26*Ibid.,* 125.

27Clowes, *op. cit.,* IV, 113; Greenwood, *Manley,* 64.

28*Independent Chronicle* (Boston), June 19, 1777.

29Greenwood, *op. cit.,* 64.

30*Boston Gazette,* June 16, 1777.

31Clowes, *op. cit.,* IV, 113.

32*Amer. Archives,* 5th ser., II, 427-429; *Marine Committee Out-Letters,* I, 12-15.

33*Amer. Archives,* 5th ser., III, 1335.

34Allen, [ed.], *Captain McNeill,* 32-34.

35Manley to Heath, March 24, 1777, MS, Massachusetts Historical Society, Boston, Massachusetts.

36Allen, [ed.]*Captain McNeill,* 39.

37*Ibid.,* 35.

38*Ibid.,* 36.

39Greenwood, *op. cit.,* 50-51.

40*Journals of Cont. Cong.,* VII, 183.

41Greenwood, *op cit.,* 68.

42William J. Morgan, "The Stormy Career of Captain McNeill, Continental Navy," *Military Affairs,* XVI (Fall, 1952), 119.

43*Ibid.,* 120.

44*Boston Gazette,* June 16, 1777.

45Morgan. *op. cit.,* 120.

[46]*Ibid.*

[47]Clowes, *Royal Navy*, IV, 5.

[48]Beatson, *Naval and Military Memoirs of Great Britain*, IV, 279.

[49]Allen, [ed.], *Captain McNeill*, 57.

[50]*Ibid.*, 60-62.

[51]Log of the *Boston*, Friday, June 27, 1777, MS, Mariners Museum, Newport News, Virginia.

[52]Manley to McNeill, June 27, 1777, MS, *Simon Gratz Collection*, Historical Society of Pennsylvania, Philadelphia, Pennsylvania.

[53]Morgan, *op. cit.*, 120.

[54]Allen, *Naval History*, I, 214. The British had recently made a prisoner of General Charles Lee.

[55]Greenwood, *Manley*, 73.

[56]Morgan, *op. cit.*, 120.

[57]Allen, [ed.], *Captain McNeill*, 65.

[58]Greenwood, *op. cit.*, 99.

[59]Allen, [ed.], *Captain McNeill*, 63.

[60]*Ibid.*, 67.

[61]*Ibid.*, 69.

[62]*Ibid.*, 72.

[63]*Ibid.*, 7-8.

[64]*Ibid.*, 75.

[65]Eastern Navy Board Resolution, October 3, 1777, MS, *Votes and Resolutions, September* 12, 1777 *to January* 3, 1778 *and Letter Book, November* 3, 1779 *to February* 6, 1782 *Navy Board of Eastern Department*, Library of Congress, Washington, D. C. Hereafter referenced as *Votes and Letter Book, Eastern Navy Board.*

[66]Allen, [ed], *Captain McNeill*, 83.

[67]*Marine Committee Out-Letters*, I, 171. Palmes apparently was a bad actor. Two years later he was again in trouble and the Eastern Navy Board was authorized to hold a court martial. Nevertheless, on the list of commissioned officers sent to President Washington in 1794 is the name of Marine Captain Richard Palmes with no indication that he had suffered disciplinary action.

[68]Allen, [ed], *Captain McNeill*, 84.

[69]*Marine Committee* Out-Letters, I, 170.

[70]*Votes and Letter Book, Eastern Navy Board*, MS, Dec. 27, 1777.

[71]*Marine Committee Out-Letters* I, 129.

[72]*Ibid.*, I, 126.

[73]Allen, *Naval History*, I, 222-223.

[74]Although it has been stated in some accounts, that the *Alfred* joined the *Raleigh* at sea, actually Hinman came into Portsmouth, N.H. He was there with the *Alfred* on Aug. 12, 1777, when he signed a receipt for ship supplies received of John Langdon. *John and Woodbury Langdon Papers*, MS, New Hampshire Historical Society, Concord, New Hampshire.

[75]*Marine Committee Out-Letters*, I, 125-129.

[76]*Raleigh* completed her gun needs in France. A ship's articles inventory made "at her arming in France, January 1778" shows her to have 32 cannon — twenty-six 12 pounders, six 6 pounders. "Inventory of the Con-

tinental Frigate Raleigh, Captain Thomas Thompson," MS, *Josiah Fox Papers,* Peabody Museum, Salem, Massachusetts.

[77]*Marine Committee Out-Letters,* I, 155.

[78]British accounts do not mention the *Grasshopper* as being present.

[79]Almon, *Remembrancer,* V, 403-405.

[80]*Ibid.,* V, 401.

[81]*Ibid.,* V, 405.

[82]*Marine Committee Out-Letters,* I, 127.

[83]B. F. Stevens, comp., *Facsimiles of Manuscripts in European Archives Relating to America* 1773-1783 (London: Chiswick Press, 1898), no. 274. Hereafter referenced as *Stevens Facsimiles.*

[84]Francis Wharton, ed., *The Revolutionary Diplomatic Correspondence of the United States* (Washington: Government Printing Office, 1889), II, 436.

[85]Hinman, *Descendants of Edward Hinman,* 819.

[86]John Bigelow, ed., *The Complete Works of Benjamin Franklin* (New York: Putnam's, 1888), VI, 112-113.

[87]Allen, *Naval History,* I, 159.

[88]*Journals of Cont. Cong.,* VII 90.

[89]*Amer. Archives,* 5th ser., I, 755. A letter written in London Aug. 10, 1776, about Johnson mentions his house in Portsmouth, New Hampshire, being destroyed the year before when the British burned Portsmouth. Since it was Falmouth and not Portsmouth which was put to the torch in 1775, I assume that the writer confused the two localities, and that Johnson resided in Falmouth, Maine.

[90]Edgar S. Maclay, *A History of American Privateers* (New York: Appleton, 1899), 70.

[91]*Amer. Archives,* 5th ser., I, 754-755.

[92]*Ibid.,* 5th ser., I, 755.

[93]*Ibid.,* 5th ser., I, 684.

[94]*Ibid.,* 5th ser., III, 1088.

[95]Benjamin Harrison and Richard Henry Lee to Johnson, Feb. 24, 1777, *Stevens Facsimiles,* no. 1437.

[96]Lupton to Eden, April 8 and 10, 1777, *Stevens Facsimiles,* no. 681.

[97]*Ibid.,* June 4, 1777, no. 168.

[98]Wickes to Johnson, May 23, 1777, *Stevens Facsimilies,* no. 1539.

[99]William B. Clark, *Lambert Wickes, Sea Raider and Diplomat* (New Haven: Yale University Press, 1932), 220-239.

[100]*Ibid.,* 239.

[101]Commissioners to Johnson, July 25, 1777, *Stevens Facsimilies,* no. 1586.

[102]Johnson to Amer. Commissioners, Sept. 16 or 17, 1777, *Stevens Facsimiles,* no. 1686.

[103]The *Reprisal* foundered off the Newfoundland Banks. Lambert Wickes, one of the best captains in the Continental Navy, perished.

[104]Bazely to Philip Stephens, Secretary of the Admiralty, Sept. 24, 1777, *Stevens Facsimiles,* no. 1695.

[105]Allen, *Naval History,* I, 276.

[106]Beaumarchais to Vergennes, Oct. 1, 1777, *Stevens Facsimiles,* no. 1708.

[107]*Marine Committee Out-Letters,* I, 274.

[108]See page 56.

[109]*Marine Committee Out-Letters,* I, 97.

[110]Files of the Early Records Section, Naval History Division, National Archives, Washington, D.C.

[111]*Papers of Cont. Cong.,* MS 78, XXIII, 443, National Archives, Washington, D.C.

[112]*Journals of Cont. Cong.,* X, 193n.

[113]I have been able to find no record that Elisha Warner engaged in privateering.

[114]*Marine Committee Out-Letters,* I, 140.

[115]Caulkins, *History of New London,* 540n. Joseph Chew, brother of Captain Samuel, was said to be a Tory; not an uncommon situation within families.

[116]Beck, ed., *Hopkins Correspondence,* 59; *Marine Committee Out-Letters,* I, 1.

[117]*Marine Committee Out-Letters,* I, 138.

[118]*Ibid.,* I, 142.

[119]Shaw to Daniel Tillinghast and John Bradford, July 6, 1777, MSS, Letter Book No. 9, *Nathaniel Shaw Papers,* Yale University Library, New Haven, Connecticut.

[120]Middlebrook, *Maritime Connecticut,* II, 267; "Papers of William Vernon and the Navy Board 1776-1794," *"Publications of the Rhode Island Historical Society,* VIII (1901), 231. Hereafter referenced as *Vernon Papers.*

[121]Ernest F. Rogers, *Connecticut's Naval Office at New London During the War of the American Revolution* (New London: New London County Historical Society, 1933), 307-308.

[122]Beatson, *Naval and Military Memoirs of Great Britain,* IV, 291.

[123]Isaac Schomberg, *Naval Chronology* (London: T. Egerton, 1802), IV, 327-328.

CHAPTER FIVE

[1]"Trevett's Journal," 38-40 and 151-155; Thomas Clark, *Naval History,* I, 74-76. This was the *Providence* sloop's third wartime assignment in the British West Indies: in 1775 as the *Katy* under Rhode Island direction, 1776 with Commodore Hopkins, and now under Rathbun in 1778.

[2]*Marine Committee Out-Letters,* I, 212.

[3]*Vernon Papers,* 217-220.

[4]*Ibid.,* 240.

[5]*Ibid.,* 241.

[6]*Papers of Cont. Cong.,* MS, 157, 204, National Archives, Washington, D.C.

[7]Eastern Navy Board to Marine Committee, Dec. 9, 1778, MS, *Letter-Book Navy Board Eastern Department, October 23, 1778 to October 29, 1779,* New York Public Library, New York, New York. Hereafter referenced as *Eastern Navy Board Letter Book.*

8Chew to -----, Jan. 15, 1777 [*sic*], MS, *Simon Gratz Collection, Histor-*ical Society of Pennsylvania, Philadelphia, Pennsylvania. Chew dated this letter "1777" although it had to be written in January 1778. Like most of us, the Captain apparently required a little time to adjust to writing the new year correctly in his correspondence.

9*Records and Papers of the New London County Historical Society* (New London: New London County Historical Society, 1893), I, 9; *Independent Chronicle* (Boston), Apr. 23, 1778.

10*Marine Committee Out-Letters,* I, 241.

11*Ibid.,* I, 251.

12Greenwood, *Manley,* 35-36 and 48.

13*Amer. Archives,* 5th ser., III, 626.

14*Massachusetts Soldiers and Sailors of the Revolutionary War* (Boston: Wright and Potter, 1896), II, 853; *Papers of Cont. Cong.,* MS, 162, I, 41. Burke claimed to have escaped from Halifax and does not mention being in New York. However, the weight of evidence seems to indicate clearly that he was transferred to New York.

15---- to Samuel Adams, July 5, 1778, MS, Massachusetts Historical Society, Boston, Massachusetts; *Journals of Cont. Cong.,* X, 412.

16----- to Samuel Adams, July 5, 1778, MS, Massachusetts Historical Society; *Journals of Cont. Cong.,* XI, 621. Manley and Waters were prisoners in New York the same time as Burke. They could have been the accusers.

17*Amer. Archives,* 5th ser., III, 625.

18*Vernon Papers,* 255.

19Beatson, *Naval and Military Memoirs of Great Britain,* IV, 355-356.

20*Eastern Navy Board Letter Book,* MS, Oct. 28, 1778.

21*Ibid.,* MS, Feb. 22, 1779.

22*Independent Chronicle* (Boston), Apr. 9, 1778.

23*Continental Journal* (Boston), April 30, 1778.

24*Ibid.*

25*Papers of Cont. Cong.,* MS, 78, XI, 355-357.

26*Vernon Papers,* 240.

27*Ibid.,* 237.

28*Continental Journal* (Boston), April 30, 1778.

29*Marine Committee Out-Letters,* I, 238. Command of the *Raleigh* was given to Captain John Barry of Pennsylvania, and the vessel passes from the purview of this study.

30Hinman, *Descendants of Edward Hinman,* 818-819.

31Hinman, *op. cit.,* 819; Benson J. Lossing, *The Pictorial Field-Book of the Revolution* (New York: Harper, 1860), I, 640n.

32*Marine Committee Out-Letters,* I, 209.

33*Vernon Papers,* 214 and 229.

34*Continental Journal* (Boston), Mar. 26, 1778; *Vernon Papers,* 229.

35*Vernon Papers,* 236.

36*Marine Committee Out-Letters,* I, 270; *Vernon Papers,* 254.

37*Vernon Papers,* 230.

38*Ibid.,* 233.

39*Independent Chronicle* (Boston), April 16, 1778.

⁴⁰*Vernon Papers,* 215 and 230. The added advance was 90 dollars to able seamen and 50 dollars to ordinary seamen and landsmen to be deducted out of future prize money.

⁴¹Arthur Lee and John Adams to Vergennes, May 4, 1778, *Stevens Facsimiles,* no. 820.

⁴²Whipple to Congress, June 10, 1786, MS, *Abraham Whipple Papers,* Rhode Island Historical Society, Providence, Rhode Island.

⁴³Jones to Whipple, June 6, 1778, MS, *Abraham Whipple Papers,* Rhode Island Historical Society.

⁴⁴The Marine Committee's first choice was Captain Joseph Olney, but the Eastern Navy Board given authority to appoint a captain for this ship named Tucker on Dec. 27, 1777. *Marine Committee Out-Letters,* I, 170; John H. Sheppard, *The Life of Samuel Tucker* (Boston: Alfred Mudge and Son, [1868]), 71.

⁴⁵Sheppard, *op. cit.,* 31.

⁴⁶*Journals of Cont. Cong.,* VII, 183.

⁴⁷Eastern Navy Board to Tucker, Feb. 10, 1778, as quoted by Sheppard, *op. cit.,* 73.

⁴⁸Adams, *Works,* III, 97-98.

⁴⁹*Ibid.,* III, 200.

⁵⁰Sheppard, *op. cit.,* 81.

⁵¹Adams' account of his passage in the *Boston* is in his *Works,* III, 90-120.

⁵²Log of the *Boston,* April 5, 1778, appended to Sheppard, *op. cit.,* 282.

⁵³Commissioners to Tucker, July 22, 1778, as quoted by Sheppard, *op. cit.,* 96-97.

⁵⁴Commissioners to Whipple, July 13, 1778, MS, *Abraham Whipple Papers,* Rhode Island Historical Society.

⁵⁵Log of the *Boston,* Aug. 8, 1778, in Sheppard, *op. cit.,* 305-306.

⁵⁶Remick, *Commissioned Officers and Enlisted Men of Kittery and Eliot, Maine,* 15; Lawrence S. Mayo, *John Langdon of New Hampshire* (Concord: Rumford Press, 1937), 146.

⁵⁷Allen, *Naval History,* I, 352.

⁵⁸[Robert C. Sands], *Life and Correspondence of John Paul Jones* (New York: A. Chandler, 1830), 103.

⁵⁹*Papers of Cont. Cong.,* MS, 102, IV, 1415.

⁶⁰Wharton, ed., *Revolutionary Diplomatic Correspondence,* II, 604-605.

⁶¹*Ibid.,* II, 616.

⁶²Wharton, ed., *op. cit.,* II, 683-684; Jones to Whipple, Aug. 18, 1778, MS, *Abraham Whipple Papers,* Rhode Island Historical Society.

⁶³Wharton, ed., *op. cit.,* II, 692.

⁶⁴*Ibid.,* II, 689.

⁶⁵As a result of being left in France without a vessel, Jones accepted command on an East Indiaman renamed the *Bon Homme Richard,* in which on Sept. 23, 1779, he defeated the *Serapis* in one of the most celebrated victories in U. S. Naval History.

⁶⁶Log of the *Boston,* Aug. 22, 1778, in Sheppard, *Tucker,* 309; Whipple to Congress, June 10, 1786, MS, *Abraham Whipple Papers,* Rhode Island Historical Society.

[67]Robert W. Neeser, *Statistical and Chronological History of the United States Navy* (New York: Macmillan, 1909), II, 288. Several years after the war Whipple wrote that six prizes were taken but the record indicates that he was mistaken.

[68]Louis H. Bolander, "The Log of the Ranger," *United States Naval Institute Proceedings*, CXII (Feb. 1936), 205-208.

[69]*Papers of Cont. Cong.*, MS, 78, XI, 355-357.

[70]*Ibid.*, MS, 78, XXII, 605.

[71]Anonymous, *The Life and Surprising Adventures of Captain Talbot* (London: Barnard and Sultzer, [1803]), 1-56.

[72]Laurens to Talbot, Nov. 17, 1778, MS, *Silas Talbot Papers*, Rhode Island Historical Society.

[73]Anonymous, *Life of Talbot*, 56.

[74]*Marine Committee Out-Letters*, I, 213.

[75]*Ibid.*, I, 179.

[76]Greenwood, *Manley*, 45 and 51.

[77]*Massachusetts Soldiers and Sailors*, XIV, 275.

[78]*Marine Committee Out-Letters*, I, 283.

[79]*Journals of Cont. Cong.*, XII, 909 and 946.

[80]*Marine Committee Out-Letters*, II, 2.

[81]See page 119 .

[82]*Marine Committee Out-Letters*, I, 262-263.

[83]*Ibid.*, I, 273.

[84]James L. Howard, *Seth Harding Mariner* (New Haven: Yale University Press, 1930), 68.

[85]Trumbull to Marine Committee, April 2, 1778, as quoted by Howard, *op. cit.*, 61-62.

[86]*Marine Committee Out-Letters*, I, 229.

[87]*Papers of Cont. Cong.*, MS, 78, XI, 333-335.

[88]*Journals of Cont. Cong.*, XII, 951.

[89]Howard, *op. cit.*, 68.

[90]*Eastern Navy Board Letter Book*, MS, Dec. 16, 1778.

[91]This year two other ships were added to the Navy but neither was commanded by a New England captain: the *Alliance* built in Massachusetts, Captain Peter Landais, a Frenchman; the *Deane* built in France, Captain Samuel Nicholson of Maryland.

[92]*Vernon Papers*, 214-215.

[93]*Ibid.*, 229-230.

[94]*Marine Committee Out-Letters*, I, 240.

[95]*Ibid.*, II, 28.

[96]*Vernon Papers*, 247.

[97]*Ibid.*

[98]Morgan, "Stormy Career of Captain McNeill," 122.

[99]Clark, *Gallant John Barry*, 185-186.

[100]*Journals of Cont. Cong.*, XI, 749; *Papers of Cont. Cong.*, MS, 78, XI, 355-357.

[101]Joseph Foster, *The Soldiers Memorial* (Portsmouth: n. pub., 1923), 63.

[102]*Vernon Papers*, 237.

[103] Allen, *Naval History*, I, 363-364.
[104] *Eastern Navy Board Letter Book*, MS, Oct. 28, 1778.
[105] *Ibid.*, MS, Dec. 25, 1778.
[106] *Massachusetts Soldiers and Sailors*, I, 381; Greenwood, *op. cit.*, 36.
[107] *Amer. Archives*, 5th ser., III, 1078.

CHAPTER SIX

[1] *Eastern Navy Board Letter Book*, MSS, Dec. 9, 1778 and Jan. 16, 1779.
[2] *Ibid.*, MSS, Dec. 9, 1778 and Dec. 16, 1778.
[3] *Continental Journal* (Boston), Feb. 18, 1779.
[4] *Eastern Navy Board Letter Book*, MSS, Jan. 26, 1779, Feb. 5, 1779, March 12, 1779. Harding was not the only one "encouraging" French seamen. The French vice consul at Boston complained of the same practice by captains in that port.
[5] *Eastern Navy Board Letter Book*, MS, Jan. 13, 1779.
[6] *Ibid.*, MS, Feb. 5, 1779.
[7] *Ibid.*
[8] See page 141-2.
[9] *Eastern Navy Board Letter Book*, MS, Jan. 15, 1779; *Evening Post* (Boston), Jan. 16, 1779; *Independent Chronicle* (Boston), Jan. 21, 1779.
[10] *Vernon Papers*, 257-258.
[11] *Eastern Navy Board Letter Book*, MS, Feb. 22, 1779; *Vernon Papers*, 257.
[12] *Eastern Navy Board Letter Book*, MS, Feb. 22, 1779; *Marine Committee Out-Letters*, II, 54.
[13] See page 122-3.
[14] *Continental Journal* (Boston), Feb. 18, 1779.
[15] *Ibid.*, March 18, 1779.
[16] In 1797 when the first frigates of the new United States Navy were built President John Adams is said to have offered Captain Elisha Hinman command of the USS *Constitution*. Hinman declined because of his advanced age. See Lossing, *Pictorial Field-Book* of the Revolution, II, 640.
[17] *Marine Committee Out-Letters*, II, 48.
[18] *Eastern Navy Board Letter Book*, MS, March 1, 1779.
[19] *Marine Committee Out-Letters*, II, 43.
[20] *Ibid.*, II, 41-43.
[21] Bolander, "Log of the Ranger," 211.
[22] *Eastern Navy Board Letter Book*, MS, Mar. 3, 1779.
[23] *Ibid.*, MS, Mar. 13, 1779.
[24] *Eastern Navy Board Letter Book*, MS, Apr. 17, 1779; *Pennsylvania Gazette* (Philadelphia) Apr. 28, 1779.
[25] *Eastern Navy Board Letter Book*, MS, Apr. 17, 1779.
[26] *Marine Committee Out-Letters*, II, 72.
[27] This is the same Marine officer Captain McNeill had trouble with on board the *Boston* in 1777.
[28] *Eastern Navy Board Letter Book*, MS. Apr. 28, 1779.
[29] *Ibid.*
[30] *Ibid.*, MSS, Apr. 28, 1779 and June 2, 1779.
[31] *Ibid.*, MS, May 3, 1779.

[32]*Ibid.,* MSS, Apr. 23, 1779 and May 18, 1779.

[33]*Marine Committee Out-Letters,* II, 75.

[34]*Eastern Navy Board Letter Book,* MS, May 7, 1779.

[35]*Ibid.,* MSS, June 4, 1779 and June 8, 1779.

[36]*Ibid.,* MSS, Sept. 22, 1779 and Sept, 29, 1779.

[37]Charles H. Lincoln, [ed.], *Naval Records of the American Revolution* 1775-1788 (Washington: Government Printing Office, 1906), 350 and 466.

[38]*Marine Committee Out-Letters,* II, 75.

[39]*Eastern Navy Board Letter Book,* MSS, Mar. 9, 1779 and Apr. 17, 1779.

[40]*Marine Committee Out-Letters,* II, 84.

[41]*Eastern Navy Board Letter Book,* MSS, Apr. 3, 1779 and Apr. 17, 1779.

[42]*Marine Committee Out-Letters,* II ,47.

[43]*Eastern Navy Board Letter Book,* MS, Apr. 6, 1779.

[44]*Ibid.,* MSS, Apr. 22, 1779 and Apr. 28, 1779.

[45]Thomas Clark, *Naval History,* I, 96; Allen, *Naval History,* II, 395.

[46]*Eastern Navy Board Letter Book,* MSS, May 13, 1779 and May 19, 1779.

[47]*Ibid.,* MSS, June 10, 1779 and June 16, 1779.

[48]Deshon to Huntington, Apr. 10, 1779, as quoted by Howard, *Seth Harding,* 82.

[49]*Marine Committee Out-Letters,* II, 67-68.

[50]*Ibid.,* II, 63-64.

[51]*Ibid.,* II, 81-82.

[52]Samuel Tucker *Journal,* MS, *The Adams Papers,* Massachusetts Historical Society, Boston, Massachusetts.

[53]*Marine Committee Out-Letters,* II, 91.

[54]*Ibid.,* II, 89-91.

[55]*Eastern Navy Board Letter Book,* MS, Sept. 8, 1779; *Boston Gazette,* Sept. 13, 1779; Samuel Tucker *Journal,* MS, *The Adams Papers,* Massachusetts Historical Society.

[56]*Eastern Navy Board Letter Book,* MS, Sept. 9, 1779; See page 98.

[57]*Ibid.,* MSS, June 8, 1779 and June 10, 1779.

[58]*Ibid.,* MS, June 8, 1779.

[59]*Ibid.*

[60]*Marine Committee Out-Letters,* II, 76.

[61]Navy Board to Whipple, June 12, 1779, MS, *Abraham Whipple Papers,* Rhode Island Historical Society, Providence, Rhode Island; *Eastern Navy Board Letter Book,* MS, June 24, 1779.

[62]Whipple address to Congress, June 10, 1786, MS, *Abraham Whipple Papers,* Rhode Island Historical Society; *Eastern Navy Board Letter Book,* MS, Aug. 26, 1779; Thomas Clark, *op. cit.,* I, 94-95. Clark's account of this cruise was personally received from a participant, John Peck, midshipman in the *Queen of France.* He states that the Jamaica fleet was 150 sail. However, this was the recollection of a midshipman many years later. The Eastern Navy Board writing contemporaneously with the event says 60 sail. I have accepted the more conservative figure.

[63]*Eastern Navy Board Letter Book*, MS, June 16, 1779.

[64]*Ibid.*, MSS, July 14, 1779 and Aug. 18, 1779.

[65]*Ibid.*, MSS, Aug. 18, 1779, Sept. 9, 1779, and Sept. 23, 1779.

[66]*Marine Committee Out-Letters*, II, 120.

[67]In 1781 James Nicholson lost the *Trumbull* to the British frigate *Iris*, ex-Continental frigate *Hancock*, and the *General Monk*, ex-American privateer *General Washington*.

[68]This is the site of modern Castine, Maine.

[69]Almon, *Remembrancer*, VIII, 356-358; Beatson, *Naval and Military Memoirs of Great Britain*, IV, 509-511.

[70]*Evening Post* (Boston), July 10, 1779.

[71]Brigadier General Peleg Wadsworth's Deposition, Sept. 29, 1779, *Papers Relating to the Penobscot Expedition*, 1779, Transcripts from the Massachusetts Archives, New-York Historical Society, New York, New York. Hereafter referenced as *Penobscot Papers*.

[72]*Eastern Navy Board Letter Book*, MS, June 30, 1779.

[73]*Marine Committee Out-Letters*, II, 95.

[74]Massachusetts General Council to Navy Board, July 3, 1779, MS, *Penobscot Papers*.

[75]*Eastern Navy Board Letter Book*, MS, July 9, 1779.

[76]List of Ships of War on the Penobscot Expedition, n. d., MS, *Penobscot Papers*.

[77]Navy Board to Saltonstall, July 13, 1779, MS, *Penobscot Papers*.

[78]*Eastern Navy Board Letter Book*, MSS, July 19, 1779 and July 14, 1779.

[79]Beatson, *op., cit.*, IV, 511.

[80]Lieutenant George Little's Deposition, Sept. 25, 1779, MS, *Penobscot Papers*.

[81]Lovell to Saltonstall, Aug. 6, 1779, War Council on board the *Warren*, Aug. 7, 1779, Hacker's Plan of Attack, Aug. 8, 1779, MSS, *Penobscot Papers*.

[82]Navy Board to Saltonstall, Aug. 12, 1779, MS, *Penobscot Papers*.

[83]Allen, *Naval History*, 432-433.

[84]Intelligence from Gilbert Richmond, first mate of the *Argo*, Aug. 9, 1779, MS, *Penobscot Papers*.

[85]War Council on board the *Warren*, Aug. 14, 1779, MS, *Penobscot Papers*.

[86]Captain Daniel Waters Deposition, Sept. 28, 1779, MS, *Penobscot Papers*.

[87]Lieutenant George Little's Deposition, Sept. 25, 1779, MS, *Penobscot Papers*.

[88]Clowes, *Royal Navy*, IV, 113, states in error that the Continental sloop *Providence* was captured. Her destruction is confirmed by Commodore Collier in his operation report to the Admiralty. See Almon, *Remembrancer*, VIII, 354.

[89]*Eastern Navy Board Letter Book*, MS, Sept. 2, 1779.

[90]Edward E. Hale, "The Naval History of the American Revolution," in Justin Winsor, ed., *Narrative and Critical History of America* (Boston: Houghton Mifflin, 1888), VI, 603.

[91]Depositions of George Little and Jonathan Williams, MSS, Sept. 25, 1779, *Penobscot Papers.*

[92]Report of the Investigating Committee of Both Houses of the Massachusetts Legislature on the Failure of the Penobscot Expedition, Oct. 7, 1779, MS, *Penobscot Papers.*

[93]Report of the Committee of Both Houses of the Massachusetts Legislature on the Conduct of Colonel Paul Revere, n. d., MS, *Penobscot Papers.*

[94]General Court of Mass. to Congress, Sept. 21, 1779, MS, *Penobscot Papers.*

[95]*Eastern Navy Board Letter Book,* MS, Oct. 28, 1779.

[96]Lincoln, [ed.], *Naval Records,* 393.

[97]*Eastern Navy Board Letter Book,* MS, Sept. 8, 1779.

[98]Navy Board to Hacker, Nov. 4, 1779, MS, *Abraham Whipple Papers,* Rhode Island Historical Society.

[99]Gates certificate to Talbot, July 17, 1783, MS, *Silas Talbot Papers,* Rhode Island Historical Society; Anonymous, *Life of Talbot,* 65-97.

[100]Marchand to Talbot, Aug. 9, 1779, MS, *Silas Talbot Papers,* Rhode Island Historical Society.

[101]Congressional resolve, Sept. 17, 1779, MS, *Silas Talbot Papers,* Rhode Island Historical Society.

[102]*Eastern Navy Board Letter Book,* MS, Oct. 28, 1779; Talbot's Letter of Marque Commission, April 14, 1780, MS, *Silas Talbot Papers,* Rhode Island Historical Society.

[103]In 1794 President Washington named Talbot third captain in the new United States Navy. He commanded the Santo Domingo Squadron in the Quasi-War with France and flew his flag in the USS *Constitution.*

[104]*Marine Committee Out-Letters,* II, 109-110.

[105]Howard, *Seth Harding,* 100-102; Clark, *Gallant John Barry,* 181-183.

[106]*Secret Journals of the Acts and Proceedings of Congress* (Boston: Thomas B. Wait, 1820), II, 265-266; *Marine Committee Out-Letters,* II, 122.

[107]The description of the *Confederacy's* grim experience is from reports by Jay and Harding to the President of Congress. *Papers of Cont. Cong.,* MSS, 110, I, 1-23 and 78, XI, 487-489, National Archives, Washington, D.C.

[108]Whipple *et al.,* to Navy Board, No. 19, 1779, MS, *Abraham Whipple Papers,* Rhode Island Historical Society.

[109]Navy Board to Whipple, Nov. 19, 1779 and Nov. 20, 1779, MSS, *Abraham Whipple Papers,* Rhode Island Historical Society.

[110]Navy Board to Whipple, Nov. 20, 1779, MS, *Abraham Whipple Papers,* Rhode Island Historical Society.

[111]Alfred T. Mahan, *The Major Operations of the Navies in the War of American Independence* (Boston: Little, Brown, 1913), 115.

[112]Allen, *Naval History,* II, 488.

CHAPTER SEVEN

[1]David Ramsay, *The History of the Revolution in South Carolina* (Trenton: Isaac Collins, 1785), II, 45-62.

[2]Whipple to Marine Committee, Jan. 8, 1780 and Jury of Inquest to Whipple, Dec. 5, 1779, MSS, *Abraham Whipple Papers,* Rhode Island Historical Society, Providence, Rhode Island. All manuscripts relating to the Charleston operation which are referenced in this chapter are to be found in the Whipple collection unless otherwise indicated.

[3]Whipple to Marine Committee, Jan. 8, 1780, MS. Apparently unaware of the change in naval administration, Whipple continued to direct his reports to the Marine Committee rather than the new Board of Admiralty.

[4]Simpson to Whipple, Jan. 11, 1780 and Whipple to Simpson, Jan. 12, 1780, MSS.

[5]Lincoln to Whipple, Jan. 16, 1780 and Whipple to Marine Committee, Feb. 13, 1780, MSS.

[6]Beatson, *Naval and Military Memoirs of Great Britain,* V, 10; Schomberg, *Naval Chronology,* IV, 359.

[7]Beatson, *op. cit.,* V, 10.

[8]Almon, *Remembrancer,* X, 45.

[9]Lincoln to Whipple, Feb. 8, 1780, MS. It is of interest to note that during World War II the major U. S. Navy fleet and area commanders were ordinarily based ashore.

[10]Rutledge to Lincoln, Feb. 8, 1780, Rutledge warrant to Whipple, Feb. 18, 1780, and Whipple to Curling, Feb. 18, 1780, MSS.

[11]Lincoln to Whipple, Jan. 30, 1780, Hacker, Rathbun, Tucker, Simpson, *et al.,* to Whipple, Feb. 1, 1780, MSS.

[12]Lincoln to Whipple, Feb. 13, 1780 and Whipple to Tucker and Simpson, Feb. 19, 1780, MSS.

[13]Whipple to Rutledge, Feb. 13, 1780, Rutledge to Whipple, Feb. 13, 1780, and Whipple to Tucker and Simpson, Feb. 15, 1780, MSS.

[14]Whipple to Rathbun, Feb. 13 and 22, 1780, MSS.

[15]Whipple *et al.,* to Lincoln, Feb. 27, 1780, MS.

[16]Lincoln to Whipple, Feb. 28, 1780, MS.

[17]Whipple to Hacker, Mar. 9, 1780 and Whipple *et al.,* to Lincoln, Mar. 11, 1780, MSS.

[18]Whipple to Lincoln, Mar. 6, 1780, Letiff to Whipple, Jan. 3, 1780, Thaxter to Whipple, Mar. 11, 1780, Pursers of Continental ships to Whipple, Apr. 6, 1780, MSS.

[19]*Board of Admiralty Out-Letters,* II, 159. Heretofore referenced as *Marine Committee Out-Letters.* The Marine Committee was superseded by a Board of Admiralty in October 1779.

[20]Almon, *Remembrancer,* X, 45.

[21]Lincoln to Whipple, Mar. 9, 1780, War Council on board *Providence,* Mar. 20, 1780, and Lincoln to Whipple, Mar. 20, 1780, MSS; Almon *op. cit.,* X, 45-46.

[22]Almon *op. cit.,* X, 46-47.

[23]Clowes, *Royal Navy,* IV, 113.

[24]*Votes and Letter Book Eastern Navy Board,* MS, July 7, 1780.

[25]Whipple, *et al.,* to Arbuthnot, May 15, 1780, MS.

[26]Whipple to Congress, June 10, 1786, Board of Admiralty to Eastern Navy Board, July 10, 1780; MSS, *Votes and Letter Book Eastern Navy Board,* June 26, 1780, MS.

[27]Lincoln, [ed.], *Naval Records,* 474 and 491; Remick, *Commissioned Officers and Enlisted Men of Kittery and Eliot, Maine,* 214; Whipple to Congress, June 10, 1786, MS.

[28]*Board of Admiralty Out-Letters,* II, 215 and 264; Clark, *Gallant John Barry,* 239.

[29]*Papers of Cont. Cong.,* 78, XI, 487-489, MS, National Archives, Washington, D.C.

[30]*Papers of Cont. Cong.* 78, XI, 487-489, MS; "Private Journal on Board the 'Confederacy' Frigate Kept by Captain Joseph Hardy in Command of Marines" appended to Howard, *Seth Harding,* 213-277. Hereafter referenced as "Hardy's Journal."

[31]*Papers of Cont. Cong.,* 78, XI, 487-489, MS.

[32]*Board of Admiralty Out-Letters,* II, 163-164.

[33]"Hardy's Journal," in Howard, *op. cit.,* 244-245.

[34]*Ibid.,* 247.

[35]*Ibid.,* 247, 249, and 255-256.

[36]*Ibid.,* 256.

[37]*Board of Admiralty Out-Letters,* II, 244.

[38]Howard, *op. cit.,* 129.

[39]*Journals of Cont. Cong.,* XVII, 602-603.

[40]*Ibid.,* XVIII, 963.

[41]*Ibid.,* XVIII, 1148-1149.

[42]"Hardy's Journal," in Howard, *op. cit.,* 257. Harding was certainly not the only Continental captain to use the press gang, but he seems to have been one of the staunchest and most persistent employers of the system.

[43]*Papers of Cont. Cong.,* 37, II, 525, MS.

[44]See page 144.

[45]*Journals of Cont. Cong.,* XVIII, 1050n.

[46]*Board of Admiralty Out-Letters,* II, 268.

[47]"Hardy's Journal," in Howard, *op. cit.,* 260.

[48]*Ibid.,* 259-261.

[49]*Ibid.,* 263.

[50]Allen, *Naval History,* II, 545.

CHAPTER EIGHT

[1]"Hardy's Journal," in Howard, *Seth Harding,* 263-264.

[2]Howard, *op cit.,* 136-137; "Hardy's Journal," in Howard, *op. cit.,* 265-267.

[3]*Papers of Cont. Cong.,* 42, II, 118, MS, National Archives, Washington, D. C.

[4]*Journals of Cont. Cong.,* XXII, 1013-1014.

[5]*Papers of Cont. Cong.,* 19, III, 47, MS.

[6]"Hardy's Journal," in Howard, *op. cit.,* 274.

[7]William B. Clark, *The First Saratoga Being the Saga of John Young and His Sloop of War* (Baton Rouge: Louisiana State University Press, 1953), 136.

[8]Unknown to Harding the *Saratoga* had foundered on Mar. 18, 1781, with the loss of Captain Young and all hands.

[9]Beatson, *Naval and Military Memoirs of Great Britain,* V, 303; Howard, *op. cit.,* 144-145.

[10]*Royal Gazette,* (New York), Apr. 21, 1781.

[11]*New York Gazette,* Apr. 30, 1781.

[12]*New York Gazette,* Apr. 21, 1781; Clowes, *Royal Navy,* IV, 63.

[13]Middlebrook, *Maritime Connecticut,* II, 262.

[14]*Votes and Letter Book Eastern Navy Board,* MS, May 13, 1781.

[15]Howard, *op. cit.,* 151-154; Lincoln, [ed.], *Naval Records,* 269 and 495.

[16]Greenwood, *Manley,* 103-124.

[17]*Journals of Cont. Cong.,* XXI, 943.

[18]Allen, *Naval History,* II, 608.

[19]*Independent Chronicle* (Boston), Sept. 26, 1782; *Pennsylvania Packet* (Philadelphia), Oct. 8, 1782.

[20]Greenwood, *op. cit.,* 129.

[21]*Boston Gazette,* Jan. 27, 1783.

[22]*Independent Chronicle* (Boston), Feb. 27, 1783.

[23]*Ibid.*

[24]*Ibid.,* Mar. 20, 1783.

[25]See pages 8-9.

[26]*Journals of Cont. Cong.,* XXIV, 210-211.

[27]Greenwood, *op. cit.,* 136.

[28]*Columbian Centinel* (Boston), Feb. 16, 1793.

[29]Greenwood, *op. cit.,* 138.

[30]McNeill to Saltonstall, Feb. 27, 1777, as quoted by Middlebrook, *Maritime Connecticut,* II, 325-326.

[31]Hinman to Saltonstall, May 2, 1777, MS, *Gratz Collection,* Historical Society of Pennsylvania, Philadelphia, Pennsylvania.

[32]*Journals of Cont. Cong.,* VI, 909.

[33]Whipple to Commanders of Private Armed Ships or Merchantmen, Oct. 18, 1779, MS, *Abraham Whipple Papers,* Rhode Island Historical Society, Providence, Rhode Island.

[34]Washington to Lafayette, July 15, 1780, as quoted by Dudley W. Knox, *The Naval Genius of George Washington* (Boston: Houghton Mifflin, 1932), 64.

[35]Lincoln, [ed.], *Naval Records,* 217-495.

[36]Hale, "Naval History of American Revolution" in Winsor, ed., *Narrative and Critical History of America,* VI, 585.

[37]Gardner Allen, *Massachusetts Privateers of the Revolution* (Cambridge: Harvard University Press, 1927), 53.